HOLY HULLABALOOS

*A Road Trip to the Battlegrounds
of the Church/State Wars*

JAY WEXLER

BEACON PRESS

BOSTON

Beacon Press
25 Beacon Street
Boston, Massachusetts 02108-2892
www.beacon.org

Beacon Press books
are published under the auspices of
the Unitarian Universalist Association of Congregations.

12 11 10 09   8 7 6 5 4 3 2 1

This book is printed on acid-free paper that meets the uncoated
paper ANSI/NISO specifications for permanence as revised in 1992.

Text design by Yvonne Tsang at Wilsted & Taylor Publishing Services

Wexler, Jay.
Holy hullabaloos : a road trip to the battlegrounds
of the church/state wars / Jay Wexler.
p. cm.
Includes bibliographical references.
ISBN-13: 978-0-8070-0044-1 (pbk. : alk. paper)
1. Church and state—United States. 2. Freedom of religion—
United States. 3. Religious minorities—Legal status, laws, etc.—
United States. I. Title.

KF4865.W48 2009
342.730852—dc22   2008047405

For my mother

Contents

Prologue to a Road Trip

The drive from St. Louis to Ellsinore, a tiny Missouri town near the Arkansas border, takes about three hours and is about as exciting as a butter sandwich. I made the trip one dreary October morning not because I thought my life was just getting too unbelievably fun, but because I wanted to talk to Adin Yutzy, a Mennonite who is the sole living plaintiff from a famous religious freedom case decided nearly forty years ago. Back when Yutzy was much younger and Amish and living in Southern Wisconsin, he and two other Amish men violated Wisconsin's compulsory education laws by keeping their teenage kids out of school for religious reasons. Wisconsin fined the Amish for their intransigence, and with the help of some lawyers working pro bono, Yutzy and his fellow plaintiffs took the case all the way to the Supreme Court, which ruled that Wisconsin had violated their First Amendment rights. The decision, called *Wisconsin v. Yoder*, still stands as the high-water mark for religious freedom in the nation's history.

A few months earlier, when I first started making trips to places where landmark church/state cases had started, I had no intention of talking to Yutzy. It hadn't even occurred to me. But while I was doing some research in Wisconsin into the *Yoder* case, I was talking with Richard Dawley, the country's preeminent expert on the Wisconsin Amish, and he happened to have Yutzy's address in Missouri. The two of them had met in Pinecraft, Florida—a winter retreat for the Amish and Mennonites—while Dawley was there researching a book called *Amish Snowbirds*, which I hope will soon become a Hollywood blockbuster starting Sharon Stone and James Gandolfini. Dawley gave me the address, and as soon as I got back to my office in Boston, I wrote Yutzy a letter asking if I might come see him when I was in St. Louis. My wife, Karen, and I were planning to be in town for a couple of days to drop my three-year-old son Walter off with my in-laws so we could take a vacation by ourselves for the first time in three years, and it seemed like the perfect time to go and talk to a guy whose famous case I had been thinking about and writing about and teaching to my students for nearly a decade.

Who knew, though, whether Yutzy would have any interest in talking to me? And even if he wouldn't mind talking to me, who knew whether he would want to write me back? Do these guys even use the mail? I decided to send along a self-addressed stamped envelope just in case it might help. When I hadn't heard back in a couple of weeks, I cursed myself about the SASE. Maybe he thought I was patronizing him. After all, Mennonites are more comfortable with modernity than the Amish, and I knew from Dawley that Yutzy drove a car, so why did I think Yutzy would have wanted any help sending me back a letter? Probably he saw the SASE and threw the whole thing in the trash, figuring I was some smart-ass northeastern elitist jerk who wasn't worth spending five seconds talking to. I decided my book was doomed and started making plans to write a multivolume academic treatise on the Constitution's weights and measures clause.

Then one day I got the SASE back in my office mailbox.

I couldn't believe it. I danced back to my office, waving my arms around like an idiot. I tore open the envelope, and inside was a tiny scrap of lined notebook paper that said, in its entirety, "To Jay Wexler. Yes you may come to visit us and talk about the school issue. Sincerely, Adin Yutzy." A man of few words. I whooped and hollered. And I immediately sent Yutzy back a short note saying that I would try to visit him on a particular day at about a particular time, so he would have some idea when I might show up. Since I had no phone number for him, and since he hadn't given me one, maybe because he didn't have one, there was no other way to contact him, so that was going to have to do.

When I showed up in Ellsinore, my most pressing problem was that I didn't really know where Yutzy lived. What I had for an address was a "Rural Route" number, which it turns out is some sort of post office designation rather than a real street location, as I was informed by the lady behind the counter at the gas-station-sub-shop-furniture-store-pool-hall where I stopped to ask directions. *Aha*, thought the guy from the city, this explained why Google Maps had been no help in pinpointing Yutzy's exact location. Only about four hundred people live in Ellsinore, though, so I figured, how hard could it be to find one of them? I took a random right turn off the highway and immediately started coming across addresses that were sort of close in number to the one I had for Yutzy. A few houses down the road, I thought I was getting closer, but then the houses stopped. Only after realizing that I had gone two miles since last seeing any sign of human life and finding myself surrounded by a flock of about a thousand angry-looking buzzards did I think: *Time to turn around!*

My next stop was the town post office, a minuscule building located directly across from a house with a giant bleeding Jesus poster and the slogan, "This Blood's for

You." Luckily, all I had to do was tell the postmaster that I was looking for Adin Yutzy, and she told me exactly where he lived. Kind of frightening, I thought, from a personal privacy perspective, but what did I care? The house was just a couple of miles down the road, and I knew I was on the right track when I passed one of those roadside signs announcing that "Yutzy Realty" had adopted the two-mile stretch of road that I was on. "Yutzy has a real estate agency?" I wondered aloud. I bet he really needed that SASE to write me back.

I found the house and flipped on my blinker. Of course, I had no idea whether anyone was expecting me, or indeed, whether anyone was even home. It was totally possible that my knocks on the door would be met with complete silence, in which case I would have no alternative but to get back into my father-in-law's 1999 Lincoln Continental, put another four hundred dollars' worth of gas in the tank, and make the boring, three-hour ride back to St. Louis. As I turned into the driveway, I hoped for the best.

Congress shall make no law respecting an establishment of religion, or prohibiting the free exercise thereof...

The opening passage of the First Amendment to the United States Constitution has only sixteen words, many of which are short, but don't let its brevity fool you. Perhaps no other clause in our history has raised so many problems or created so much controversy. Consider some of the issues it perennially raises. Can a town place Christmas symbols on public property? How about a Ten Commandments monument? May students pray in class? At a football game? What if the teacher leads the prayer? The mascot? Was George W. Bush's "faith-based initiative" somehow constitutional? And what's going on with the

Pledge of Allegiance's "under God" provision? When can tax dollars fund religious education? May religious believers opt out of legal requirements, like sending their kids to school, or evade legal prohibitions, like those against drug use or human sacrifice?

It would be hard enough to figure out what the First Amendment should mean in a nation that is religiously homogeneous—say, one where everybody is either a devout Baptist with conservative political views or an atheist with liberal ones—but it becomes *really* hard in a country like the United States, which is blessed with enormous religious diversity. This diversity manifests itself in lots of ways. Most obviously, people in this country identify with all sorts of religious groups and institutions. The majority of Americans would describe themselves as Christian (though there is incredible variety even within this broad designation), but many hold Jewish, Muslim, Taoist, Zoroastrian, Buddhist, Hindu, Shintoist, and a whole bunch of other views. Some belong to new sects, like the Raelians, who believe that aliens created life thousands of years ago, while others hold what are often described as "New Age" beliefs or treat nature as the ultimate reality. Still others—as many as 14 percent, by some estimates—have no religious beliefs at all.

Americans also hold their beliefs with different levels of intensity. Some believe devoutly, while others attend religious services once a year. For some, religious beliefs are incredibly important to their everyday lives, while for others, religion is more a form of cultural identity than anything else. The same is true for nonbelievers. Some just don't know what they believe, while others affirmatively believe that there is no ultimate reality whatsoever. And some are truly offended by religious ideas.

People think all sorts of things about the nature of reality as a result of their religious beliefs. Some think that miracles occur. Others think the world is flat or was created ten thousand years ago. Some believe we go to heaven (or hell) after death; others think we are reincarnated. Some think that trees and streams have active thoughts and communicate with us. Others believe that if they focus hard enough, they can walk through walls or fly. Still others think they can communicate with the dead.

Finally, Americans hold all sorts of ethical and political views as a result of their beliefs or nonbeliefs. Some people hold so-called "liberal" views because of their religion ("we should recognize gay marriages"), while others hold "conservative" views ("we should oppose abortion") or even views generally understood as abhorrent ("the white race is superior to all others"). One scholar has famously argued that the primary distinction among religious Americans these days is not whether they are Christians, Jews, Muslims, or members of some other religion, but whether they are so-called "orthodox" believers or "progressive" ones, with the former holding far more traditional and conservative views than the latter. Nonbelievers also differ in their political and ethical beliefs. Of course, many agnostics and atheists are political liberals, but then again, some of the most repressive ideologies in recent history have vehemently denied the existence of the divine.

I think it is because so many people believe so many things in so many ways that I have always been fascinated by religion, even though I've been an atheist since I was eighteen. As the son of two New York Jews, I was raised Jewish and attended Hebrew school unwillingly for years. My bar mitzvah was memorable mostly because the rabbi had to push me out of the way after I was done croaking out my haftarah so he could get to the microphone. Like many who were taught Judaism by mean Hebrew school teachers, these years were enough to put me off Judaism forever, but I still think that if you had asked me during those days whether I believed in some sort of god, I would have said that I did. I started changing my mind in high school. I vividly remember declaring that I did not believe in God during a meeting of my freshman English class, although when I broke my collarbone playing dodgeball later that very day (don't ask), I decided to put off my disbelief for another couple of years.

It wasn't until college that I dared openly disbelieve again, but at the same time, I found myself thinking about religion more and more. After my sophomore year in high school, I had spent a summer in Tokyo with my father, who had moved there temporarily for work. I was drawn to Asia, and in college declared myself an East Asian studies major at the end of freshman year. All Asian studies majors had to learn something about the great Chinese and Japanese religions, and soon I found myself enamored with Buddhism, Confucianism, and especially Taoism. I wrote my senior thesis on Chuang Tzu, a brilliant and playful oddball who was the second most prominent Taoist in Chinese history, after the great Lao Tzu. If you haven't read the *Chuang Tzu*, you should, although when you're done you may no longer believe that there is any real distinction between life and death, or dreaming and being awake, or anything else. I can't say that I ever considered myself an actual Taoist (Chuang Tzu's philosophy is not an easy one to live by in the modern world, especially when you're raising a child or driving a car in downtown Boston), but I do like to think that from time to time, I put his lessons into practice.

My original idea after graduating from college was that I would get a PhD in religious studies and teach Chinese religion to college students. I went to the University of Chicago Divinity School, where I studied Christianity for the first time in my life, as well as a bunch of other stuff about religion. In many ways I loved the Div School, but ultimately I decided that the overwhelming academic atmosphere was too much. There were just too many people talking about "problematiques" and "epiphenomena" and "Wittgenstein's Weltanschauung" and other way too heady stuff. I quit after getting my master's and decided to apply to law school. Before long, though, I started gravitating back toward issues involving religion, and I wrote my first article as a law student, back in 1996, on whether schools can constitutionally teach the purportedly scientific theory of "intelligent design" in science classes as an alternative to evolution. When a court finally got around to considering the same question ten years later, it came to the same conclusion that I had, which is to say: *No way*.

After law school, I clerked for Supreme Court justice Ruth Bader Ginsburg and worked as an attorney at the Justice Department for a couple of years. But then Al Gore sort of lost the presidential election of 2000, and George W. Bush took over, and I knew I had to leave. It's a good thing, too, because the office where I worked turned out to be the one responsible for writing such revered classics as the so-called "Torture Memo" and other quasi-legal justifications for the president's unprecedented expansion of executive power. I've been at Boston University ever since and have spent most of my time writing and speaking about church/state law, with an emphasis on thinking about how these issues play out in the public school classroom, and drinking beer with students.

After ten years of thinking about church/state issues from an academic perspective, though, what I really wanted to do was write a book for people who want to understand, in plain terms, exactly what the Supreme

Court has said about church/state law. That is sort of what this book is. Over the next eight chapters, I discuss nearly all the major issues of church/state law: the exercise of government power by religious institutions, religious discrimination, religious liberty, religious symbols and displays, legislative prayer, school prayer, funding of religious schools, and religious influences on public school curricula.

I also explain my own views about what the Supreme Court has done. I actually think the Court has gotten a lot of things right in the area of church/state law. It is an extremely difficult area that does not admit to many easy answers, and the Court should get credit for struggling thoughtfully with some really hard issues. On the other hand, the Court has made a couple of mistakes. For one thing, I think the Court has wrongly decided that believers do not deserve exemptions from general laws that burden their religion. The Court has also wrongly failed to protect nonbelievers from government endorsements of religion that make them (us) feel excluded from our pluralistic society. Though I'm not shy in stating my opinions, I have tried not to let them get too much in the way. Whenever I felt like ranting, I tried to make sure that I had already explained what the Court has said fairly and accurately, so that even if you end up disagreeing with my personal views on the issues, you will at least finish the book with a basic understanding of the details of church/state law.

When I was first thinking about writing a book, I figured that, like most professors, I would end up spending most of my time in my office or the library. Just as I was getting started, however, I found myself for some reason reading all of these books by writers who had hit the road in search of their obsessions. In *Candyfreak*, Steve Almond toured the country to learn about his favorite sweets. In *Killing Yourself to Live*, Chuck Klosterman morbidly visited the grave sites of dead rock stars. And in *Assassination Vacation*, the brilliant (and even more morbid) Sarah Vowell went looking across America at places having anything to do with the assassinations of Presidents Lincoln, McKinley, and Garfield. These books were hilarious and terrific, and I suggest reading all of them (after you finish this one).

Halfway through *Assassination Vacation*, the idea came to me. Maybe I should travel around the country to visit some places where big Supreme Court church/state cases started. If nothing else, I would be getting out of the office and into the world. I could actually see these places that I've been teaching about and talk to the people whom I've been writing about. I would get some great anecdotes to spice up my classes. And I was pretty sure that I would learn a lot about the substantive legal issues, not to mention about religion itself. I figured, what was stopping me? I had a sabbatical coming up. My wife, Karen, a high school teacher for the past dozen years, wanted a break. My son, Walter, hadn't started school yet. I owned a partially reliable 1997 Honda Civic. The road trip was on!

For the next six months, I traveled around the country and visited all sorts of fascinating places, from a high school football field in East Texas to the gallery of the U.S. Senate, from a Wisconsin Amish farm to a spooky South Florida cemetery, from an Islamic elementary school in downtown Cleveland to the grounds of the Texas state capitol. I went to a mosque, a Jewish temple, a Buddhist shrine, a grungy pub, and a museum filled with animatronic biblical figures. I talked to the Senate chaplain, a Jewish rabbi, a Muslim imam, a Buddhist abbot, an Amish elder, an atheist minister, a Santeria priest, and a world-famous scientist. I learned countless things that I didn't know, and I learned that a lot of the things I thought I knew were wrong. It was a priceless trip, and it made writ-

ing the book feel almost effortless. I only hope that reading it proves to be at least a fraction of the fun that it was
to write.

Though I loved the places I visited, there are a lot of
other places that I would have liked to visit but didn't.
Every person I told about this project had terrific sugges-
tions about where I could or should or must go, and I wish
I could have gone to all of them, but it wasn't possible. For
example, I would have loved to have spent a week with
snake charmers in the hills of Tennessee, but that wasn't
in the cards. More seriously, I wish I could have visited
some Mormons, Jehovah's Witnesses, and Native Americans, three groups that are indispensable to fully understanding American religious history, but I did not have
the time or the resources. I probably should have spent
some more time in the Deep South, but I didn't get the
chance. I want to make it clear that I don't intend this book,
by any means, to be a comprehensive summary of American religiosity or even of American church/state law. I had
to make some choices about where to go and whom to talk
to. I tried to choose places that were connected in some
interesting way to big church/state cases or issues, that
I thought would be fun to visit and read about, and that
were practically possible, given my various limitations,
which include, among other things, a pretty serious fear
of snakes.

Well, was Adin Yutzy home? Did he have anything interesting to say about his landmark case? Did he make me
a grilled cheese sandwich with a side of peas? Did he tell
me I was going to hell and advise me to start living my life
through Jesus Christ? All I can tell you for now is: maybe
he did, and maybe he didn't. Read on, and you will find out
soon enough.

1

HASIDIC HULLABALOO

Destination New York State

Of all the places where a major church/state controversy heading to the Supreme Court might erupt, a grungy pub on a side street in a large city is probably not the first place you'd think of, but that's exactly what happened in the mid-1980s at a hole in the wall in Cambridge, Massachusetts, called Grendel's Den. The case was about the constitutionality of a Massachusetts law that gave churches the power to prevent nearby bars and restaurants from getting liquor licenses. When Grendel's applied for the twenty-seventh liquor license in the vicinity of the Holy Cross Armenian Parish, the church decided that enough was enough and vetoed the application.

Perhaps it should have surprised nobody that a bar named after a monster who allegedly descended directly from Cain and is described alternatively in *Beowulf* as a "demon corpse," "hell-serf," and "captain of evil" wouldn't shrink from a fight with a church. After all, if you believe the scholars (and goodness knows you should always believe the scholars), Beowulf—the hero who pulls off Grendel's arm, leaves him to crawl off to a cave and bleed to death, decapitates him, and then kills his mother for good

1

measure—might very well have been meant to exemplify Christian values. With this in mind, who could really have blamed Grendel's Den for being so sensitive to the church's veto?

Whether it was out of revenge or simply good business sense, Grendel's Den sued the church, arguing that the Massachusetts law violated the First Amendment. The Supreme Court agreed with the bar. The problem with the law was that it gave the power to make official decisions directly to religious institutions. As Justice Burger, no great champion of secularism, wrote, the law "substitutes the unilateral and absolute power of a church for the reasoned decisionmaking of a public legislative body acting on evidence and guided by standards, on issues with significant economic and political implications. . . . Ordinary human experience and a long line of cases teach that few entanglements could be more offensive to the spirit of the Constitution." In other words, whatever the separation of church and state may or may not mean, it's got to mean that the church cannot *be the actual state*. In this chapter, I will explain this point, and then when I'm done with that, I'll tell you all about my visit to what might be the weirdest place in the entire country.

I actually spent a lot of time in Grendel's during college, drinking too much cheap beer and acting like a total moron. I'm pretty sure the last time I was there, I ended up puking. I guess I have the First Amendment to thank for that opportunity. Our founding fathers would be so proud! Since I now live only fifteen minutes away from Grendel's by subway, I figured it would be fun to go back and check the place out. I also thought it would be interesting to see how the church had fared following its defeat. I wondered whether it had managed to thrive despite the generations of drinkers who had slaked their thirst, according to the Supreme Court decision, a mere ten feet from its back wall.

I made it to the bar about ten minutes before I was supposed to meet my friends, so I had some time to look around. I walked up and down the nearby streets looking for anything that resembled a church, but all I could see was a restaurant called Upstairs at the Square, a funky Indian place across the street, and an office building. I thought that maybe the office building was really a church, but when I smushed my face up against the glass door and looked inside, it was clear that the office building was just an office building. Something had changed. There was simply no church anywhere in the vicinity. Unless I had read the opinion wrong (had it said ten miles?), it appeared that I had a little mystery on my hands.

Descending into the bar, I passed on my left a framed copy of an article from the *New York Times* written the day after the Court announced its decision. Next to the article was a picture that also appeared in the paper; in it, the bar's owners are celebrating the victory by drinking champagne right outside the bar's entrance. I took a seat at the bar, ordered a Harpoon IPA, and looked around. I hadn't been to this place for at least fifteen years. The bar was still the dive that I remembered from college—crowded, low ceilinged, packed with tables, and kind of clammy. It actually smelled sort of like a cave where a monster might crawl in to die.

I was curious about why there didn't seem to be a church around anywhere, so I called over to the bartender and asked him. He was probably in his late twenties, with a scraggly beard on his cheeks and a well-worn Red Sox cap on his head. I resisted the urge to call him "barkeep," which is something I've always wanted to call a bartender, usually when I want to "settle up" or order a "double." He was somewhat familiar with the case, though not the details, and he told me that the church had been torn down years before, though he didn't know exactly when. He suggested that the church used to stand where there was now a Peet's coffee shop. This seemed questionable. The court opinion says that the church and bar stood back to back, but the part of the bar that faced Peet's didn't seem to me to be the back, although who can really say what counts as the back of a tiny dive? In any event, it didn't matter. The key point was that the church had long ago ceased to exist, while the bar was still thriving. Mystery solved. Satan 1, Jesus 0.

Before long, my friends Miriam and Aaron arrived. Both had been students in my Law and Religion seminar a few years before. Both were practicing Jews, smart, and very funny. Indeed, I quickly decided to steal several of their jokes. Like, remember that joke about "Satan 1, Jesus 0"? That was Miriam's.

At the time, Aaron had a job that gave him unlimited access to a binding machine, and so he had taken the liberty of putting together three bound copies of *Larkin v. Grendel's Den*, complete with a nifty cover that utilized several fonts to stunning effect. When the barkeep came over to take their drink orders, he saw the opinion and asked for a copy, which Aaron kindly turned over. Aaron engaged him in some banter about the case, and we learned a couple more tasty tidbits. For one thing, the very bar our drinks were resting on had apparently been constructed from the old pews of some long-abandoned church. Not the church that tried to veto the bar's liquor license, we were assured, but some other church. We all found this a little creepy. Also, we learned that Laurence

Tribe, the famous Harvard law professor who had argued the bar's case in the Supreme Court many years ago, continued to come in all the time to eat and drink. I asked the bartender if Tribe had to pay, and the young guy waved his hands around as if to take in the entire place. "Everything is free. Anything he wants," he said. Pretty good deal, I figured, for a guy who probably makes one and a half gazillion dollars a year in legal fees.

The bar made out of church pews seemed to be just one aspect of Grendel's general uneasiness with religion. Even the religious symbols strewn about the bar seemed to reveal a passive-aggressive distaste for religious faith. We were there on the seventh day of Hanukkah, only four days before Christmas, and there were holiday lights hung up around the bar, but not many. Miriam found a fake Christmas tree about a foot and a half tall hidden away in a corner behind some newspapers and dirty plates. Instead of a star on the top, there was a dreidel. The dreidel looked authentic enough to me, but then again I hadn't picked up a dreidel since losing in the finals of the National Dreidel Tournament back in 1982. Aaron and Miriam, however, really knew their way around a dreidel, and they pointed out that the letters on this one were questionable. The hei and the gimel were written more or less correctly, but the other two letters looked more like an indecipherable scribble and maybe the number "7" than any letter that belonged on any self-respecting Hanukkah top.

I found another instance of this hostility to religion when I excused myself to use the men's room. Hanging on the wall next to the bathroom door was a framed document entitled "Declaration in Defense of Science and Secularism," signed by a bunch of famous Harvard scientists and other intellectuals. The document, which I also found later on the Internet, complains that "far too many Americans, including influential decision-makers, [fail] to understand the nature of scientific inquiry" and that "this disdain for science is aggravated by the excessive influence of religious doctrine on our public policies." Specifically, the declaration calls for political leaders "to maintain a strict separation between church and state and, in particular, not to permit legislation or executive action to be influenced by religious beliefs."

Now, I'm a strong separationist myself, and just as much as the next guy who has taken first-grade science, I think it's sad that 20 percent of Americans think that the sun revolves about the earth (as the declaration notes). But this secularist view that religion should be a private matter of little relevance to public decision making kind of drives me nuts. For one thing, it is perfectly clear that the First Amendment does not prohibit citizens, legislators, or even presidents from consulting their religious beliefs when making decisions about public policy. Moreover, we should probably be glad that people rely on their religious beliefs when making important decisions. If they couldn't, or didn't feel free to, we might not have had abolitionism or the civil rights movement or the Endangered Species Act, all of which drew some of their strongest support from religious people acting on their most deeply held beliefs.

I'll get back to this issue of religion and public decision making in a minute, but first things first. Why did Grendel's Den rightly win its lawsuit against the state? Remember that the *Grendel's* case involved a simple and quite narrow question, which is this: is it okay for the government to delegate its actual decision-making authority to a church? The Court's answer, with which I agree, was no.

For all sorts of reasons which have been written about in dusty volumes by academics and aren't worth mentioning here, government actors delegate their powers to other actors all the time. Congress delegates its lawmaking powers to administrative agencies, such as the Food and Drug Administration and the Environmental Protection Agency. State legislatures do the same. Agency heads delegate their powers to subordinates. Subordinates delegate to their subordinates. Agencies themselves delegate their policy-making powers to subagencies, and even sometimes to private parties. And so on. Whether, and under what conditions, these delegations are legal is a convoluted topic that in law schools is covered in a course called Administrative Law, which most students find excruciatingly boring, and not only when I'm teaching it. But whatever the merits of delegation of governmental power might be in general, acts of delegation like the one involved in the *Grendel's Den* case are surely invalid. If courts are going to interpret the establishment clause ("Congress shall make no law respecting an establishment of religion") to prevent anything at all short of the government setting up an official state religion, then delegation of actual governmental power to religious institutions should not be allowed.

The Massachusetts law challenged in *Grendel's Den* said that "premises . . . located within a radius of five hundred feet of a church or school shall not be licensed for the sale of alcoholic beverages if the governing body of such church or school files written objection thereto." The term "church" was defined broadly, as it always is in these kinds of statutes, to encompass all sorts of religious buildings, so the problem with the law wasn't that the statute preferred some religions over others. The problem was that it gave complete power and discretion to the church to decide which liquor licenses to approve and which to reject. The church, in other words, was acting as the government, and its decisions had official governmental effects on private parties like Grendel's Den.

The Supreme Court worried that a church could reject a liquor license for any reason at all, no matter how discriminatory or stupid that reason might be. So, in his opinion, Justice Burger complained that a church could theoretically reject someone's license application "for explicitly religious goals [such as] favoring liquor licenses for members of that congregation or adherents of that faith." During oral argument, the justices wondered about even more dastardly motives. "What happens if the church . . . only allows bars in its neighborhood that sell Irish whiskey?" one justice asked. When the lawyer representing Massachusetts tried to head off the question with an Irish-whiskey-specific response, the justice threatened to rephrase the question in terms of tequila.

If the Court had upheld the law in *Grendel's Den*, we might have a very different-looking government, one much more dangerous than the one we already have. Nothing would stop the legislature—federal, state, local —from giving power to a church (or a temple, or a mosque, or an organization of Taoists or Hare Krishnas) to decide who should enjoy a tax break or who should get a broadcast license or who deserves unemployment benefits or disability accommodations. Can you imagine if a Jew had to go to the corner Protestant church to contest a parking ticket, or a Catholic had to visit the local Buddhist temple to ask for a tax extension? Maybe if it were still the fifteenth century or something. But these days we expect the government to apply its laws in the same way to everyone, regardless of our religious beliefs or nonbeliefs. We might not trust that the government will in fact do this in every situation, but we should trust the inclination of religious groups to be impartial far less. If the Court had decided that the government could delegate its core functions to religious groups, then it would have been saying that churches could basically run the country. If that's not an "establishment of religion," then what would be?

It is important, however, to keep in mind exactly what the Massachusetts statute said. That statute was unique in that it gave actual decision-making power to churches. Most statutes don't do that. So compare the following two laws:

Law 1: The state shall grant no liquor licenses within five hundred feet of a church or school.

Law 2: The state shall grant no liquor licenses within five hundred feet of a church or school, if the church or school objects to the license.

The second law is the one that the Court struck down in *Grendel's Den*. The first law, on the other hand, is just a simple zoning law, like ones that exist in communities all over the country and that are without question constitutional. Unlike Law 2, Law 1 does not give any actual decision-making power to any religious institution. In the first law, the legislature, not the church, has made the determination about what bars can go where.

Maybe you've come across one of these zoning laws, or at least heard of a controversy involving some new bar or adult bookstore or strip club that can't open because it's too close to a school or hospital or church. News stories about these disputes pop up all the time. In 2003 a neighborhood group in Old West Lawrence, Kansas, objected to a bar called Rick's Place moving into a nearby strip mall, because it would have been too close to an Orthodox church in the same strip mall. According to one news account, "Rick's Place . . . is a blue-collar bar with a regular clientele, sort of a Lawrence version of Cheers, the fictional bar from the popular television series." Of course, the proximity to the church was probably not the real reason the neighbors objected to the bar. Most likely, they just didn't want drunk people in the neighborhood screaming at lampposts and throwing up in the bushes. The bar's opponents were happy enough to use the "no bar too close to a church" law to serve their purposes. For its part, the church wasn't so sure. It would have preferred the sandwich shop that had previously intended to move into the strip mall, but as to whether the bar should be allowed to move there, the parish president told a reporter, "We'd prefer it not go there. But who are we to decide what God has in mind?"

Then there was the 2002 brouhaha in Wichita over whether an "Adult Superstore" could continue to exist despite standing next door to a church. For years, neighborhood residents had tried to drive the store out of town, passing out antipornography leaflets to customers and holding prayer vigils on the sidewalk. The upright citizens of Wichita argued that "this type of business seems to attract people with no scruples" and claimed that "children would find sex toys when they mowed the lawn." Finally, the neighborhood organizers successfully urged the city to deny the store a new license. In May 2002, a police officer gave employees thirty minutes to close the store or face being arrested. Preferring to stay clear of the local prison, the employees gave in and closed the store. The victorious neighbors planned a party to celebrate their success, and apparently to give thanks to God. As one activist put it, "We are elated and we give the Lord all the credit on this one." It turned out their celebration was premature. When the owner challenged the procedure the city followed in closing the store, the city decided to settle the lawsuit. The result? Two months after the city closed the store down, it allowed the store to reopen and gave the owner over sixty thousand dollars to make up for her lost business. Satan 2, Jesus 0 (this time in OT).

Although zoning laws may not always be politically viable, they generally *are* constitutionally acceptable. The point here is not to say whether these zoning laws are good policy. They might be, or they might not be. Defenders generally argue that they are necessary to protect children from the harmful "secondary effects" of having a bar in the neighborhood. Are they right? I don't know. I'm not a child psychiatrist. I hope they're wrong, since I live with my son in a building that contains a bar. My only point is that such zoning regulations do not violate the First Amendment.

Why is this? It's because the primary purpose and effect of your typical zoning law is not to help or promote or advance religion. In the late sixties, in a case brought by a guy with the unfortunate name of Lemon, the Court crafted a crude test, known forever after as the *"Lemon* test," that says a law violates the establishment clause only if it has the primary purpose or the primary effect of promoting religion, or if it involves excessive entanglement between government and religion. Many scholars have pointed out, often in incredibly long articles with inexcusable titles like "The Future of the *Lemon* Test: A Sweeter Alternative," "Making *Lemon*-Aid from the Supreme Court's *Lemon*," and *"Lemon* is a Lemon," that the *Lemon* test is unsatisfactory in many ways. How much "entanglement" is too much? What counts as "promotion," anyway? These commentators are right, and indeed the Court itself, while continuing to mention the test in nearly every church/state case, has molded specific versions of the *Lemon* test to fit differing situations. But there is really no need to do much tinkering to understand why zoning laws such as the one in Wichita that almost, but not quite, spelled doom for the Adult Superstore are constitutional.

For one thing, zoning laws don't involve any entanglement of government and religion. While the *Grendel's* law completely entangled governmental and religious functions by giving churches the official power to veto liquor licenses, the typical zoning law does no such thing. Moreover, the purpose of these zoning laws is not to promote religion, and that's not their main effect. As one court upholding such a zoning law explained, "It is difficult to see how religion is advanced at all by the ordinance in light of the fact that no financial support is involved, no sponsorship of religious activities is created, and no government involvement with religion is incurred." It is true that a zoning law might confer some incidental benefit on churches. A church protected by a zoning law does not have to take its own steps to protect visiting children from drunk guys and sex toys. But a church protected by the city fire department doesn't have to fight its own fires either, and nobody thinks that's a problem. Why should the zoning law be any different?

I hope that the distinction I'm drawing between zoning laws and laws that delegate government authority to churches is clear. This will not be the last distinction in the book, and it is by no means the trickiest. But some of these things can get confusing, especially to those who don't spend all day doing this law stuff. Maybe it would help to go through an example. This may seem like a surprise quiz, but don't worry, you won't be graded on it. Imagine a state legislature passes the following four laws:

Law A provides for trash pickup around large churches three times a week, but around small churches only twice a week.

Law B criminalizes the possession of a firearm or sharpened blade within a "rock's throw" of any school or church.

Law C provides that nobody shall park their Hummer in front of any church during services without a permit.

Law D authorizes the head of any church congregation to issue an enforceable fine of one thousand dollars to anyone who litters within city limits.

Which one of these violates the rule set out in *Grendel's Den*?

The correct answer is D. Only Law D confers actual governmental authority and discretion upon a religious actor. Law C is almost certainly fine; it's basically just like the zoning laws in Wichita and Old West Lawrence, except that it wisely discriminates against obnoxiously giant trucks instead of beer drinkers. Law B likewise gives no power to churches and thus poses no establishment clause problems. The "rock's throw" part is idiotic and perhaps invalidly vague, but that's not a First Amendment problem. Law A might run into trouble for distinguishing among types of churches, but even that distinction might be all right, since large churches are likely to generate more trash than smaller ones. In any event, there's no delegation of government power in Law A, so it's not a *Grendel's Den* issue.

Now that that's over, let's return to Grendel's itself and its proudly displayed Declaration in Defense of Science and

Secularism. Some pages ago, I took issue with the declaration's view that the principle of separation of church and state means that public officials should refrain from consulting their religious beliefs when making public policy decisions. But then a few pages later, I said the Court will strike down laws whose primary purpose is to promote religion. Maybe you're thinking that these two positions are inconsistent. They are not. The Court's point is only that the predominant purpose of a statute may not be religious. So long as the legislature or mayor or president or whoever also has some serious secular purpose in enacting a law, courts will not strike down the law because it was also inspired by religion. Laws that are incidentally motivated by religion pose no greater constitutional problem than laws, like the church zoning statutes, that give religion an incidental benefit. As a result, courts rarely invalidate a law because it has a religious purpose.

It's true that, every once in a while, a court will strike down a law because it finds that the law was motivated solely by religion. Back in 1978 the state of Alabama had a statute on the books that required teachers, at the beginning of the first class of the day, to give their students a one-minute moment of silence "for meditation." In 1981 the state legislature amended the law by adding the phrase "or voluntary prayer" after the phrase "for meditation." At trial, when explaining why he wanted to change the original law, the bill's sponsor, state senator Donald G. Holmes, explained that the bill was "an effort to return voluntary prayer to our public schools." When pressed as to whether he had any other goal in proposing the amendment, Holmes replied on the stand that he had "no other purpose in mind." Oops. With these facts, the Supreme Court had little choice but to conclude that the government's sole purpose in adding the phrase "voluntary prayer" was religious. It therefore struck down the statute. As a general matter, however, legislators are not as daft as Mr. Holmes, and so usually it's hard for the court to conclude that the legislature's sole goal was to promote religion. What this means is that if the president thinks that stem cell research conflicts with his faith, or if a state legislator thinks that abortion violates the law of God, he has every right to say so (indeed, the free speech clause of the First Amendment guarantees this), and the resulting law will stand, so long as there is some other, secular reason behind the policy. If a nonbeliever disagrees about banning stem cell research or restricting abortion, then by all means she should object to the policies. But she should object to the substance of the policies, not to the fact that they were motivated somewhat by religion. After all, the next policy supported by a religious leader might involve something more palatable, like limiting the death penalty, protecting the environment, improving health care for the poor, or putting an end to an unjust war.

I suppose that the most persuasive reason for excluding religious opinions from politics might be that in the United States, as a practical matter, allowing religious voices into the public square basically means having to listen to people talk about what Jesus would do all the time. For those of us who are not Christians—say, those of us who were raised Jewish but were terrorized by Hebrew school teachers and are now atheists with a slight Taoist bent, for example—hearing about the New Testament all the time can be a drag. But I think non-Christians should see this as a challenge rather than a principled objection to talking about religion in public. Regardless of our beliefs—whether we are Christian, or believe in some other religion, or don't buy religion in the least—we should all seek to inject our voices into the public square, and we shouldn't shy away from making our most fundamental views known to our fellow citizens. If we try, we might be able to create a public square that is truly inclusive, one that is framed broadly enough to include everyone, no matter what we think or don't think.

Wouldn't it be great if instead of just hearing what the Christian view or the biblical view of this or that issue is all the time, we also learned about the Buddhist view and the Taoist view and the Hindu view and the Raelian view of the issue? What is the Rastafarian perspective on abortion rights, anyway? What do the Confucians think about social welfare policy? And beyond this, are there nonreligious groups with strong, principled, and novel beliefs we should be hearing from on these issues? Where are the people, for example, who think that promotion of pleasure should be a legitimate goal of public policy, and what do these neo-Epicureans think about the movement to legalize marijuana?

Now back to constitutional law. The *Grendel's Den* case, then, means that the government cannot delegate its decision-making authority to religious institutions. One of the main ideas behind this prohibition is that religious institutions may not always be impartial to those who do not share their beliefs. What should happen, then, if the power delegated by the government gives the religion the power to govern only itself and not others? Since the delegation does not affect nonbelievers, should it survive despite the rule set out in *Grendel's Den*? In a way, this is the question posed by a bizarre series of facts involving a community of Hasidic Jews in the incorporated village of Kiryas Joel in lower New York state.

The Satmar Hasidim are a small, extremely close-knit

group of super-duper conservative Jews who dress distinctively, raise large families, avoid television and many other adornments of modernity, and speak mostly Yiddish. Almost all the community's children attend private religious schools. About twenty years ago, however, some Satmar parents sent their children with disabilities to local public schools so the kids could receive the disability services they were entitled to under state and federal law. For anyone acquainted with public schools, or children in general, or the human race, it will come as no surprise to hear that this experiment turned out to be an unmitigated disaster. When it became clear that the children were suffering "panic, fear, and trauma" (to quote the Court opinion), the Satmar parents withdrew their kids and tried to find another solution.

The solution they settled on was convincing the state legislature to designate the village of Kiryas Joel as its own public school district, with its own school board and everything. When he signed the law, governor Mario Cuomo noted that the residents of the school district all happened to be "members of the same religious sect," but justified the law as a "good faith effort" to "solve [a] unique problem." The district started running a program for disabled Hasidic Jews that served about forty students, two-thirds of whom actually came from outside the village. A couple of taxpayers sued, saying this was an impermissible mingling of religion and government. In a case called *Board of Education of Kiryas Joel v. Grumet*, the Supreme Court agreed.

Although the Court believed the Kiryas Joel situation was "subtle," the majority held that it was governed by the principles set out in the *Grendel's Den* case. By "delegat[ing] its civic authority to a group chosen according to a religious criterion," the Court wrote, the state had created a "purposeful and forbidden fusion of governmental and religious functions" just like in *Grendel's Den*. The very act of giving official governmental power (the power to run a school district) to some group (the members of the village of Kiryas Joel) based on that group's religion (Hasidic Judaism) was unconstitutional.

In a separate concurrence, Justice O'Connor hinted at how the state could solve the problem. She explained that instead of writing a law just for the Hasidim of Kiryas Joel, New York could probably accommodate their needs by enacting a general and neutral law that would have the incidental benefit of allowing the village to operate its own public school district. For example, she said that the state could allow any existing village to create its own school district, or it could allow some subset of those villages to create their own districts, so long as the subset was defined by secular criteria (population, population density, square miles, income of residents, and so on) rather than religious criteria. The state and the village took Justice O'Connor up on her suggestion and tried several times to draft a sufficiently neutral law that would allow Kiryas Joel to have its own public school district. Twice the high court of New York struck down the state's attempts. Finally, in 1999, the state passed a law that was broad enough, and as a result, the village of Kiryas Joel has operated its own public school district ever since.

When you drive north up Route 44 in Monroe, New York, and cross over Seven Springs Road into Kiryas Joel, it's like you've landed on planet Neptune or something. All of a sudden, the single-family houses with big yards and tank-top-wearing women smoking cigarettes on front stoops disappear, replaced by an endless series of ugly, identical, four-story tan apartment buildings and a bunch of tractors and other construction vehicles that are paving the way for even more nondescript housing to hold the village's ever-burgeoning population. The roads are hilly and curvy and have names like Satmar Drive and Stropkov Court and Schunnemunk Road and Mordche Sher Boulevard. Because there are no signs pointing you where to go, and because all you see everywhere are these apartment buildings that all look the same, it's easy to get lost. Karen timed it once, and it took us eighteen minutes of driving around in circles like numskulls to get out of the village, which is a lot, considering the area of the village is only 1.1 square miles. Over eighteen thousand people live there, though, which means that in terms of population density, Kiryas Joel is more dense than almost every major city in the United States except New York. Boston, for example, is like a Nebraska cornfield compared to Kiryas Joel. And every single resident in the village, save for a very few live-in helpers and the like, are Satmars.

As you drive around, it's not just the weird houses that make the place look so different. For one thing, there's really no public space in the village. No parks or playgrounds. As a result, the kids have to play with their Big Wheels and scooters and wagons in the front yards of the apartment complexes. Since the toys are strewn willy-nilly all over the place, it looks like every house is having a yard sale. Also, there's a lot of Hebrew writing everywhere. Most striking, though, are the people. Everywhere you look, men walk around with beards and heavy black suits and the long side curls that male Hasidic Jews tend to cultivate beginning on their third birthday. Everyone wears a black hat. Some of the hats are furry, and a few of them, I swear, are as big as a wedding cake. Women aren't allowed to drive here, so they walk and push their strollers every which way up the big hills. They dress distinctively as well, with long dresses and long sleeves despite the hot weather. Married women wear head coverings—hats or scarves, mostly black, but some in varied colors that don't necessarily seem to match their dresses.

I came here to speak with Joel Petlin, the superintendent of the Kiryas Joel school district, to see what I could learn from him about the community and its reaction to all the litigation. I turned onto Forest Drive, the main drag of the village; drove past the impressive main synagogue on my left; and pulled into the parking lot of the central, and pretty much only, shopping center in town. The long two-story building had maybe ten shops on the ground floor. There were two groceries, a deli, a butcher, a toy shop (which looked like Grand Central Station with all of the women and little kids and strollers milling outside), a "dairy restaurant," and a couple of other things. The top floor had a few more shops and some administrative offices. I went in through the center door of the complex and up the stairs to Room 315. It turned out that the office of the Kiryas Joel public school district sat behind a single, windowless door the color of old calamine lotion. I pushed the door open and went inside.

After introducing myself to a woman working behind a thick glass partition like you might find at a sketchy check-cashing storefront in inner-city Detroit, I took a seat on one of the four brown chairs in the waiting room and watched the ladies behind the glass. They did not seem to be speaking English. Once in a while, a Satmar guy shuffled in and looked skeptically in my direction. The office itself seemed totally bland, the only decoration a tiny poster taped to the wall with two wine glasses and the words "Mazel Tov" on it.

Waiting for Petlin to come get me, I have to admit I was

pretty nervous. As I've suggested, I have some real ambivalence about being Jewish. When I was a kid, there was nothing I hated more than going to Hebrew school. The teachers were mean, and I didn't believe anything they said. I always wished I were at home playing soccer or kiss chase with the Christian kids. At the time, I remember I would say to my parents, "I hate Hebrew school. Hebrew school sucks." In response, they would generally say something like, "You may not like it now, but when you are older, you will appreciate what you learned, and you will be glad you went to Hebrew school. And also, watch your language." Now, of course, I am "older," but I don't appreciate what I learned, and I still think Hebrew school totally sucked.

I was always getting in trouble at Hebrew school for saying the wrong things. Once we were studying the holiday of Sukkoth, and I made fun of both the etrog *and* the lulav. The principal called my mother. Another time I asked why my Christian friends got to celebrate fun holidays featuring jolly fat men and cheery egg-toting bunnies while our repeated "celebrations" of various narrow escapes from complete extermination were marked by gloomy chanting, painful fasting, and other excruciating forms of psychic self-flagellation. This got me another phone call home. And then there was the whole "maybe the PLO isn't so bad after all" incident, which was really the last straw, from the temple's perspective.

Perhaps because of this experience, I have never felt comfortable with my own Jewishness, much less other people's. The idea of sitting one-on-one with a very serious Jew talking about things Jewish was, frankly, scaring the crap out of me. Of course I've had a million Jewish friends, like Miriam and Aaron, and even a couple of Orthodox ones, but I hadn't been so close to a serious Jew *acting in his capacity as a Jew* since Rabbi Morheim pushed me out of the way twenty-five years ago at my own bar mitzvah ceremony.

So I have to say, I was a little relieved when it turned out that Joel Petlin is not a Satmar. He's not even Hasidic. He is an Orthodox Jew, but he's not from Kiryas Joel, and his beliefs and practices differ a lot from the Satmar. He put me at ease immediately. He was wearing a yarmulke, but other than that pretty much looked like me, though with a better tie. He seemed like someone who would have been fun to have a beer with, if he hadn't made it so clear that he was a Yankees fan.

Petlin told me how he had come to Kiryas Joel as a lawyer for the school district just a few years out of law school and a couple of years before the case made it to the Supreme Court. Mementos from the case were all around. A drawing of the oral argument was taped to the wall; he pointed out an entire filing cabinet devoted to the various stages of the litigation. A sign on his door, though, read "Educate more, litigate less," or something like that, which seemed like a pretty apt sentiment.

Now I feel the need to point out that the whole time since I left our hotel, I had been feeling like a complete doofus because I was wearing a brown beach hat with my Brooks Brothers suit and Italian shoes. I don't own a yarmulke, so when it came time to go to Kiryas Joel, and I realized that it was probably the respectful thing to do to wear something on my head, the only thing I had was this one brown beach hat—the kind with a big, droopy brim, spotted with sand and salt water and other remnants of beach visits gone by. It made me look like a total moron, but I figured it was better to look like a moron than to offend the people in the community, particularly the guy I was going to interview. This was bad enough, but then when it turned out that Petlin was a totally regular guy and was wearing just a yarmulke rather than the whole Satmar getup, I kept wondering to myself whether I should ask if it was okay to take off the hat, or whether maybe I should just take it off, or point to it and make a joke, or what. Would he be offended if I took it off? Was I offending him keeping it on? I had no idea, so ultimately I decided to forget about it, which was difficult because, after all, *I was wearing a beach hat with my suit and tie!*

I talked with Petlin about the community and his school district and the case for a good while. I was curious about whether a non-Satmar could live in Kiryas Joel and feel comfortable there, so I asked him about it. "This is still America," he said. "If you wanted to, you could move here." But, he added, "what would be the advantage?" He explained that the cultures are so different, and there are so many local ordinances restricting things like television antennae and swimming pools, that it would be pretty difficult for a non-Satmar to feel comfortable living there.

According to Petlin, the Kiryas Joel community had been very upset about how the Court's decision came out. The residents feared they would have to close their public schools and send their kids with special needs back to the other public schools in the area. He relayed a couple of the horror stories that had come out during the case about what happened in those schools. One Hasidic child was dressed up by her teachers as Rudolph the Red-Nosed Reindeer for a school performance. Not cool. Another was taken to McDonald's, which, for those readers who are not completely familiar with all of the details of keeping kosher, does not really cut the mustard with Orthodox Jews. When I raised the suggestion, made by a few of the justices, that the whole problem could have been solved if only the non-Satmars could have gotten a little sensitivity training, it looked like he was working hard not to cackle. Instead, he smiled faintly and said this was just "not realistic."

I pressed him a little bit, asking whether the Court's decision might have been a good thing for Jews. If the case had come out the other way, what would stop southern states, for example, from handing over governmental functions to entirely Christian communities? He seemed unimpressed with that scenario and claimed that the "balkanization fear was theoretical" because Kiryas Joel raised a totally unique situation. If I were a clever interviewer, maybe I would have figured out how to get him to say something I could have pounced on, but I'm not. I am about as good at interviewing as I am at using the "Socratic method" in the law school classroom, where the professor is supposed to lead the students toward understanding some point through a series of subtle questions. The best I can do there is to repeatedly ask "ARE YOU SURE?" really loudly in response to some student's answer, but this would have been a really strange thing to do in Petlin's small, windowless office with only the two of us present, so I just jotted down his answer and moved on.*

I wanted to hear what he thought about the hostility that nearby communities feel toward Kiryas Joel. He suggested that this has more to do with land use issues than the public school district and is largely rooted in anti-Semitism. The prejudice point is certainly a big part of it. A quick look at the comments people post online whenever the local paper publishes a story about Kiryas Joel confirms this. One says, "If they would stop interbreeding they wouldn't have so many handicapped kids and need

---

*It's a pretty strange thing to do in the classroom, too, by the way.

a larger rehabilitation center. How long before there's a whole genetic pool of deformed aliens?" Another genius writes, "Why don't they go out to some deserted island someplace where they can overbreed at will. Put the overflow on sampans in the ocean. Typhoon? So solly."

On the other hand, the land use issues seem like a legitimate concern. Because the Satmars believe in having big families (many have six or more kids; Petlin said some have as many as fifteen) and because they live close together, their community looks completely different from its surroundings, from a purely architectural, density, and open space perspective. It seems normal that people who live in the area because they like grass, trees, and running around with the wind blowing through their hair might be worried about the growing size of Kiryas Joel. I wouldn't want to live near these hideous apartment buildings if they were filled with Playboy Bunnies and generous pastry chefs. I raised this with Petlin, and he answered by saying that the village exemplifies the currently hot idea of environmentally friendly "smart growth," which seems like an ingenious response until you realize that having six or eight or fifteen kids per family is not really consistent with the concept.

So did the Supreme Court get this case right? Justice Scalia mocked the majority in his ~~maniacal rant~~ dissent when he wrote that the Grand Rebbe Joel Teitelbaum, the founder of the Satmar, "would be astounded to learn that after escaping brutal persecution and coming to America with the modest hope of religious toleration for their ascetic form of Judaism, the Satmar had become so powerful, so closely allied with Mammon, as to have become an 'establishment' of the Empire State."

Scalia's snide and uncharitable beside-the-point observation notwithstanding, I think the Court's decision was correct, although it was surely a very close case. As in *Grendel's Den*, the Kiryas Joel arrangement involved the delegation of core governmental power to a religious group. In this sense, the case was just like *Grendel's*, except maybe a little worse, if you think that the power to manage a school district is more substantial than the power to veto nearby liquor licenses.

Of course, the cases are different in the way I mentioned earlier. Here, the students within the district were all members of the same religious faith and likely wouldn't have suffered because of the arrangement. Should this matter? During the many years I've taught this case, I always assumed that some non-Satmar families might reasonably want to move to Kiryas Joel, perhaps because it is an affordable suburb within commuting distance of Manhattan or because of the nearby scenery or even because the strongly religious character of the community makes it a safe place to raise a family. If this were true, then the premise of the distinction—that the only ones affected by the arrangement are Satmars—would collapse. After visiting Kiryas Joel, though, I've decided this is wrong. Nobody who is not a Satmar would want to live there. Petlin is right. The place is so comprehensively tailored to a specific set of incredibly unique religious beliefs that nobody who does not share those beliefs could possibly feel comfortable living there.

So why not allow the state to directly give this religious group the authority to run its own school district? Admittedly, the specific facts of the case were pretty unique, and the community's situation was compelling, especially since the kids who needed help were suffering from various disabilities. But when the Supreme Court decides cases, particularly constitutional ones, it tries to see beyond the specific controversy before it to understand the general principles involved and how those principles will affect future cases. If the Court had upheld this arrangement, it would have been saying that the government can delegate its core functions directly to religious groups so long as the affected community is homogeneous. I think that Petlin was too quick to dismiss the possible dangers of such a rule, and that the justices in the majority had it right when they worried about the stigma and animosity that could come of it.

What if other communities around the country started imitating the original arrangement between New York and Kiryas Joel? There are a lot of places in the country where the population is religiously homogeneous. Should the powerful religious institutions in these areas be allowed to manage all of the secular aspects of the community (law enforcement, education, health care, and so on) in addition to the religious ones? Should religious groups be able to basically secede from society and create their own little homogeneous communities from which nonbelievers feel excluded? Are these the kind of arrangements we want our constitutional law to encourage? Without the rule of *Kiryas Joel*, we might find ourselves living in a loose collection of religious fiefdoms instead of a nation. Does that sound like the kind of place you want to live in?

This isn't just idle speculation. Recently, the Roman Catholic founder of Domino's Pizza basically built a brand new town in Florida called Ave Maria, which is supposed to have as its centerpiece a Roman Catholic university and law school. Tom Monaghan, the pizza mogul, originally stated that town pharmacies wouldn't be allowed to sell contraception and that pornography would be banned within town limits. Under threat from the ACLU,

Monaghan backed down somewhat, but his original plans demonstrate that it's not crazy to think some religious groups might try to create little religious towns outside society's mainstream.

When I was in Miami investigating Santeria animal sacrifice (see Chapter 2), I took a day off to ride out to Ave Maria and have a look around. It's in the middle of nowhere. Actually, to get there, you first have to take Alligator Alley out to the middle of nowhere, and then get off and drive another fifteen miles even further into nowhere. For twenty minutes, the only evidence of human intervention in the surrounding landscape is the occasional sign announcing "Danger: Panther Crossing" and pointing out that only thirty panthers remain. The pressure is enormous. Who wants to take his eyes off the road for even a second and risk reducing the total panther population by 3 percent? After lots and lots of nothingness, however, all of a sudden you run into this little constellation of real estate developments and storefronts surrounding a gigantic church. This is Ave Maria.

I have to say that the town turned out to be a lot less interesting than I had hoped. It was around Christmas time, and I saw a constitutionally questionable nativity scene, as well as a just-plain-bizarre, forty-foot-high lit-up display of Santa Claus kneeling in front of baby Jesus, but for the most part the town did not seem hostile to non-Catholics. Even the holiday signs said things like "Season's Greetings" and "Happy Holidays" rather than "Merry Christmas." Still, though, I worry about the possibilities hinted at by Ave Maria. Perhaps the *Kiryas Joel* case, and the *Grendel's Den* one that came before it, can even be thanked for its relative mildness.

Now does anyone have a yarmulke I can borrow?

②

SANTERIA SKIRMISH

Destination South Florida

The last chapter explained how the First Amendment stops churches and other religious organizations from wielding actual government power. The next question is: how does the same amendment limit the power of the government to do things to religion? Imagine for a moment being arrested, fined, imprisoned, tortured, or even killed because of your religious beliefs. Fortunately, this kind of official government discrimination and punishment of religious belief or practice does not generally happen here in the United States. Sure, it has happened from time to time. Those who like to tout the glories of the early Republic, for example, tend not to mention that a few Quakers were hanged on the Boston Common in the mid-1600s. And we've certainly had our share of anti-Catholic and anti-Semitic and anti-Islamic periods too. Nonetheless, for the most part, we don't see all that much official religious discrimination in the United States these days.

Not so in other countries around the world. Every year the State Department issues a report on international religious freedom, singling out those countries that haven't quite recognized that religious freedom is a fundamen-

29

tal right. Those countries that have "engaged in or tolerated particularly severe violations of religious freedom" are designated as "countries of particular concern." The 2006 report identified Burma, China, Eritrea, Iran, North Korea, Saudi Arabia, Sudan, and Vietnam as falling into this category. The report also listed twelve other countries where serious religious freedom issues regularly come up, including Russia, Cuba, and Egypt. In many of these countries, it is simply not safe to hold certain beliefs. All over the world, governments arrest, detain, and punish religious leaders and religious believers for doing nothing more than taking their religion seriously.

As we in the United States engage in our perennial debates over such matters as whether the government may display a cross next to a smiling reindeer on public property or whether it's okay for the Senate to start every session off with a little prayer, we should probably remember that in the global scheme of things, our issues are a little, shall we say, "subtle." This isn't to say that they are not important. They are. In crucial ways, how we resolve these church/state controversies defines who we are as Americans and can have real effects on how religious believers and nonbelievers live their lives. But the bread-and-butter issues of U.S. constitutional law—such as what kind of funding government can provide to religious organizations, or whether a public high school can invite a rabbi to give its commencement address—are simply not the kind of life-and-death issues that so many people across the world have to face every day.

Intellectual and social historians could give us all sorts of answers as to why official religious discrimination is relatively uncommon in the United States, but surely we have the Constitution to thank, at least partially, for this happy state of affairs. A number of different provisions in the document protect us from such dastardly governmental badness, including the due process clause, which, if you're not suspected of being involved in terrorism, prevents the government from arbitrarily taking away your rights. Most obviously, the equal protection clause mandates, more or less, that the state treats us all the same. That clause, which says that "no State shall . . . deny to any person . . . the equal protection of the laws," would seem to be the one best suited for preventing official religious discrimination. But for whatever reason, the Supreme Court has said that the First Amendment's free exercise clause, which prohibits the government from "prohibiting the free exercise" of religion, is the primary source of the Constitution's anti-religious-discrimination proscription.

Every once in a while, even here in the United States, we do see a state or local government attempting to discriminate against some religion or other, generally one that is not particularly popular and engages in some practice that many people find gross or just plain weird. These attempts at discrimination don't usually resemble the crude "arrest the worshipper" or "torture the priest" versions practiced in some other countries; they tend to be somewhat more restrained and covert, even nefarious. Nonetheless, as I explain in this chapter about beards, bears, and my trip to the animal sacrifice capital of America, the courts have done a pretty good job of seeing these efforts for what they are and striking them down.

Back in 1978, you will recall, disco was all the rage; *Mork and Mindy* premiered to great acclaim on NBC; *The Deer Hunter* took home top honors at the Oscars; and Bucky Dent tragically hit the most unlikely home run in the history of baseball, propelling the Yankees over the Red Sox and into the playoffs.* Somewhat less memorably, perhaps, 1978 was also the year that the Minnesota legislature amended its Charitable Solicitation Act—a law that required most charitable organizations to disclose their activities—to exempt religious organizations receiving more than 50 percent of their total contributions from their members. That is, religious groups that relied more heavily on soliciting contributions from nonmembers (in other words, less established faiths) had to file an extensive and cumbersome report, while more long-standing religious groups that got most of their money from members did not. Why would Minnesota pass such a law? Comments from the legislators shed some light. "What you're trying to get at here is the people that are running around airports and running around streets and soliciting people," one said. According to another, the goal was to "deal with the religious organizations which are soliciting on the street and soliciting by direct mail, but who are not substantial religious institutions." A third Minnesotan got right to the point: "I'm not sure why we're so hot to regulate the Moonies anyway."

The Holy Spirit Association for the Unification of World Christianity, or Unification Church, was founded by the Reverend Sun Myung Moon in the mid-1950s in Seoul, South Korea. The church expanded quickly and established a not infinitesimal presence in the United States. Referred to by skeptics and detractors (but not by themselves) as "Moonies," Unificationists believe that through family and traditional "family values," God's power can

---

*I was at that game—I was nine—and I think my belief in God started dissipating about two seconds after the ball sailed over the Green Monster.

bring true love to the world (or something like that). Unificationists have a lot of unique beliefs and rituals, but they are best known for their mass wedding celebrations, in which thousands of men and women, some of whom have met only days before, are married in huge stadiums and other public venues. A lot of Americans, needless to say, find this ritual kind of weird.

Shortly after the registration law was amended, Minnesota's Commerce Department sent the Unification Church a notice ordering it to comply with the new law. The agency even included an "information sheet" and the "proper forms" for the church to fill out. The church had no interest in complying, however, and a group of followers filed suit in federal district court saying that the new law unconstitutionally discriminated against their religious organization.

The case went all the way to the Supreme Court, and as in so many 1970s Super Bowls, Minnesota lost. Noting that the First Amendment's "clearest command . . . is that one religious denomination cannot be officially preferred over another," the majority of justices thought that the 50 percent rule "sets up precisely the sort of official denominational preference that the Framers of the First Amendment forbade."

Again, it is important to note what the Minnesota law did and did not do. The key problem with the law was not simply that it burdened religion, but that it burdened some religions and not others. The analysis would have been completely different if the law had included all religious organizations in the set of charitable and other nonprofit groups that had to file the cumbersome disclosure forms. On the other hand, if the law had required only religious groups, and not other similarly situated charitable organizations, to file the forms, this too would have been problematic, because it would have singled out religion generally for special treatment. Okay, this is complicated, I realize, but it is important, so let's linger on it for a bit. Consider three different laws:

> Law 1 requires all charitable organizations, including all religious organizations, to file complicated and burdensome forms.

> Law 2 requires all religious organizations, but not other similarly situated charitable organizations, to file complicated and burdensome forms.

> Law 3 requires all charitable organizations, including religious organizations, to file complicated and burdensome forms, but religious organizations that get more than half of their contributions from members do not have to file these forms.

Law 1 is known as a neutral and generally applicable law, and as we will see in great detail in the next chapter, these laws are usually fine, even if they happen to place enormous burdens on religious groups or individuals. Laws 2 and 3, on the other hand, are both problematic because they discriminate against religion. Law 3 is the Minnesota law and is invalid because it discriminates against certain types of religious groups. Law 2 discriminates against religion as a whole and would also be unconstitutional. The key point is to recognize the distinction between generally applicable laws that happen to burden religion (usually okay) and laws that discriminate against either specific religions or religion generally (not okay).

Because this distinction is really important, and because these cases usually come up when the government tries to criminalize or penalize some action or behavior, it is probably worth running through the examples again, this time using a criminal prohibition. Imagine that as part of its idiotic war on drugs, the government decides that too many of its citizens are trying to get around antimarijuana laws by smoking catnip. Imagine also, however, that most of the people doing this are members of a new and genuine religious group called the Lebowskians who use the catnip in their religious ceremonies. The government could go about solving this "problem" in a variety of ways. Again, consider three laws:

Law 1: It shall be illegal to smoke catnip.

Law 2: It shall be illegal to smoke catnip for religious purposes.

Law 3: It shall be illegal for Lebowskians to smoke catnip.

As in the previous example, Law 1 is a neutral law of general applicability and is therefore probably okay, even though it might have the effect of making it impossible for Lebowskians and other religious groups who believe they must smoke catnip to practice their religion. Laws 2 and 3 are both unconstitutional, Law 2 for discriminating against religion generally, and Law 3 for discriminating specifically against Lebowskians.

Now of course, states are usually not so dumb as to enact a law that reads like Law 3, and so sometimes cases come up where it's kind of hard to tell if the state was really trying to discriminate against a specific religion. Let's assume that the Lebowskians always use big bongs to smoke their catnip. Let's also assume that one other group smokes catnip for religious purposes, except that group always uses hollowed-out apples instead of bongs. What should happen if the state enacted a law, call it Law 4, that says, "It shall be illegal to smoke catnip using big bongs"? The state justifies the law on the grounds that smoking out of bongs is more dangerous than using hollowed-out apples. The Lebowskians, however, say that the state is discriminating against them because they're the only religious group that uses big bongs. Now what happens?

The classic Supreme Court case dealing with such a scenario is the memorably named *Church of the Lukumi Babalu Aye, Inc. v. City of Hialeah*. Like so many religious believers before them, followers of the Santeria faith kill animals for sacred purposes. To show their devotion to certain important spirits known as "orishas," Santeria followers sacrifice animals such as chickens, ducks, sheep, goats, or turtles in religious ceremonies and then generally eat the sacrificed animals. Santeria developed in Cuba as a combination of traditional African religion and Catholicism back in the 1800s and then spread to the United States, particularly southern Florida, following the Cuban revolution in the early 1960s.

Most of the time, Santeria rituals take place in secret, but in the late 1980s Ernesto Pichardo, the leader of a prominent Santeria church in the city of Hialeah, Florida, decided to bring Santeria more into the open. He announced the opening of a church building in a prominent downtown location, and he went around getting the necessary permits and what have you so the church could start practicing its religion without sneaking around. As you might imagine, residents of the town (not to mention the neighborhood turtle population) flipped out. At a series of meetings, various city leaders expressed their disgust for the planned sacrifices. The police department chaplain called Santeria a sinful and foolish "abomination to the Lord." Santeria followers "are in violation of everything this country stands for," barked one council-man. The city council president asked, "What can we do to prevent the church from opening?"

The town couldn't prevent the church from opening, so instead it decided to craft a series of laws targeting the Santeria practice of animal sacrifice. The details are too complicated to explain fully here, but the main point is that without actually coming out and writing a law say-ing, "It shall be illegal to kill animals within the city lim-its, but only as part of a Santeria religious ceremony," the city pretty much made it illegal to kill animals within the city limits, but only as part of a Santeria religious ceremony. Want to exterminate the mice in your cup-board? Sure, go ahead. Slaughter chickens for food? No problem. Hunt deer? Boil a lobster? Knock yourself out. Just don't kill animals for religious purposes. Actually, you could kill animals in connection with your religion, so long as your religion wasn't Santeria. One of the laws en-acted by the city, for example, prohibited animal sacrifice but defined "sacrifice" as unnecessarily killing an animal in a ritual "not for the primary purpose of food consump-tion," which made it clear that the town was not banning kosher killings. In fact, a number of the ordinances passed by the city council were flawed in this way. The town wanted to ban religious animal killing, but only when done by Santeria followers and not when done by kosher Jews. The Court later found this to be pretty clear evidence that the laws discriminated against the followers of San-teria.

The other thing that bit the city in the ass was that under state law, it was not considered animal cruelty for greyhound owners to use live rabbits to train their dogs. Why did this matter? One thing the city did was to pass a law adding to the penalties for anyone violating the state's animal cruelty laws within city limits. In other words, if it would have cost you a fifty-dollar fine for doing something bad to a hamster in Fort Lauderdale, maybe you would have had to pay a thousand dollars or go to jail for doing the same thing in Hialeah. To make sure this law would serve its purposes, the city asked the state's attorney general whether Florida's animal cruelty law would prohibit religious animal sacrifices. The attorney general said yes, pointing out that such a sacrifice would be "unnecessary" because it would not be "in any sense beneficial or useful to the person killing the animal." But a few years earlier, a Florida appeals court had held that using live rabbits to train greyhounds was not "unnecessary" under the same statute.

So basically the government was saying that killing rabbits to train racing dogs was more important than killing animals as part of a religious ceremony. To see why the Supreme Court might have found this problematic, consider this account from the greyhound case of how trainers used these live rabbits:

> To train the dogs, appellants engage in two training operations. In one, appellants release live rabbits in an enclosure from which they cannot escape. Greyhounds are then turned into the enclosure where they run the rabbits down and chew them to pieces. The other training operation consists of attaching live rabbits to mechanical lures. The lure and rabbit are then propelled around a racetrack with the dogs in hot pursuit with a mechanical device emitting a wailing sound. The testimony was that during the course of the trip the rabbit's eyes bulge and his mouth is open. The dogs are allowed to catch the rabbit and thereafter, if enough life is left in him, he is given another run around the track on the mechanical arm.

How could it be more unnecessary to sacrifice an animal as part of a ceremony that is central to your entire world view than to do this? Especially since the Santeria followers (usually) used a relatively quick and humane method of killing their animals? For the Court, this discrepancy showed that the city was not really concerned with protecting animals, but rather just wanted to stop the Santeria rituals. "[The city's] application of the ordinance's test of necessity devalues religious reasons for killing by judging them to be of lesser import than nonreligious reasons," said the Court. "Thus, religious practice is being singled out for discriminatory treatment." Or to put it another way, by targeting the Santeria faith, the Hialeah laws were neither neutral nor generally applicable, and they were therefore unconstitutional.

In early December, with a bitter chill making its cruel return to the northeast air, I made a pretty significant sacrifice of my own and bought a plane ticket for south Florida. What I originally wanted to find out was whether the Supreme Court's decision had really affected the communities in and around Miami. How often did the local Santeria church sacrifice animals, and what kind? Were the streets littered with goat carcasses and turtle carapaces? Did the majority of the townspeople hold a grudge against the Santeria followers, or vice versa?

In preparing for my trip, however, I learned about a shocking event that had occurred in Miami just months earlier. A group of Santeria adherents had been sacrificing some animals (forty-four chickens and some goats) as part of a ceremony in a house in Coral Gables, one of Miami's most ritzy areas, when a swarm of police officers descended on the house with guns drawn and stopped the ceremony. Only after keeping the twenty Santeria faithful (including children and old people) holed up in the house like a bunch of criminals for hours did the cops finally realize that they couldn't arrest anyone for performing a religious ceremony. So remember all that stuff I said before about there not being any actual official religious discrimination or hostility in the United States? Well, scratch that.

Ernesto Pichardo wasn't at the Coral Gables house that day, but as the leader of Miami's Santeria community, he had plenty to say about it, both in the press and to me, when we met in front of a botanica somewhere out in west Miami. A botanica is a store that sells items used in religious ceremonies, both Santeria and otherwise, and Pichardo wanted us to meet there because he claims that the federal government has recently started targeting these places because of hostility to his faith. While I waited for Pichardo to finish up a cigarette outside, I wandered around the store and looked at the vats of shells and plants and bottles of "Dragon Blood" bath/floor wash and big statues of maybe Catholic saints with cigars and other offerings lying in front of them. I tried my best to ignore the squawking and other animal noises coming from behind the door in the back. A few minutes later Pichardo came in. He was wearing brown khakis and a Miami-ish turquoisey button-down shirt and a cool pair of glasses, and as he started talking angrily about the feds, I got my first taste of the guy's passion and energy for his cause. He's short and compact, but he's not someone you want to mess with. I cringe typing it, but I feel the obligation to describe him as "fiery."

"The feds come in here, they say what's this, what's that?" Pichardo blurted, pointing to the various buckets of what look like bulbs and roots. "They ask for import records on the agricultural items, and they take them away. They say, 'I think it's imported.' I say, 'Well, I think you're stupid, where does that leave us?'"

I don't think I'm much cut out for journalism, because I'm drawn to everyone I meet on my journey. I'm sure I should have been more skeptical, but I was taken in immediately by Pichardo's manner. He showed me around the shop a little more, and then we went next door to talk over coffee.

We chatted for a good while about the history of the *Lukumi Babalu Aye* case. Pichardo said that the plan had been to open a museum in Hialeah dedicated to education about Santeria, not to sacrificing animals, which was going to be done elsewhere. Educating people about Santeria has been an ongoing project of Pichardo's; he used to train police officers about the faith, and he recently finished teaching a course on the subject at Florida International University. On the Friday before the building was set to open, Pichardo made an announcement about the building, and by Monday morning the community was already talking about how to close down the place. Pichardo was not surprised by the reaction, which he called "silly and predictable." He and the others involved in the decision had been thinking about opening a place for a dozen years, and they were quite familiar with the "rules of engagement" (a phrase Pichardo used repeatedly over the course of the day). They had strategies to deal with the media, the politicians, and even the electricity inspectors who tried to shut the building down because of alleged problems with the wiring of an air conditioning unit. "The air conditioning wasn't even attached to the wires," he pointed out, although the church did end up rewiring the entire building.

Pichardo and his lawyer were also quite prepared for

the legal battle they knew was coming. I asked if he had been surprised that the case went all the way to the Supreme Court, and he said no. "We created the case from day one to go to the Supreme Court. We had nothing to lose." Pichardo explained that they figured they wouldn't win at the trial court level, so they went to great lengths to get stuff into the record that would help them on appeal. Pichardo himself, for example, testified that Santeria was a religion rather than a cult. The legal team had identified a series of factors that appellate judges look to when deciding what counts as a "religion," and Pichardo provided testimony on each one of them. When I suggested that he was the model client, however, Pichardo scoffed. "None of this client bullshit," he said, pointing out that he was a full member of the legal team. He had to be part of all the decisions because he was the one who knew about the faith and because he was fighting a public relations war himself. He wasn't going to let the lawyers talk on his behalf, at least to the public. "I own the media," he told me. "Don't speak for me. That's best."

After about an hour and a half, we left the coffee shop, me in my rented Ford Focus and Pichardo in his sleek black Jaguar, and went to visit Jesus Suarez, the priest who was there when the cops burst into the house in Coral Gables. The day we visited happened to be the one day each year when Suarez celebrates the anniversary of becoming a priest, so when we arrived at his apartment in a very typical-looking complex, trays of food were being prepared for guests and Suarez himself was behind closed doors ritually washing various parts of his body.

The apartment may have seemed typical on the outside, but the inside was a whole different story. As Pichardo put it, "You've got a religious museum in here, man." There were religious paintings on the walls and a candlelit shrine in a corner and a bunch of spiritual dolls on a side table. A painting of a Santeria ceremony, complete with a dead goat oozing blood from its neck, occupied the place of honor on the wall over the couch. Suarez used to study with a Hindu guru, and he had built a sort of a mini-shrine to the guy on one of the other living room walls. Pichardo kept pointing out, rightly I think, that the guru looked just like Al Sharpton. A machete was leaning against the wall right next to the front door. An offering of chicken feet and the internal organs of a variety of animals that would soon be cooked for dinner had been arranged in a bowl on the kitchen counter. I wondered who the neighbors were. What did they think about the machete-wielding family next door? And what did the machete owners think about them?

Pichardo was demonstrating how to crack open a coconut (tap it quickly, firmly, and repeatedly with a hammer at an angle around the top of the fruit, which ideally you will have kept in the freezer for a while) when Suarez appeared, big and jolly and all dressed in priestly white. For some reason there was a little Pillsbury Doughboy doll in the kitchen, and Suarez picked it up and declared they were twins. There was some joking about how maybe they should pray to the Doughboy—for prosperity and merriment, and presumably flaky crescent rolls as well. As much as I liked Pichardo, I realized quickly that I would like Suarez even more. He was smoking with one of those metal cigarette holders that I sort of knew existed but had never actually seen before. He swore freely but also greeted people as "sweetie." He immediately started talking about his pants and mentioned that in Miami it's really hard to find any white pants in the stores because everyone wants them. He said he was lucky to pick up the pair of Dickies he was wearing at a Walmart or something, and then he once again disappeared to do some priestly duties in the back room where he keeps the shrine to his orisha.

While we were alone in the living room, Pichardo explained to me that the anniversary day is like an open house when visitors come and socialize and give respect to the priest and his orisha, a day of merriment rather than anything too serious. I asked him what a priest does in the faith, and he explained that the priest is a respected member of the community, but not an "above everyone holy man of the cloth" kind of guy. He said that when the priest is actually ordained, he or she has to stay in a room for seven days, but he was quick to point out that the priest can have visitors. His point was to dispel the stereotype that Santeria is all about secrecy.

Pichardo can be intimidating. Talking about his experiences with discrimination, he occasionally got so worked up and loud and almost menacing that I had to silently reassure myself that he wasn't angry (I didn't think) at me and that I shouldn't worry that he was going to use his martial arts ability to break my skull. We were having one of these moments as he was telling me about a memorable encounter with an anthropologist in the 1970s, when suddenly from the back room came a burst of chanting and banging and other sounds of worship. Pichardo stood up and motioned for me to do the same. Pichardo's wife came into the living room, put some chalk on both of our foreheads, and then returned to the back room. We sat down a minute later when the chanting stopped and continued our discussion as if nothing had happened. Stuff like this happened all afternoon.

Occasionally I found that I had no idea what Pichardo was talking about. He's an intellectual, and at times talking to him was like reading a book in a foreign language. At one point, he was saying something about "false premises" and the "rules of engagement" and the "frame of study" and I wrote in my notes, "Am I Stroking Out?" because I was afraid maybe I was losing my mind. Then Pichardo started talking about the Holocaust, and I got even more confused.

Though he had a lot of friends to talk to and a lot of religious duties to attend to, Suarez kindly made time to talk to me about the Coral Gables incident. According to him, they had been doing a "higher initiation" when a neighbor called the police and reported that there was some animal killing going on next door. Both he and Pichardo are convinced from listening to the 911 tapes that the police knew they were getting involved in a religious ceremony when they headed out to the Coral Gables address. Suarez said that at least twenty cops showed up, which may or may not have included the SWAT team and the chopper flying around overhead. The media, too, swarmed all over the neighborhood, and the streets were closed off to other traffic.

Suarez says he was working in the "ritual room" when the police came in with guns drawn and demanded that everyone put his or her hands in the air. A guy who was relatively new to the country screamed back in Spanish, "Don't shoot . . . we're doing Santeria," and Suarez had to tell the guy (and his son) not to move or the police would indeed shoot him. The cops moved them out of the house at gunpoint and onto the porch. Suarez told the police that they were making a big mistake, because it was a religious ceremony, and he produced a church identification card to prove it. According to Suarez, the card got passed around to every cop at the scene for inspection. The police finally left a couple of hours later, but only after taking pictures of everything in the house, moving everything around, and otherwise violating the community's sacred space. They did not, however, offer any apology for what happened. As Suarez put it, "Not even 'Here's a piece of paper, wipe your ass with it.'" Instead, the police simply told them they had permission to continue their ritual. "Gee," said Suarez. "Thanks for the privilege."

Obviously, Suarez and Pichardo were angry with the police, but they had it in for the media as well, who they believe reported the story as being about animal sacrifice rather than the civil rights of the Santeria followers. As Pichardo put it, "The news is the injury, the victimization; why is animal cruelty worse than cops raiding little kids at gunpoint?" I asked why the media reported it that way, and Suarez blurted out, "Because they're a bunch of fascists." Pichardo quickly took a milder tack, saying that there's a new media crew in town that thinks "if it's not Christian, it's voodoo." He pronounced it "voooodoooo." He said that the media treats them differently because, as a Catholic reporter once said to him, they look "weird." "This," Pichardo pointed out, "from a guy who wears a crucifix, a dead guy on a cross, around his neck."

I asked Suarez whether he had experienced anything like the Coral Gables incident before, and he said no, that this was the "only time in my frickin' life." He said he couldn't sleep for four days, that he had dreams about "Nazis and all kinds of shit." He still couldn't believe it happened. "Politically, it makes you feel like a big nothing," he said. "We just want to get on with life—pay rent, go grocery shopping, buy Dickies. Who has time for this?" I asked whether he's pessimistic about the future, and he said he feels like the government doesn't think he's a person who deserves rights in this country. Pichardo was also pessimistic. "You sort of have to be," he said.

We started talking about animal sacrifice itself. Pichardo made the interesting point that it's a Hispanic cultural norm to have dead animals hanging around in food stores. In the United States, though, we have a sanitized idea of animals, and we don't want to know where our food really comes from. Several times over the course of the afternoon, Pichardo and Suarez questioned the distinction between animal sacrifice (not okay) and slaughtering cows to make hamburgers for McDonald's and Burger King (somehow okay). In any event, Pichardo said, Catholics engage in ritual cannibalism every week. They spend their lives eating Jesus's flesh and blood. "They're not weird, though," he scoffed.

It had been a long afternoon, but I was delighted when at the end, Suarez invited me to take a look at the orisha room where he and his friends had been worshipping all day. I won't make any attempt to describe it, except to say that it was impressive and interesting and very blue (the orisha, I believe, is connected to the ocean), and it was an honor to get to see it. When I emerged from the room, though, a woman who had been cooking all day and who introduced herself as a priest and called me "Boston" and was extremely tall (in my memory she appears to be about eight feet tall) kind of waylaid me and loomed over me and told me that although I didn't recognize it now, this had been a very special day for me. She spoke to me for a while, but although I wish I could recall what she said, the whole experience was so unnerving that all I really remember about it is sweating a lot and twitching. In that way, it was a lot like my wedding.

People who want to regulate Santeria often say that laws are needed to stop the disposal of animal carcasses on street corners and in parks and other public places. This was one of the arguments made during the Supreme Court litigation in the nineties, and you still hear it today. Pichardo has had to respond to the allegations so many times, he can barely stand it anymore. When I mentioned the issue, he went into a tirade in which he threw out about four or five separate compelling counterarguments in the space of a few minutes. According to Pichardo, usually the sacrificed animals are eaten; he pointed to the tray of cooked goat on the counter as evidence. In some cases, however, after rituals that involve transferring some badness from a human to an animal, the entire animal must be disposed of. But the religion requires that the animal be disposed somewhere where it can decay in its "natural course," like near a sacred tree in a forest or something. The religion never requires that anyone dump a goat on a lawn or a sidewalk. If it did, Pichardo pointed out (noting that a lot of people practice Santeria in Miami), you wouldn't be able to walk anywhere in Miami without tripping over a goat every five minutes. Pichardo admitted that once in a while, some irresponsible member of the community might dispose of an animal in the wrong way, but disposal in a public area is already illegal. Moreover, nobody would be more angry with a member of the faith who did this than Pichardo himself, since to him, the disposal would be not only a public health hazard and a legal violation, but a violation of the sacred requirements of his religion as well.

Before arriving in Miami, I had some vague idea that I would walk around the city and see if I found any animal carcasses lying around. The notion that anyone would "walk around Miami," however, turned out to be ludicrous, since the city is gargantuan and spread out and hot, and also because nobody even walks to the corner grocery store in Miami, much less all around the city. Instead, I decided to pick a place where there had been allegations of improper disposal and see if I could find anything.

In reading about the Coral Gables incident in the *Miami New Times*, I came across an article reporting that a Coral Gables woman had complained to city hall that she had found a "headless chicken and other religious relics" in Pinewood Cemetery, a small historic graveyard in the southern part of her neighborhood. I would tell you her name, but she wouldn't give it to the newspaper because she was afraid of being cursed. "I really believe in their hexes," she told the paper, "and I don't want them after me."

So one afternoon I took a walk around Pinewood Cemetery in search of dead animals. The cemetery itself is a very creepy place, even if you're not worrying about finding a rotting goat. It's kind of like a little jungle of lush trees and twisted branches, with an occasional gravestone put in here and there. For Miami, it's really old, which means that it was established sometime around 1900. For about half an hour, I walked around the little place with a long stick in my hand, which I used to push around bushes and rocks and stuff in search of anything that might have resembled a dead chicken. I saw a lot of little lizards and some cool headstones, but I'm pretty sure I didn't see any dead animals. There was one thing near a brick wall that at first I thought maybe looked a tiny bit like a chicken—it was kind of lumpy and appeared to have some feathery-looking things on it—but after poking it for a while with my stick and turning it over and even reluctantly looking at it real close, I'm pretty sure it wasn't a chicken. It may have been a moldy cantaloupe.

Getting back to the law, then, remember that the key question is whether the challenged law is neutral and generally applicable. If the law is neutral and generally applicable, then it's most likely going to be upheld, even if it happens to harm religion. Otherwise, it will most likely be struck down. But how can you tell the difference? The Santeria case was pretty easy, because it was clear what was really going on there. A religious group announced it was going to do something that a lot of people found nasty, and so the city responded by trying to outlaw the nastiness. The town leaders came right out and called the group nasty, and the laws they passed went after just the specific nastiness they didn't like while leaving all sorts of similar nastiness untouched. The law was not neutral (it targeted Santeria followers), and it was not generally applicable (it only outlawed Santeria animal killing and not other kinds of animal killing).

Not all cases, however, are so easy. Sometimes the government will enact a law that seems applicable to everyone, but then it makes so many exceptions that the law is no longer generally applicable. So imagine if the Hialeah city council passed this statute:

Section 1: It shall be illegal to kill animals within the city limits.

Section 2: The prohibition set out in Section 1 of the statute shall not apply to hunting, fishing, pest control, euthanasia, kosher killing, or the slaughter of cute fluffy rabbits for the purpose of teaching dogs how to run faster.

See the problem? If you just looked at Section 1, you'd think the law is fine. Only when you look at the exceptions do you see that the law is not generally applicable. Again, though, this is not a hard case, because the exceptions (1) are so numerous, (2) specifically include one type of religious practice but not others, and (3) have that thing in there about the rabbits that makes it clear the city doesn't really care about protecting animals. But some cases are, in fact, hard. Going back to the catnip-smoking example, what would happen if this law came before Congress?

Law 5: It shall be illegal to smoke catnip; however, it shall not be illegal to smoke catnip for legitimate medical reasons under instructions from a licensed physician.

Assume for a moment that there might be some legitimate medical reason for doctors to prescribe catnip smoking to some patients. Assume also (and this might be harder to imagine) that the federal government is willing to let a tiny bit of compassion get in the way of its drug war and actually enacts this piece of proposed legislation. The Lebowskians appreciate the government's slight concession to human freedom, but they also think that by exempting medical use but not religious use of catnip, the government has crafted a law that is no longer generally applicable. Should they win? Has the government violated the free exercise clause by devaluing religious reasons for catnip use as compared to other kinds of uses? Does the law discriminate against religion?

The Supreme Court hasn't considered a case like this, but the lower federal courts have considered several. Two of the most influential decisions have come from the U.S. Court of Appeals for the Third Circuit, one of the federal courts right below the Supreme Court, which decides cases in Pennsylvania, New Jersey, Delaware, and, for some reason unknown to me, the Virgin Islands. I will refer to the two cases as the "beard case" and the "bear case," because they involve beards and bears, respectively.

Back in 1971 the police department of Newark, New Jersey, issued an order barring its officers from wearing beards. The idea was that to promote safety and morale, everyone on the force should look basically the same. Because some men, however, suffer from a serious skin condition, called *pseudofolliculitis barbae*, that makes shaving painful and debilitating (do a Google image search if you don't believe it), the department exempted those guys from the no-beard rule. For many years, the policy posed no legal problems. It might have been dumb, much like the Yankees' no-facial-hair policy, but nobody claimed it was unconstitutional. Then in the mid-1990s, two Sunni Muslim officers, who believed it was their religious obligation to grow beards, refused to follow the order. You'd think the police department would have just said "fine," but then again, if we didn't have unreasonable people in the world, we probably wouldn't have any interesting legal cases either. The department said "no way" and threatened to fire the two officers. "Zero tolerance for facial hair!" the Department proclaimed (except for mustaches and sideburns and people with certain medical conditions). Again, one might think the officers could get a break from their religious obligation if they were ordered by someone else to cut their beards, but alas, the Sunni faith was not so forgiving. According to an affidavit filed by a Sunni imam in the case, "a Sunni Muslim male will not be saved from this major sin because of an instruction of another." And so off to court everyone went.

Perhaps surprisingly, the Muslim officers won. The court said that, at least in this situation, if the city was going to make an exception for medical reasons, it had to make an exception for religious ones as well. The department tried to argue that a religious exemption would undermine its interest in having a "monolithic, highly disciplined force," but the three-judge panel was unimpressed. "We are at a loss to understand," wrote the court, "why religious exemptions threaten important city interests but medical exemptions do not." The court gave even shorter shrift to the borderline brain-dead alternative argument advanced by the city, which was that "other officers and citizens might have difficulty identifying a bearded officer as a genuine Newark police officer," thus posing safety problems. The judges were rightfully skeptical that the no-beard requirement had any relationship to public safety. As the court pointed out, people generally look to whether a person is *wearing a police uniform*, not whether he has a beard, when deciding whether that person is a police officer.

If you think that case was interesting, wait until you hear about the bear case. Most people in the world think that bears are a little scary, or maybe some mixture of cute and scary, but for the Lakota Indians, black bears are sacred creatures that protect the earth. When a guy named Blackhawk, who had been raised by the Lakotas, started seeing black bears in his dreams, tribal leaders decided that he had a special gift related to bears. Blackhawk bought two bears, which he named Timber and Tundra, and started performing religious ceremonies with the bears at his home in Pennsylvania. Native Americans from all over the country would come to take part in these ceremonies. Some thought Blackhawk was a holy man.

Then along came the decidedly unholy Pennsylvania Game Commission. Under Pennsylvania law, anyone who possessed "exotic wildlife," which was defined by the relevant statute as "all bears, coyotes, lions, tigers, leopards, jaguars, cheetahs, cougars, wolves and any crossbreed of these animals which have similar characteristics in appearance or features," had to get an annual permit at the price of fifty dollars. Blackhawk sought an exemption from having to get the permit, under a section of the statute that allowed the state to waive the permit requirement "where hardship or extraordinary circumstance warrants." After all, Blackhawk probably figured, a separate section of the law excluded zoos and circuses from having to obtain permits, so why should he have to get one? Apparently in dire need of Blackhawk's fifty bucks, the game commission denied him the waiver. Blackhawk refused to pay and then challenged the $6,442 fine that the commission imposed for his recalcitrance.

Once again, the government lost, because the court thought the exemptions for circuses and zoos showed that the state was discriminating against religion. If Pennsylvania wanted to exempt circuses and zoos from getting a permit, then it had to exempt owners who used their animals for religious reasons too. To put it another way, if a state wants to give financial benefits to shady showmen who train bears to ride bicycles and juggle beach balls, then by all means the state can do this. But it can't treat religious or sacred uses of bears as less important than those other lofty pursuits.

So the upshot of the bear and beard cases is that, in at least one part of the country, if the government sets up some legal requirement or prohibition and it makes an exemption for basically anything, it has to make a religious exemption as well. I said earlier that these cases were influential, to which you might ask why. After all, it's just one court governing a few states, and the Supreme Court could one day decide that the Third Circuit's approach to the question is incorrect. Well, this is true, but the decisions are quite carefully reasoned and, more importantly, written by Samuel Alito, who now sits on the Supreme Court. As I mentioned before, the Supreme Court hasn't taken up this "If there's an exception for one thing, does there have to be an exception for religion?" issue yet, but if it ever does, one could expect that Justice Alito will speak pretty powerfully about how it should be addressed.

That, then, is pretty much the current state of the law on religious discrimination. Now it's worth pausing for a bit to consider whether the law has developed the right way. Was the Santeria case decided correctly? How about the bear and the beard cases? My view is that while the beard case was really close, all three decisions were probably right.

We have to start with the premise that it is unconstitutional to discriminate against people because of their religious beliefs. If straight-out discrimination is unconstitutional, then it isn't much of a leap to agree that the Court rightly decided the Santeria case. The difference between passing a law saying that Santeria followers shall not be allowed to sacrifice animals as part of a religious ceremony and doing what Hialeah actually did is basically one of form rather than substance.

Now maybe you think that sacrificing animals is gross or weird. That's fine, but it's not the point. We all do weird and gross things that other people can't understand. You know you do. I know *I* do. I'll spare you most of them, but here are a few: I like to eat slaughtered chicken, cows, and pigs, often slathered in cheese sauce, even though I could get by just fine eating fruits and nuts and even though there are plenty of vegetarians and kosher Jews out there who think that my eating habits are weird and gross. To PETA's dismay, I wear a leather jacket sometimes, even though I'd probably look less like a pathetic middle-aged man trying to regain his lost youth if I would just wear a windbreaker from Lands' End. If a mouse finds its way into my apartment, I will stand on a desk and squeal and beg my wife to call the exterminator, even though the mouse is unlikely to eat me while I sleep. Hell, when I was in East Texas researching school prayer (see Chapter 7), I lost fifty bucks at the dog track, even though I myself think that dog racing is weird and gross (I did, however, resist buying a "Show Me the Bunny" T-shirt).

If the government wants to ban an activity that it finds immoral, unsafe, gross, or unpalatable, it can usually do so. But if the state makes such a choice, then it has to follow through and prohibit the thing in a comprehensive manner, not just when someone takes the action for religious reasons. So if the City of Hialeah had wanted to ban the killing of animals within city limits, it was free to do so. As a political matter, such a law would have been impossible to pass, because there are too many people out there like me who like cheeseburgers and are afraid of mice. But trying to get around this reality by banning only a certain type of religious killing of animals amounted to religious discrimination, and the Court's close examination of the city's laws rightfully smoked out the government's improper object.

The bear and beard cases are harder. In these cases, the government didn't target a particular religious group or act hostile to religion generally. Chances are, the Pennsylvania legislature never thought anyone would want to employ exotic animals in religious ceremonies when it decided to exempt circuses and zoos from its permit requirement. But even though Pennsylvania and Newark weren't nearly as mean as Hialeah, they nonetheless treated religious motivations as less important than other motivations. I think that Judge (now Justice) Alito and his brethren were right to call them on it. Whether you share this view or not, and whether you fully understand it or not, it is a plain fact that for many, many, many people, religion is among the most important things in their lives, perhaps the most important. Religion is a large part of who they are, gives them identity, provides them with meaning, and guides every aspect of their existence. Religion has played this role for zillions of people for zillions of years, and it still does, and whether you like it or not, it almost surely always will. By singling out religion for special treatment, the words of the First Amendment emphasize religion's unique importance. It makes sense for judges to interpret the amendment to make the government take religion as seriously as it takes its other interests.

This is not to say that I think there *always* needs to be a religious exemption if the government exempts something else. The bear case is pretty easy, because circuses and zoos, fun though they may be, are not as important as religion and certainly not *more* important. The beard case is harder, because the government should be able to treat at least some medical reasons as categorically different and more important than other types of reasons, including religious ones. If shaving were life threatening, for example, I think the Newark police department would have been safe exempting medical reasons for having beards but not religious ones. As it is, since the skin condition aggravated by shaving is debilitating but not devastating, religious reasons for not shaving should have also been exempted. But the case is certainly a close one and could have gone either way.

It is probably worth noting that the "if you make exceptions for other things, then you must make an exception for religion" approach also helps safeguard minority religious beliefs, those that are in greatest need of protection from democratic majorities. Notice that none of the cases

I've described involve any mainstream religious tradition. Christians do not bring these cases. They don't have to. Democracy is about majority rule, and majorities rarely vote to require themselves to do things they don't like. If Christian services all involved a sacred bear dance instead of that awkward thing where you have to shake hands with total strangers and say "May peace be with you," I'll bet that Pennsylvania would already have exempted religious bears from its permit requirement, or there wouldn't have been a permit requirement in the first place.

Also, Christian ceremonies would be more fun if they involved bears.

3

AMISH AGITATION

Destination the Cheese State

All this stuff in the last chapter about when a law counts as discrimination wouldn't matter so much if the Supreme Court didn't insist on minimizing the threat to religion posed by neutral general laws that happen to burden religious freedom. It's true that laws targeting religion for special negative treatment may seem particularly mean and offensive, but is there really any practical difference between a law that discriminates against a religion and a law that just happens to make practicing the religion impossible? What if Hialeah had banned all animal killing within city limits? What if the Newark police department had not made an exemption from its no-beard policy for medical reasons? Or if the Pennsylvania Game Commission hadn't exempted zoos and circuses from its exotic animal permit requirement? Would the Santeria adherents, Sunni officers, and Blackhawk really be any better off? The Santeria adherents wouldn't have been able to conduct their ceremonies; the two police officers would have lost their jobs or been condemned to hell; and Blackhawk would have had to put Tundra and Timber up for sale on eBay. Discriminatory or not, the laws would have prevented all of these believers from freely exercising their religion.

So can the government really do this? The answer is mostly yes. More specifically, the answer is that for many years the answer was yes, and then for about thirty years the answer was not really, then for a couple of years the answer was yes again, followed by a very short period of time when the answer was no before it became yes once more, becoming mostly yes instead of completely yes only very recently. In this chapter, I will recount this fascinating and ridiculous roller-coaster-ride story. Also, I will tell you about my conversation with a smoking Amish guy who was recovering from a motorcycle accident.

Before you can understand the story of the free exercise clause, though, we must make a quick detour through some general principles of constitutional law. Specifically, you need to know about the various levels of "scrutiny" that the Supreme Court applies to different kinds of laws. As I will explain, the Court applies different levels of scrutiny to different types of laws, and the Court's choice of which level of "scrutiny" to apply—whether it be "strict scrutiny," "intermediate scrutiny," or "rational basis scrutiny"—will generally have a big effect on whether the law survives judicial review.

One of the problems of making this detour, however, is that I hate the word "scrutiny" and can barely stand typing it. It sounds like a combination of "scrotum" and "mutiny" and should be retired from the English language immediately. In fact, I hate the word so much that in the first draft of this book, I replaced it every time it appeared with the word "fluffernutter," which of course is a word that seven-year-olds with Boston accents use to refer to a peanut butter and marshmallow creme sandwich and that is kind of funny to say and think about. Unfortunately, however, this gave my editor a pretty serious migraine, so for the time being anyway, we're stuck with the awful word "scrutiny."

In many areas of constitutional jurisprudence, the first question that the Court will ask when reviewing a challenged law is what level of scrutiny to apply. The two most important levels of scrutiny are strict and rational basis scrutiny. The Court reviews laws that allegedly infringe on our most basic and fundamental rights with strict scrutiny. For example, laws that discriminate on the basis of race get strict scrutiny, as do laws that regulate speech on the basis of the speech's message (such as "it shall be illegal to make pro-union speeches outside the factory" or "it shall be illegal to burn the American flag"). If the Court uses strict scrutiny, it will uphold the challenged law only if the government can show that the law serves a "compelling state interest" and is "narrowly tailored" to accomplish that interest. This is difficult to show. What this means is that if the Court applies strict scrutiny to a law, the law almost certainly will not survive. As my own constitutional law professor once famously put it, "Strict scrutiny is strict in theory but fatal in fact."

On the other hand, if the Court applies rational basis scrutiny, the law will survive if there is any rational basis whatsoever to support it. This is very lenient, and courts rarely strike down laws under this standard. All of your typical, garden-variety laws are subject to rational basis scrutiny. Perhaps most importantly, laws that simply regulate the economic activity of businesses to protect workers and promote safety and the like get this standard of review these days, though this wasn't always the case.

In between strict and rational basis scrutiny are a number of other levels of scrutiny. Most prominently, in the 1970s, the Court started applying "intermediate" scrutiny to laws that discriminate on the basis of gender. The idea was that discriminating on the basis of gender was bad, but not quite as bad as discriminating on the basis of race. Under intermediate scrutiny, a law will be upheld if the government can show that the law serves "important" (rather than "compelling") interests and that it is "reasonably" tailored (rather than "narrowly" tailored) to achieve those interests. In the wake of the gender decisions, the Court has applied intermediate scrutiny to other types of laws, such as those that regulate advertising. When a court applies intermediate scrutiny, it basically balances all of the interests and circumstances it can think of and decides however it feels like deciding. Sometimes laws survive intermediate scrutiny, and sometimes they don't.

Cynics who study the Court are prone to claim that this whole scrutiny thing is a bunch of horseshit. To some degree, they are certainly right. There is no scientific method for distinguishing intermediate scrutiny from rational basis scrutiny from strict scrutiny. On the other hand, the basic decision of whether a certain category of laws should get strict, intermediate, or rational basis scrutiny is an important one because it often determines what will happen to that category of laws. Laws that get strict scrutiny usually do not survive, while laws receiving rational basis scrutiny almost always survive. Laws getting intermediate scrutiny sometimes survive and sometimes do not.

The free exercise clause saga revolves around what level of scrutiny courts should apply to general and neutral laws that substantially burden somebody's religious practice.

In such a situation, the believer will generally sue to get an exemption from the law or policy that is burdening his or her religious practice. The scrutiny question is critical because if strict scrutiny applies to laws that burden religion, then the government will often have to grant these exemptions. On the other hand, if rational basis scrutiny applies, then the government will basically be able to deny the requests as it pleases.

The Court first considered this issue in 1878. The controversy back then was Mormon polygamy. Most Americans have always hated polygamists, and it has pretty much always been illegal to be one in the United States. Following the Civil War, Congress passed several laws outlawing polygamy, and in the mid-1870s, a test case was arranged between the U.S. government and a Mormon named George Reynolds who admitted to having several wives. The Mormons agreed to take part in the case because they wanted to prove that the law was unconstitutional.

The Mormons lost. The Court had not yet started talking about levels of scrutiny, so the opinion wasn't phrased in those terms, but the basic idea was that while the government may not infringe on religious "belief and opinions," it is free to prohibit those religious practices that it finds "subversive of good order." The Court was willing to assume that Reynolds believed he would face "damnation in the life to come" if he failed to marry more than one woman, but it wasn't moved by his plight. Rather, it found compelling the government's need for uniformity. Granting a religious exemption "would be to make the professed doctrines of religious belief superior to the law of the land, and in effect to permit every citizen to become a law unto himself," the Court wrote. "Government could exist only in name under such circumstances."

And so that's how the law remained for the next eighty-five years. The government was free to place enormous burdens on religion so long as it did so through general laws. That all changed, though, when Adell Sherbert, a South Carolina mill worker, finally convinced the Court, in the early sixties, to start applying strict scrutiny to laws burdening religion. Sherbert was a Seventh-day Adventist and so refused to work on Saturdays. For a couple of years, this was fine because her mill let her work five days a week. But when production increased, the mill told her she had to work on Saturdays as well. Sherbert refused and was fired. She tried to find a job at some other nearby mills but couldn't find one that would let her have Saturdays off. When she applied for unemployment compensation, the state wouldn't give it to her, because it said that she had turned down perfectly fine jobs without "good cause." The Supreme Court ruled in Sherbert's favor. It agreed with her that the state's ruling had burdened her religious practice because it made her "choose between following the precepts of her religion and forfeiting benefits, on the one hand, and abandoning one of the precepts of her religion in order to accept work, on the other hand." Then it ruled against South Carolina because the state could demonstrate no "compelling interest" to justify the burden.

The high-water mark for the free exercise clause came nine years later, when the Court held in *Wisconsin v. Yoder* that three Amish families could ignore Wisconsin's compulsory education law and keep their fifteen-year-olds home from school to work on their farms. Whenever people ask me to rank the top ten Supreme Court cases of all time, I always place this case pretty high up, because it's so interesting and the result is so correct, and because I have a weird fascination with the Amish people.

Although Wisconsin might not be the first state that comes to mind when you think of the Amish, quite a few of the technology-shunning, German-speaking, buggy-driving, mustache-rejecting, button-not-liking, quirky characters do indeed make their home in the Cheese State. In the early 1960s, a group of Amish who were living in northeastern Iowa left when the authorities there started basically chasing around Amish children whose parents refused to send them to public schools. Some of the fleeing families settled in the small town of New Glarus, Wisconsin, also known as America's "Little Switzerland," which must have been attractive to members of a religious group that can trace its origins back to the Swiss Anabaptists of the sixteenth century.

Before long, though, the Amish started running into trouble with the authorities in New Glarus. They clashed over a variety of issues, including whether Amish girls had to take gym class in the public schools, whether an Amish woman known for baking delicious pies and dinner rolls could operate a bakery out of her family's farmhouse, and whether Amish dairy barns had to comply with state sanitary regulations that might have required Amish farmers to use some frowned-upon technology. But the biggest dispute in New Glarus revolved around whether the Amish could take their kids out of school after the eighth grade. The Amish are okay with sending their kids to school for a while, but they think that after about age fourteen or fifteen, the teenagers should be working in the Amish community rather than learning too much in a classroom about worldly things like evolution and literary criticism and pre-calc.

Initially, the New Glarus authorities didn't think this was all that big a deal. What they were really worried about was losing public funds when the Amish moved their littler kids from public schools into newly established Amish schools. In the fall of 1968, the superintendent of the New

Glarus school system realized that he was going to lose over eighteen thousand dollars if the Amish had their own schools running by the beginning of the school year. He came up with the brilliant idea of asking the Amish to keep their kids in the public schools for a couple of weeks in September, just long enough for them to count for per-pupil public funding. The Amish, well known for their eagerness to pull financial scams in close cooperation with high government officials, politely declined.* The superintendent got pissed off and charged three Amish families with taking their kids out of school altogether, contrary to Wisconsin's compulsory education laws. The Amish took the case all the way to the Supreme Court.

Once again, the Court applied strict scrutiny to the state's insistence on requiring the Amish teenagers to attend school. It agreed that the state's interest in universal compulsory education was pretty important, but it didn't think that requiring Amish kids to spend a couple more years in school was necessary to prepare these kids for adult life. As the justices put it:

> The evidence adduced by the Amish in this case is persuasively to the effect that an additional one or two years of formal high school for Amish children in place of their long-established program of informal vocational education would do little to serve those interests. . . . It is one thing to say that compulsory education for a year or two beyond the eighth grade may be necessary when its goal is the preparation of the child for life in modern society as

---

*Since the Amish might not be much for sarcasm either, I'll just point out here, in the interest of avoiding any sort of misunderstanding, that the "eagerness to pull financial scams in close cooperation with high government officials" thing was not meant seriously.

the majority live, but it is quite another if the goal of education be viewed as the preparation of the child for life in the separated agrarian community that is the keystone of the Amish faith.

In other words, Wisconsin lost because it could not prove that requiring Amish teenagers to attend school was necessary to further a compelling interest, and it thus could not fulfill the rigorous requirements of the strict scrutiny test.

There are a couple of quirky aspects of the *Yoder* case that are worth mentioning. For one thing, the opinion was very narrow, meaning that it was exceedingly focused on the specific attributes of the Amish, who the majority believed were highly responsible, law-abiding, admirable members of the community. This is nice for the Amish, but it means that it's not clear whether the justices would have come out the same way if the case involved a somewhat more sketchy religious group. The opinion is filled with gushing praise for the Amish, at one point going so far as saying they "singularly parallel and reflect many of the virtues of Jefferson's ideal of the 'sturdy yeoman' who would form the basis of what he considered as the ideal of a democratic society." This was just too much for Justice Douglas, the lone dissenter, who felt compelled to point out in a footnote that the Amish in fact drink a lot, commit suicide as much as anyone else in the country, and are preoccupied with "filthy stories" and "rowdyism."

The other quirky thing, probably a little more important, was what to do about the rights of the kids, as opposed to the rights of the parents. It was the parents who were suing to keep their kids out of the schools, not the kids themselves. What if the kids had *wanted* to go to high school? One of the kids—Frieda Yoder—actually testified at trial that she did not want to go to school, but the others didn't say one way or the other. For Justice Douglas, this made a big difference. Because he thought that the Amish children should have the right to choose to go to school in case they end up leaving the Amish community to become "a pianist or an astronaut or an oceanographer," he joined the Court's opinion only as it applied to Frieda Yoder and dissented as to Vernon Yutzy and Barbara Miller. Douglas's concern is a valid one, and if there had been some indication in the record that Vernon Yutzy and Barbara Miller were being forced to stay home from school against their wills, I think the case would have posed a really difficult question. As it was, though, since there was no evidence that Yutzy and Miller were dying to go to high school, the majority was probably right to skirt the issue.

I had this question about the Amish children in my mind when Karen, Walter, and I descended on southern Wisconsin in late August to see what I could learn about the people and places involved in *Yoder*. We showed up at the tail end of a series of torrential rainstorms that had turned several Wisconsin counties into mush. In our rented Chrysler, we made the seventeen-hour drive from Milwaukee to New Glarus, which sits in northern Green County, about one hundred miles from the Milwaukee airport. Okay, so it didn't take seventeen hours, but it sort of felt like it. For one thing, drivers in Wisconsin go slowly. Really slowly. Karen—who herself hails from the Midwest—explained to me the concept of the "Wisconsin roadblock," which occurs when two cars, each going about forty-five miles an hour, take up both of the lanes ahead of you. This happened a lot. The other problem was that once we got off the main road and started taking weird windy country roads, like County Highway D and Local Rustic Road PB and Dirty Ditch with Lots of Rocks on It QL, we got lost a lot. For instance, without knowing it until we passed the Mount Horeb junior varsity football team's afternoon practice for a second time, we once actually made a twenty-five-mile circle on these crazy roads that added something like three hours to the trip.

I shouldn't be so hard on Wisconsin, though. The state is beautiful, in a bucolic way that is quite a shock to someone from the city. It looks exactly like the idealized picture of farmland you might find in a television show or on a jigsaw puzzle. Imagine an undulating green landscape of windswept grass and cornfields, punctuated here and there by an imposing red barn next to a towering gray silo, black-and-white cows munching away on the roadside, dappled horses neighing about, and farm kitties scurrying across the road to avoid oncoming traffic.

We stayed at a great farmhouse about four miles outside of New Glarus, rented out to urban strangers by a terrific family that lives a couple minutes down the road on one of the handful of real dairy farms left around town. About two thousand people live in the little village, which is indeed decked out all Swiss-like. You can tour an outside replica of a classic Swiss village. The bells on the prominent Swiss Church of Christ on the corner of Railroad and Fourth streets (or, as the signs say, the corner of Bahnhofstrasse and Engistrasse) ring out tunes like "Amazing Grace" for the entire town to hum along with. The restaurants serve dishes like Kalberwürst and Wienerschnitzel. And here and there you really do hear people speaking Swiss German, like the historic marker at the visitors' center claims.

That same marker also celebrates the town's important role in the state's cheese-making history. According to the sign, immigrants from the Swiss canton of Glarus arrived in 1848 and organized the town two years later. After that, things moved quickly: "New Glarus began to prosper; in 1851, the first store opened, in 1853 the first hotel, and in 1870 the first cheese factory." I actually shouted out "Yes!" into the chilly morning New Glarus air when I read that last part. Inside the center, I purchased, for three dollars, a little pamphlet on the history of New Glarus, written by a longtime resident named Millard Tschudy, which further outlines the town's cheesy history. Tschudy reports, for example, that in 1876 the cheese pioneer Nick Gerber operated two cheese factories in New Glarus, manufacturing almost 228,000 pounds of limburger cheese. In the next few years, limburger apparently became even more profitable in the area than swiss cheese, and so by 1879, three-fourths of the total "township cheese" (that's a direct quote, I swear) was limburger. Even now, all the limburger in the United States is manufactured in Green County. On our second day, I bought a hunk at the downtown cheese shop, and over the next twenty-four hours I ate about five cheese sandwiches, until I was finally pressured to throw the rest out when Walter asked why the car stunk so bad and Karen told him that "daddy likes to eat cheese that smells like feet."

On our first morning in New Glarus, I walked around the town by myself, looking for signs of the *Yoder* case. I realized, of course, that the town had lost, so I didn't anticipate that it would have built the village around the incident or anything. I wasn't expecting, for example, a thirty-foot statue of an Amish man thrusting his wide-brimmed straw hat triumphantly into the air while crushing a high school textbook under his boot. Still, I thought there might have been something. After all, this was the town where one of the biggest victories for religious freedom in the history of the country had its start. Maybe the town had put its pride aside and modestly commemorated the accomplishments of its courageous Amish citizens. Or maybe a private individual had put up a little celebratory plaque. At the very least, there would have to be some mention of the case, some evidence that this is where free exercise took a daring step forward. Wouldn't there?

It turns out that the citizens of New Glarus would probably commemorate the sinking of the *Lusitania* or the Battle of Bull Run before they would ever talk about the *Yoder* litigation. I visited both the tiny town library and the visitors' center, and nobody in those places knew what I was talking about when I asked if they had heard of *Yoder*. The woman working the visitors' center even looked sort of like she was going to call the cops, which I think she might have if I hadn't made such a quick exit after purchasing my copy of Tschudy's monograph. I read the little book over a cup of coffee, and although I came across references to a 1979 visit from a Swiss yodel club and the donation of a Swiss floral clock in 1964, there wasn't a mention of *Yoder* anywhere. I'm pretty sure you could walk the streets of the village until your feet fell off and still not find any trace of the famous case.

I have to admit I was disappointed. I'm not one of those law professors who thinks everything revolves around the law and can't stop talking about substantive due process and the incorporation controversy and Justice Powell's separate opinion in *Bakke* and on and on and on (there are people like this, believe me), but still, I guess I thought that a huge law and religion case that went all the way to the Supreme Court was worth at least a mention in the originating town's public life.

I wanted to talk to somebody in town who might know something about the case, so I got in touch with Nic Owen, the town administrator, and asked him whether there was a town historian or someone I could talk with. He put me in touch with Peter Etter, a German-born retired teacher and administrator who had been the superintendent of schools in New Glarus for twenty-one years, right after the guy who presided over the schools during the litigation. Etter is so famous around town that a statue of a cow named after him (it's called "Udderly Etter") stands in front of the elementary school. We talked on the phone and agreed to meet at a tavern called Puempel's to discuss the case.

Puempel's is a classic. Built in 1893, only twenty-three years after the town's first cheese factory was erected, the tavern stands in the middle of town, right next to the post office. Almost every time I went by, there was a group of people in front, often chatting in German. The bartender —at least the one I saw—is Swiss. There are ashtrays on the tables and smoke in the air, just as there should be in a bar (I'm kind of a nut-job libertarian on this point, I have to admit). A sign on each table advertises cheese sandwiches—your choice of swiss, brick, cheddar, or limburger—for $3.75. Awesome New Glarus beer, available only in Wisconsin and just about worth the trip out there all by itself, is on tap. The ceiling looks like it's twenty feet high, and for some reason I never figured out, there are dollar bills tacked to it. On the walls, enormous painted murals from 1913 depict the small village in Switzerland where Mrs. Puempel was born and a scene showing Andreas Hofer, the William Tell of Austria, being taken away by Napoleon's troops to be executed. Since nothing makes me thirstier than looking at a man about to die, I ordered up a pint of New Glarus Spotted Cow and waited for Etter to arrive.

Etter is a big man, loud and gregarious, friendly and

forthcoming. He was wearing a badge identifying him as a volunteer tour guide at the Swiss Village, and we had to talk fast, since his next tour was coming up quickly. He knew everyone at the bar and spoke to most of them in German. At one point, an ex-student came into the bar and joked that Etter must be getting old if historians were coming out to talk with him. Etter took this in stride, but when the student insisted that "BMW" stands for "British Motor Works" instead of "Bavarian Motor Works," Etter jumped out of his chair and practically tackled the guy. It was all in fun, of course, but it proved impossible to explain this with any success to the miniature dachshund that was sitting in the lap of a customer at the bar and went berserk for about five minutes at what the dog was convinced was an honest-to-goodness bar fight.

I asked Etter why there is no evidence of the case to be found anywhere in the town. His answer did not surprise me. "They don't make a big deal of the case because it looks negative for the town, that they were forcing the Amish to go to school." He told me that in Germany, only a small percentage of students go to academic high school. His point, I think, was that advertising the town's actions would look particularly bad to the German and Swiss tourists who regularly come to visit the town. On the other hand, he did say that it really wasn't the town's fault; after all, the village was just enforcing the state's compulsory education laws, which Etter clearly thinks are idiotic. "Yahoos" was how he described the state legislators who make policy for local schools boards to follow. He said he knew Russ Monroe, the superintendent who went after the Amish, and that Monroe's explanation for what he did was simply that he was doing his job. When I asked Etter what he would have done if he had been in Monroe's shoes, however, he said he probably would have "looked the other way," and I believe him. The local/state relationship somehow had not previously occurred to me, and after we spoke I wondered whether the town could embrace the religious freedom side of *Yoder* by spinning its involvement as merely carrying out the state's dumb rules. Why not? What do you say, New Glarus?

Perhaps you're wondering why the Amish themselves haven't commemorated the victory in New Glarus. There's a simple answer to the question, and a more complicated one. The simple answer is that no Amish live there anymore. Well, that's not exactly true. Although almost all the Amish moved out of town shortly after *Yoder* was decided, one Amish family remained in New Glarus at the time I was there. Luckily for me, the mother-in-law of one of the daughters of the woman who rented us the farmhouse happened to know Jay Kramer and his two sisters. She kindly asked Kramer if he would be willing to talk to me, and since he was laid up in the house recovering from a motorcycle accident, he agreed that she could give me his cell phone number.

So now you're probably thinking, what is an Amish guy doing with a motorcycle and a cell phone? What are you, the Amish police? One thing I learned from talking to the Amish, and people familiar with the Amish, on this trip is that the Amish don't think that technology is itself evil or that you go straight to hell if you happen to drive a car one day or watch an episode of *SpongeBob SquarePants*. The skepticism about technology is instrumental; when an Amish community decides not to use a particular type of technology, it does so because it thinks that the technology in question threatens to undermine the closeness of the community. Different communities feel differently about different types of technology. Phones might be totally banned in one but allowed in another. Still another community might have one phone in a booth somewhere. The booth might be out in the open or hidden away. And yes, some Amish even use cell phones. When I sat down with Kramer at a plastic table in his front yard, not so far from where some cows were munching and mooing, I asked him about the cell phone. He smiled and admitted that he has "pushed the tenets of the church somewhat." But he continued (referring to the fact that sometimes the Amish will get a non-Amish person to drive them somewhere), "I bet a lot of Amish have cell phones because they're easy to hide. I've seen a lot of Amish with cell phones, and I don't think it's their drivers' cell phones all the time."

I had no idea what to expect when I drove out to Kramer's farm. When I arrived, he was sitting at the plastic table and leafing through a book about the *Yoder* case. Mr. Kramer did not look anything like the stereotypical Amish man you might envision from a book or see in a movie starring Woody Harrelson.* For one thing, he was smoking a cigarette and drinking a can of Mountain Dew. Also, he was hatless. Don't Amish wear hats? Instead of a conservative dark shirt and suspenders, he was wearing an uncomfortable-looking back and neck brace that was holding his spine together where he had busted two vertebrae in the aforementioned motorcycle accident. His arms were muscular, and he was sporting not only the classic Amish beard but also a not-so-classic Amish mustache. And his eyes were steely blue. Or if not steely blue exactly, then at least more steely blue than anyone else's

---

*A piece of trivia that I've always found fascinating is that Gene Siskel, not long before passing away, ranked the Amish bowling movie *Kingpin* the ninth-best movie of 1996.

eyes whom I met during my travels, and since I swore to myself that I would use the phrase "steely blue" to describe someone's eyes if I ever wrote a book, this seems to be a good place to throw it in.

Maybe it's something about the New Glarus air, but like Pete Etter, Jay Kramer was an incredibly friendly guy quite willing to talk to a total stranger. We talked about all sorts of things, from computers to the effect of the herd buyouts of the 1970s on Wisconsin's dairy farms to how the town of New Glarus abandoned farmers in favor of tourism and "fake Swiss stuff." I asked him if he remembered anything about the *Yoder* case. He was really young at the time, and the thing he remembered most clearly was that a reporter was always hanging around asking the kids "dumb questions" and generally being a "nuisance." The Amish parents would tell the kids to be polite but not say anything and just go into the school or playground if they saw him or his car lingering around. As a result, the kids knew that something was going on, but they didn't really understand what it was.

I asked Kramer about his own schooling. His is a unique case because, although the Amish community set up their own schools in New Glarus when he was in second grade, his father kept him and his siblings in the English schools (the Amish refer to their non-Amish neighbors as the "English," which I think is pretty cool). They were the only Amish who stayed. He liked it there. Sure, he got picked on a bit, but there wasn't any real trouble. "We were different," he said. "Just people." He claimed his ability to make jokes and get along with people helped him fit in with both the Amish and the English. I didn't doubt it. Did he want to stop going after eighth grade? He said that he wanted to stay in school, but only because of the sports. He liked them all, especially football; but other than that, he didn't pay much attention to his schoolwork because, after all, he knew he was leaving school after the eighth grade. It wasn't like he had to keep up his grades for college or anything. Nevertheless, he said he kept up his knowledge from reading and through the news. When I mentioned Justice Douglas's concern about Amish kids who might want to become oceanographers or astronauts, he said, "Well, the way we were brought up, we have enough problems down here on earth, not to mention outer space."

Kramer made the point several times that he always felt like he had a choice of what to do with his life. Kids in most Amish communities, including Kramer's, do not automatically become members of the church when they grow up; they have to choose to join once they reach adulthood. Before they choose, these kids can explore English life and decide what they think of it. Most end up joining the church—about 90 percent, by Kramer's estimate. Kramer himself didn't join until he was twenty-six, and if he had wanted to go to school, he could have. But what was important to him was using his common sense. Book smarts, he said, were always less important. He was perfectly happy just knowing how to read and write and do arithmetic.

Finally, we chatted about the outcome of the *Yoder* case. I was curious as to how the Amish viewed their victory. Did they have a parade or something? No way. According to Kramer, there was no sense of having won a big victory, no celebration—just relief that they didn't have to look around all the time to make sure they weren't going to be arrested. He explained that the Amish just want to be left alone, and that what's important to the community is the community's own rules, not the government's. So winning a case in the government's system was nothing to be particularly proud of or excited about. This is the more

complicated reason why the Amish haven't commemorated the *Yoder* decision in New Glarus, or anywhere else.
It wasn't a big deal, because it was like winning a contest
in someone else's league.

I enjoyed talking to Jay. I knew he was probably sort
of eccentric from an Amish point of view (even he said
that some of his friends and cousins would call his family "Amish-English" as opposed to "real Amish"), but I still
felt like I had talked to someone who is pretty Amish. One
person who doesn't agree with that assessment is Richard
Dawley, a teacher and writer from New Berlin who is probably the foremost English expert on the Wisconsin Amish.
In one of his four books about the Amish, he reports telling
Adin Yutzy that Kramer is "no more Amish than I am."

With this quote in mind, I drove the hour and a half
out to the Milwaukee suburbs to talk with Dawley, and
the first thing we talked about was Kramer. "He's a sham,"
Dawley said, "not Amish anymore." I wondered if it was
because he used a cell phone, but the technology wasn't
Dawley's point. For Dawley, the problem with calling
Kramer an Amish is that there's no church congregation
or settlement in New Glarus, not even a nearby settlement
for him to visit and worship with. I guess this sounds like
a good point, and maybe Dawley is right, but still, I don't
feel qualified to make a judgment call questioning somebody's self-identification with a religious group.

For over ten years, Dawley has devoted himself to educating the English about the Amish. It's a bit of an odd
pursuit, perhaps, but I think a noble one. In the fall of
1995, Dawley told me, a pissed-off and probably drunk English guy shot up a horse and buggy and raped an Amish
girl. Dawley was moved by the incident and decided to
do whatever he could to improve understanding of the
Amish and counter the hatred that some English still har-

bor toward the group. I was kind of surprised to hear that anyone could hate the Amish. It seems as stupid as hating ducklings. Dawley, though, insisted it is true. Maybe it's because of how different the Amish are, or because they are successful farmers, or because they drive their buggies too slowly and without lights. Dawley also explained that there are a lot of myths circulating in the English world about the Amish that he wants to discredit through his books and lectures, among them that the Amish don't pay taxes.

We talked for a while about the schooling question. Dawley said that in all his time with the Amish, he's never heard an Amish person say he wished he could have gone to high school. This is hardly slam-dunk evidence, of course, that Amish kids never want to go on to study in higher grades—an Amish who did want to go to high school might be hesitant to admit her innermost longings and regrets to an outsider, for instance. But Dawley has perhaps talked to more Amish people than almost any English person, and if he's never heard a complaint, it might mean that not so many Amish wish they could have become oceanographers. Dawley also said that he's been an educator at all different levels for forty-five years and thinks that the Amish kids are well equipped for the careers they will be following. I thought this kind of begged the question, though, since the whole point is that maybe a high school education would have inspired the kids to choose some other career. I also was not sure what to make of Dawley's comment that he has "no problem with the women having their roles established as wives and mothers," or that it's nice that they "don't have to worry about matching their clothes to their earrings."

Dawley sent me on the road back to New Glarus with a terrific gift: a cassette tape of a talk given at a church in

Missouri by Adin Yutzy, in which Yutzy reminisced about the *Yoder* case and an even more hostile clash with state educational authorities that happened in Iowa before the Amish left for New Glarus. As I mentioned in the prologue, Dawley had met Yutzy in Pinecraft, Florida, a winter Amish community that was the subject of Dawley's fourth book, *Amish Snowbirds*, which features a really great cover picture of an Amish couple staring wistfully out at the quiet Florida surf. Dawley also gave me a Walkman-like thing to listen to the tape with, and I have to say that I found listening to the cracking, emotional voice of one of the original *Yoder* plaintiffs talking about the case, while I was sitting in a farmhouse in the town where the case came from, completely surreal and genuinely moving, and not just because I'm a big Supreme Court history sap.

You might say that in a sense, the *Yoder* plaintiffs didn't suffer that much from the state's actions. They were fined only five dollars, after all. But it's important to realize that many of the New Glarus Amish had just come from Iowa, where they had been seriously persecuted for their schooling practices. There, the controversy was over whether the teachers in the Amish schools had to get certified by the state; the Amish believed that this requirement violated their religious beliefs, and they refused to comply. As Yutzy tells the story, the authorities forced the Amish to ride their buggies six miles every day to the courthouse to avoid being arrested, placed liens on their crops to pay the state's accumulating fines, and even arrested and jailed a few Amish on occasion. Yutzy himself was convicted of a felony because one evening he failed to make the long ride to court. Yutzy also talks about the day that the police came to the Amish school to force the Amish children onto a bus headed for the public school, and he even claims that he is the one who told a photographer to point his camera toward the cornfields instead of the school bus, advice that resulted in a famous photograph of some Amish kids fleeing into the fields, which helped turn public sympathy toward the Amish plight. A lot of Amish left Iowa because of this clash, so you can probably imagine, even without listening to the tape, how frustrating and disheartening it must have been for them to end up in a similar battle in their new Wisconsin home.

You'll remember that when I turned into Adin Yutzy's driveway in Ellsinore, Missouri, I had no idea whether anyone was even home. I need not have worried, though, because as soon as I got out of my father-in-law's car, Adin came to the back door of his house and invited me inside. The house was modest but well appointed, backed by some farmland that Adin used to work but now leases to somebody else. He led me to his living room, where I met his wife, Fanny, and took a seat. I don't know exactly how old Adin is, but however old he is, he looked a lot younger than that in his plaid shirt and jeans. Fanny, who was wearing a white gown and bonnet, was incredibly kind and sweet. When I mentioned that I was planning to teach in Krakow the following spring, she honestly and truly said, "That's really awesome." At another point we were talking about the tourism that has swamped some of the larger Amish communities in Pennsylvania and Ohio, and Fanny said that she had recently come across an advertisement for "Amish cheese." Practically giggling at the notion that Amish cheese would not taste the same as any other kind of cheese, she wondered, "What's the difference?"

I mentioned to Fanny and Adin that I was honored to meet them, which was true. But I realized later that this must have been somewhat uncomfortable for them (thus explaining why they looked uncomfortable when I mentioned it), because they do not believe in taking pride or even credit for what they did forty years ago in Wisconsin. I asked Adin directly whether he was proud of his important victory, and he quickly and unequivocally said no. Both were glad that they did what they did, because of the benefits the case brought to the Amish and Mennonite communities, but they were definitely not proud of it. Indeed, it occurred to me on the ride home that pride is one of the seven deadly sins, which is kind of interesting, because in the parlance of our times, anyway, being proud of oneself or others is generally considered a good thing and empowering in ways that gluttony and lust, for example, are not. But to Adin, who probably believes pride is a sin, my question, "Were you proud of what you accomplished?" must have sounded like I was wondering whether he liked pigging out on cheeseburgers or drooling over *Hustler*.

Although the three of us talked for a good while, most of what we discussed was pretty much the same stuff that was on the tape, so I won't reiterate it here. I was about to say my goodbyes and head back to St. Louis when Adin asked if he could ask me a personal question. Sure, I said, and that's when Adin Yutzy tried to convert me to Christianity. He asked if I was a Christian, to which I said that I was born Jewish but don't really believe in any religion at the moment. He followed up by asking what I think happens after we die, and I responded that while I'm not particularly happy about it, I think that we turn into dust and that's about it. Obviously, I was going to be a bit of a challenge from a religious conversion point of view.

Adin said that in the Bible it says that there is a heaven and a hell, and that if you live your life right you will go to heaven. My mind was spinning as I tried to figure out what to say in return. Part of me was just surprised by the conversation's turn, and another big part of me kept saying "Wow, this is so cool that Adin Yutzy is trying to convert me to Christianity," so it was hard to focus on what to say next. I managed to ask whether Adin thought there was more than one way to heaven. He said yes, but that you have to get there through Jesus Christ. This was clearly going to be somewhat difficult for me. He urged me to read my Bible so I could recognize the truth. Okay, I figured, fair enough. I've been asking people about their beliefs for the past bunch of months, why shouldn't someone challenge my own? I decided to make Adin and Fanny a promise. I told them that if they singled out some passages, I would promise to reread them and give them serious thought. Adin said that I should look at the New Testament rather than the Old, because the Old Testament is just "history." Fanny suggested I read chapters 5 through 7 of Matthew. Adin then stood up and got his Bible so he could find a particular chapter in Luke about a rich person suffering in hell. I'm not sure why he thought I would particularly benefit from a passage about a rich person—he might have thought differently if he had seen the $67,000 outstanding student loan debt I still have twelve years after graduating from law school—but it turned out to be Luke 16, and I gave Adin my promise that I would read it.

Anyway, back to the free exercise saga. The *Yoder/Sherbert* era of applying strict scrutiny to general laws impinging on religious practice lasted for another eighteen years before Justice Scalia put a stop to it in a debacle of a decision called *Employment Division v. Smith*, which I will discuss shortly. During the years before *Smith*, though, the strict scrutiny that the Court applied was more like intermediate scrutiny than classic strict scrutiny. Recall from the previous discussion that for the most part, when the Court applies strict scrutiny to a law or government practice, the Court will just about always rule against the government. Even though the Court said it was applying strict scrutiny in the years between *Yoder* and *Smith*, it often ended up ruling in the government's favor anyway. For example, the Court once held that a Jewish pilot didn't have any right to wear a yarmulke in violation of military regulations. Another time, it let the Forest Service destroy a forest that some Native Americans used for their religious ceremonies. Still, before 1990, the Court required the government to show some kind of really good reason before it could seriously burden someone's religious liberty.

Now on to *Smith*. As a general matter, the Supreme Court decides only those issues that have been fully briefed and argued before it. This makes total sense, because the issues that end up in the Court are usually very difficult, complex, and important. The Court benefits a great deal from having an issue fully aired and discussed by all the parties before it reaches a decision. Justice Scalia, for instance, has recognized this explicitly. In a case decided in 1994 involving questions having nothing at all to do with religion, Scalia declined to weigh in on an issue that Justice Souter had spent a long time discussing in a concurring opinion, because, in Scalia's words, "The further issues perceptively discussed in Justice Souter's concurrence . . . were in my view wisely avoided by the Court, since they were inadequately presented and not at all argued. . . . As Justice Souter's opinion demonstrates, the issues are complex; they should be resolved only after full briefing and argument."

This was a bit of a weird thing for Justice Scalia to say, since four years earlier, in *Smith*, he completely reversed the *Yoder/Sherbert* strict scrutiny rule, thereby undermining religious liberty, even though none of the parties had briefed or argued the point. Alfred Smith and Galen Black were both working at a drug rehab organization when they were fired for eating peyote during a sacred religious ceremony of the Native American Church in Oregon. The state denied them unemployment benefits because they had been fired for misconduct. The Oregon Supreme Court held that the state's criminal drug laws could not be applied to Smith and Black's religious use of peyote. The U.S. Supreme Court reversed and held for the government.

The surprising thing about the decision was not that the government won. As I have mentioned, the government did win a lot of these free exercise cases, even when the Court applied strict scrutiny. The surprising thing was that out of the blue, the Court took it upon itself to get rid of strict scrutiny altogether and hold that plaintiffs can basically never get an exemption from a general and neutral law. Nobody expected such a thing. Nobody even asked for it. As Garrett Epps writes in his masterful book about the case, *To an Unknown God*, the state of Oregon itself had never asked the Court to reverse *Sherbert* and *Yoder*, and in all its briefs and arguments had simply argued that it should prevail in its case against Smith under the strict scrutiny test of *Sherbert* and *Yoder*.

This position, however, was too moderate for Justice Scalia and his brethren. In their view, it was not the recently decided *Sherbert* and *Yoder* decisions that mattered, but rather the *Reynolds* polygamy decision that the Court had issued 111 years earlier, when the country had only thirty-eight states and Rutherford Hayes was president. According to Justice Scalia, the Court in *Reynolds* was right when it said that "every citizen" would "become a law unto himself" if religious believers could ask courts to exempt them from general criminal laws. As Scalia put it, "Any society adopting such a system would be courting anarchy." Anarchy, yikes! As for *Sherbert* and *Yoder,* Justice Scalia basically deposited them in the circular file, or the trash bin of history, or the toilet bowl of jurisprudence, or whatever moniker you prefer for the place where good old cases are left to die.*

Explaining why *Smith* was a bad decision, both as a matter of principle and as a matter of legal reasoning, would take a whole separate book. What many consider the most compelling critique of the decision was written by Michael McConnell, a law professor at the time, now a federal judge but still probably the most respected church/state legal scholar in the country. His scathing article, "Free Exercise Revisionism and the *Smith* Decision," became as much of an instant classic as anything can become in the world of legal academia. One thing that's particularly interesting about McConnell's critique of Scalia is that, unlike me, McConnell is no bleeding-heart, tree-hugging, Starbucks-sipping, Al-Franken-reading liberal. In fact, he's extremely conservative. As we might say here in Boston, he's *wicked* conservative. George W. Bush put him on the court of appeals and most likely considered him seriously for a seat on the Supreme Court. What this shows is that it's not just liberals who dislike *Smith.* Just about everyone dislikes it, which explains why in its wake, religious organizations and civil liberties groups came together en masse to support a law called the Religious Free-

---

*Scalia did not actually say that those cases were overruled. Instead he offered a variety of cockamamie reasons why they weren't really applicable to the broad range of free exercise cases. These cockamamie reasons were so cockamamie that I can't bear to mention them here. Trust me, though: they're cockamamie.

dom Restoration Act (RFRA), enacted by near-unanimous majorities in both houses of Congress, that tried to reverse *Smith* and restore strict scrutiny as the standard to govern free exercise cases.

Although I won't engage in any extended criticism of *Smith* here, I do want to make one small point that I think is particularly important, and that is this: *Anarchy, my ass.* To begin with, when strict scrutiny was the rule, the government still often won by showing a compelling interest in uniformly enforcing the challenged law. It's not like the courts, after all, were inclined to let religious believers go around killing people in God's name or otherwise undermining the nation's security in the name of Buddha or the Tao.

But even assuming that Scalia meant something less radical than real anarchy—maybe something like "more people will engage in behavior that is generally considered bad"—there still seems little reason to believe this was something to worry about. Remember, of course, that the nation had lived under this horrible anarchy-courting scheme for thirty years prior to the *Smith* decision. Was the country really that bad during that time? I mean, sure, a lot of people wore a lot of bad shirts during the seventies, and Reagan kind of ruined the eighties, but can any of that be chalked up to the *Yoder/Sherbert* strict scrutiny rule? Let's take a close look at the evidence that Justice Scalia provides in his opinion to demonstrate the link. Hmm, let me just flip through the opinion to find that information. It must be here somewhere . . . Oh, wait, *he doesn't mention any evidence.* When someone argues that a long-term position should be abandoned because of its bad effects, don't they usually have the burden of actually showing that the position has caused the bad effects? And what about the evidence post-*Smith*? Does this bear out

Scalia's fears? Well, nineteen states have their own laws, either constitutions or statutes, that essentially mirror the *Yoder/Sherbert* rule. The last time you drove from Vermont or Massachusetts (with the rule) to New Hampshire (without the rule), did you all of a sudden feel anarchy breaking out around you? How about crossing the state line into Kentucky from Ohio? Did you immediately lock the doors and roll up the windows? No, of course not. And so I say: *Anarchy, my ass.*

The rest of the free exercise clause saga can be summarized fairly quickly. As I mentioned, after *Smith*, just about everyone in the country—from the ACLU to the Christian Coalition—came together to convince Congress to pass a law called the Religious Freedom Restoration Act (RFRA), which restored the strict fluffernutter (that's better than "scrutiny," isn't it?) rule of *Yoder* and *Sherbert*. Under the RFRA, the government (local, state, federal) could impose a substantial burden on someone's exercise of religion only if it could show that applying the burden to the person was necessary to achieve a compelling interest. Unfortunately, however, the Supreme Court held that the RFRA was unconstitutional as it applied to state and local governments. That holding did not directly involve the First Amendment; rather, the Court's decision turned on an esoteric aspect of constitutional law that I couldn't possibly explain here, even if I could find my notes from law school.

Undeterred, Congress came right back and passed a new law three years later called the Religious Land Use and Institutionalized Persons Act (RLUIPA), which once again restored the strict scrutiny standard for evaluating governmental burdens on religious exercise. RLUIPA, however, applies only in limited contexts, specifically to (1) burdens imposed by "land use regulations," such as zoning laws, and (2) burdens placed on people who are in prisons or mental institutions. Again, for reasons not important here, this kind of more limited law is clearly constitutional. Thus, under federal law, states can burden religious freedom through general and neutral laws with impunity *unless* they do so through land use regulations or in their prisons, in which case they must justify imposing these burdens by showing a compelling interest and the other requirements of strict scrutiny.

On the whole, RLUIPA is a good thing, in that it makes it harder for states and local governments to burden religious exercise, but it does raise a couple of problems. For one thing, it creates this weird situation where the people who get the most protection for their religious practices, at least formally, are prisoners. Not that prisoners shouldn't have rights or anything, but it does seem a bit odd that someone who has been convicted of murder should have more rights against the government to practice her religion than, say, a monk or saint or Taoist sage. As it is, the courts and casebooks are filled with all sorts of suits by prisoners, seeking special diets, religious reading material, the right to wear religious symbols or to shower every day, and all sorts of other requests. The second and more significant problem with RLUIPA is that it's impossible to say without sounding like a total idiot. Rrrrrlooooopa? Rrrlllwhooiipa? Rrrrrlweeepa? What the hell? Was this really the best our esteemed elected officials could come up with? An acronym that makes you feel like you're throwing up every time you say it?

In a way, though, given the Court's refusal to protect religious freedom, maybe it's a fitting last chapter to a story that kind of makes you want to puke.

4

RELIGIOUS DISPLAY RUCKUS

Destination Austin

Each December, as the snow begins to fall, toy store shelves fill up with those adorable Furby dolls, and the poor Detroit Lions realize once more that they'll be spending the playoff season on the golf course, controversy erupts in communities across the nation over whether the government may display religious symbols on public property. Americans have come to expect these battles; some of us even look forward to them. Indeed, these holiday hullabaloos have become nearly as much a part of our national culture as the Christmas consumer madness they accompany every year.

In December 2006, one of the biggest fracases centered on a bunch of big plastic Christmas trees at Seattle's Sea-Tac Airport. When a rabbi asked that an eight-foot menorah be displayed next to the largest of the Christmas trees in the international terminal, airport officials balked, figuring that if they added a menorah, they would have to add symbols for all sorts of other religious traditions as well. This itself might not have been a problem, but the holiday season is a busy one, and as the airport's spokeswoman put it, "the staff didn't have time to play cultural anthropologists." Instead, the airport took down all the trees. The idea was to do it under cover of night, but when employees at the airport saw what was happening, they alerted the media, which descended on the airport at two in the morning. Before long, the controversy had made international headlines.

People all over the place flipped out about the airport's decision. Some thought the airport should have put up a menorah. Others thought the airport should have kept the trees. Some airline employees bought their own trees, like the customer service workers at Frontier Airlines who pooled their cash and bought four twelve-inch trees for their ticket counter. Others had more creative ideas. A commissioner for the Port of Seattle suggested putting up a nine-foot-tall Grinch. One person posting an online comment on the news story urged the airport to put up a huge dollar bill, since "that's the biggest object of worship" during the Christmas season. An Idaho citizen suggested that since Idahoans worship potatoes, the airport "should have added a giant potato to the display, or hung potatoes as Christmas ornaments," to which another contributor added, "You could use french fries as icicles!" Still another observer said that since "in 2000 76.5% of Americans called themselves Christian, 1.3% Jewish, 13.2% non-religious, with the other religions making up less than .5% of the population each," the airport should have put up "a 7.6 foot Christmas tree, a 1.3 foot menorah, a blank area for the non-religious, and half-foot figurines for all the rest."

These bizarre disputes pop up every holiday season because the Supreme Court has said that the government violates the establishment clause whenever it puts up a symbol or display that *endorses* a religion. To understand this issue, it is necessary to move from the free exercise clause—the subject of the last two chapters—back to the establishment clause and its associated "endorsement test." What this "endorsement test" means and whether it deserves to be ridiculed as the dumbest test ever invented by the Supreme Court are the main topics of this chapter.

The Supreme Court first started talking about endorsement back in 1984, when some residents of Pawtucket, Rhode Island, challenged the town's holiday display. The display, which was erected in a public park, included, in the Court's words,

> many of the figures and decorations traditionally associated with Christmas, including, among other things, a Santa Claus house, reindeer pulling Santa's sleigh, candy-striped poles, a Christmas tree, carolers, cutout figures representing such characters as a clown, an elephant, and a teddy bear, hundreds of colored lights, a large banner that reads "SEASONS GREETINGS," and the creche . . . which . . . consists of the traditional figures, including the Infant Jesus, Mary and Joseph, angels, shepherds, kings, and animals.

The objecting citizens didn't like the fact that the town had displayed a baby Jesus on government property. The town responded that the display was just a harmless show of holiday cheer and pointed to the reindeer, clown, elephant, and teddy bear. After all, who but someone without a sense of humor could possibly object to such a delightful mix of figures on town property? The Supreme Court, in *Lynch v. Donnelly*, sided with the town. The majority opinion was written by Justice Burger and was about as interesting as my big toe. The important part of the decision was Justice O'Connor's concurrence, which introduced the so-called "endorsement test" for evaluating establishment clause challenges to government-sponsored religious displays.

According to O'Connor, the government should not be able to put up a display that endorses a religious viewpoint, because such displays "send a message to nonadherents that they are outsiders, not full members of the political community, and an accompanying message to adherents that they are insiders, favored members of the political community." The test requires the Court to give careful consideration to how a "reasonable observer" would understand the meaning of the display. As to the specific holiday display being challenged, O'Connor concluded that it did not endorse a religious belief because the various goofy things surrounding the clearly religious symbol of the crèche combined to neutralize the meaning of the display such that no reasonable observer would think that it endorsed Christianity.

Although O'Connor wrote only for herself in *Lynch*, a majority of the Court adopted her endorsement test five years later in a case called *County of Allegheny v. ACLU*. This case, decided in 1989, involved challenges to two separate displays on government property: a crèche sitting alone on the grand staircase of a county courthouse, and an eighteen-foot menorah placed next to a forty-five-foot Christmas tree and a sign reading "Salute to Liberty." In an unbelievably convoluted set of opinions, the Court struck down the crèche but upheld the tree/menorah/sign display. All of the justices who applied the endorsement test agreed that the crèche, standing alone, endorsed Christianity. Unlike the display in *Lynch*, this one had no goofy figures to "detract from the crèche's religious message." The government tried to argue that because the crèche was surrounded by a floral decoration, it was not really standing by itself. Justice Blackmun's opinion for the Court, however, rejected the defense, suggesting that "the floral frame, like all good frames, serves only to draw one's attention to the message inside the frame," which in turn inspired a dissenting Justice Kennedy to warn, "After today's decision, municipal greenery must be used with care."

The Court's opinion regarding the tree/menorah/ sign display was even weirder. Everyone had a different view about what meaning a reasonable observer would take from the display. Both Justice O'Connor and Justice Blackmun thought that the display did not endorse religion. Adding them to the four other justices who didn't accept the endorsement test at all (and thus would have upheld both displays) made six justices who voted to uphold the tree/menorah/sign display. Only Justices Brennan, Stevens, and Marshall would have struck down that display. But rather than just tell you what the various justices wrote in their various opinions, I thought I'd let them speak for themselves, in this totally fabricated dramatization of their conference table discussion:

*The justices sit around a big conference table. Some of them chew homemade beef jerky brought in by Justice O'Connor. Justice Scalia skips the jerky and gnaws on a big sharp steel nail instead.**

BLACKMUN: So now that we've decided that the crèche is unconstitutional, let's turn our attention to the other display, which clearly does not send a religious message.

BRENNAN: What? Are you kidding me?

---

*Justice O'Connor really did bring in some beef jerky. I tasted it once. Very delicious. Quite tangy.

O'CONNOR: Hey, don't talk to Blackmun like that. He's right, this display doesn't endorse religion. Mmmm, this beef jerky is good.

BRENNAN: Of course this display endorses religion. The menorah is clearly a religious symbol, and so is the Christmas tree.

Justice Stevens and Justice Marshall nod vigorously.

BLACKMUN: Whoa, hold the phone there, Brenmeister. The Christmas tree is not a religious symbol. It's secular, and since the Christmas tree is forty-five feet tall and in the middle of the display, it transforms the meaning of the menorah, which is on the side and only eighteen feet tall, from a religious symbol to a secular one. So the display just celebrates the December holiday season in a secular fashion.

O'CONNOR: I wouldn't go that far, Blackmun. I agree that the Christmas tree is a secular symbol, but the menorah? That's clearly religious. It's the central symbol in a completely religious holiday.

BLACKMUN: Hanukkah isn't completely religious. I've read several books about Jews, and they say that Hanukkah has some secular dimensions too.

O'CONNOR: I don't care how many books you've read about Jews, Harry, Hanukkah is a religious holiday. And even if it does have secular dimensions, that doesn't make it a secular holiday. I mean, Easter isn't secular just because the Easter Bunny goes hopping around hiding colored eggs.

WHITE: Easter Bunny, ha, ha. She's got you there, Blackmun.

*Justice White tries to give Justice O'Connor a high five.
She ignores him.*

BRENNAN: So wait, O'Connor, if you think the menorah is religious, then how can you say the display doesn't send a religious message?

O'CONNOR: Well, because of the sign. It says, "During this holiday season, the city of Pittsburgh salutes liberty. Let these festive lights remind us that we are the keepers of the flame of liberty and our legacy of freedom." I think that the sign, along with the tree and the menorah, combine to send a message of pluralism and freedom of belief during the holiday season. That's not endorsement of religion.

BRENNAN: Ahhhh! Where do I begin? For one thing, if you think that the sign celebrates religious pluralism, then how can you possibly say that the Christmas tree isn't religious? Pluralism means more than one, so if the menorah is the only religious symbol, how can the display be celebrating religious pluralism?

O'CONNOR: Maybe I don't mean just *religious* pluralism.

BRENNAN: What other kind of pluralism could you mean? Surely you don't mean the cultural pluralism that comes from recognizing lots of different religious and nonreligious holidays. If that were true, you'd have to say that displaying a giant menorah next to a Fourth of July firecracker would be constitutional. Or maybe you mean pluralism in the sense of a display that can mean either the secular or religious parts of a given holiday? But then you'd have to say that a city could put up a display with a Latin cross next to an Easter Bunny. You don't mean that, do you?

WHITE: Easter Bunny, ha!

BRENNAN: I mean, come on. Are you telling me that if the Christmas tree were next to a statue of the Buddha and a picture of a mosque, it wouldn't be seen as a religious symbol?

KENNEDY: (*sighing and wringing his hands and groaning like he always does*) I don't think that endorsement should be the test.

Chief Justice Rehnquist, Justice White, and Justice Scalia nod furiously. Scalia swallows the nail and starts biting a stapler.

O'CONNOR: Yeah, but since five justices think it should be the test, we don't need to hear from you again during this totally fabricated dramatization.

KENNEDY: Fine, then, we'll leave. Come on, guys. Let's go get haircuts.

The four justices get up and leave. Before he walks out the door, Chief Justice Rehnquist grabs a handful of jerky for the road.

BRENNAN: Good, now that they're gone, we can get down to brass tacks. Blackmun, do you seriously think that the Christmas tree changes the meaning of the menorah, and not vice versa?

BLACKMUN: Well, it doesn't not change the nonmeaning of the nonmenorah.

STEVENS: What?

BLACKMUN: Sorry. I don't know what got into me.

BRENNAN: It seems to me that if anything, the menorah changes the meaning of the tree, not the other way around. Even if the Christmas tree might otherwise be mostly secular, once you put it next to an eye-catching menorah that, by the way, was lit during a religious ceremony when the city first put it up, the Christmas tree starts looking a lot more religious.

BLACKMUN: But the tree is two and a half times bigger than the menorah.

BRENNAN: That's how big Christmas trees usually are. It's not unusual at all to see a giant Christmas tree. But I think that when there are two symbols next to each other, one that has a religious and secular meaning and the other that has a purely religious meaning, the purely religious symbol will predominate over the other. So it's the menorah that predominates.

BLACKMUN: I think it's relevant that there's no other secular symbol that the city could have put up to symbolize Hanukkah.

BRENNAN: What about a dreidel?

BLACKMUN: No. If the city had put up an eighteen-foot-high dreidel, it would have looked like the city was making fun of Jews. And that would be an endorsement of Christianity.

O'CONNOR: Isn't it interesting that under my endorsement test, displaying a purely religious symbol like the menorah might be less problematic than putting up a nonreligious symbol like a dreidel?

MARSHALL: Yeah, it's fascinating.

BLACKMUN: I guess that's it, then. I think the display just celebrates the holiday season, and Justice O'Connor

thinks the display celebrates pluralism of some unspeci-
fied sort. The two of us plus the four at the barber makes
six, so the display stays.

BRENNAN: I don't get it. This is the most endorsing display I've ever seen. It endorses religion over nonreligion,
Christianity and Judaism over other religions, and Christianity over Judaism, since it makes it seem like Hanukkah is the most important Jewish holiday just because
it comes in December, even though it's actually pretty
minor compared to Rosh Hashanah and Yom Kippur.
How many more unconstitutional messages could this
thing send?

*Justices Stevens and Marshall break into applause and do
a small dance.*

O'CONNOR: I'm afraid to say that reasonable minds can
differ. Lunchtime!

The End

I want to stress here that although the stuff about the
nail eating and the high fives and the small dance and all
are totally made up, the substantive arguments about the
meaning of the symbols, including the two references to
the Easter Bunny, accurately reflect the written opinions.
There really was a debate over whether the meaning of
the menorah changes the meaning of the Christmas tree
or vice versa, and Justice Blackmun indeed raised the possibility that the city could have erected an eighteen-foot
dreidel. The only thing that could have made the opinion
more bizarre is some discussion of the old "Hanukkah
Harry" character from *Saturday Night Live.*
Hopefully, it's clear from my descriptions of these cases

why lots of people think that the Court's approach to these displays is totally ludicrous. Here are these nine purportedly serious, brilliant, scholarly, powerful people sitting around a table in an ornate, mahogany-paneled conference room in the middle of a magnificent white marble building that looks like a sacred temple, and they're arguing about things like whether a menorah changes the meaning of a Christmas tree or vice versa, or whether putting an elephant next to a little Jesus makes the display more secular, or whether the bushes surrounding a religious symbol make the symbol more or less powerful. As one influential lower court judge has put it, the endorsement test makes judges render decisions that are more like interior decorating than constitutional law. I guarantee you that every single law professor who has taught these cases, no matter how otherwise boring and staid and possessing the personality of an oak tree he or she may be, has gotten the class to laugh. It's virtually impossible not to. The cases are great fodder for law professor hypotheticals. What if the menorah were fifty feet tall? What if the reindeer's antlers were shaped like a pentagram? What if baby Jesus were doing the Macarena? You get the idea.

Well, the endorsement test may not be perfect, but I don't think it's uniquely ridiculous or that it requires judges to do anything that is particularly absurd. It's true that the test requires judges to consider all the circumstances surrounding a display and to balance all sorts of factors and to come up with an overall judgment about how the display would be understood by a reasonable person. The inquiry, as we say in the law game, is indeterminate. It requires judges to exercise their judgment. There are no clear rules one way or the other. Little things like shrubbery or

JAY WEXLER · 101

a snowman might make all the difference. But applying judgment to a complicated set of facts in order to come up with the best decision possible under the circumstances is what judges do all the time, whether they're deciding if a police search is reasonable under the Fourth Amendment or if a contract really requires a company to deliver fourteen tons of peanut brittle by July 17 or if a driver acted negligently by not tying up his couch tight enough to keep it from flying into the windshield of an oncoming vehicle. The only real difference between these contexts and the religious symbol situation is that the latter lends itself to a little more goofiness, perhaps because it is so visual, or maybe because it involves the mixture of sacred symbols with everyday ones, some of which happen to have trunks where their noses should be.

Its superficial silliness aside, though, the endorsement test gets at something very significant, which is that the government should not be able to affirmatively take sides on what constitutes religious truth. In a country where so many people believe so many things, including nothing at all, why should the government, which is supposed to represent all of us, be able to send an affirmative signal that a particular view of ultimate reality is true and good and right, and other views of ultimate reality are false and bad and wrong? Some people who don't like the endorsement test say that symbols aren't that important and that the law shouldn't protect people who are "merely offended" by symbols sent by the government. This, as my son would say, is "crazy talk." Symbols are incredibly potent communicators. Why else do people flip out like the world is coming to an end when somebody even thinks about burning an American flag? And the harm that follows the official endorsement of a religious symbol is not "mere offense," as if the government had whispered a little too loudly

that someone's ass looks really big in some dress. Justice
O'Connor is right that the message the government sends
when it erects a religious symbol on public property is that
those who believe in that symbol are officially included
and favored by the political community, and those who
don't are excluded and disfavored. To me, that seems like
about as serious a harm (short of force or violence) as a
democratic government can inflict upon its own citizens.

While I was staying in Wisconsin, I took a day off from researching *Yoder* to visit Freethought Hall, the world head-
quarters of the Freedom from Religion Foundation (FFRF),
a nonprofit organization whose two main purposes are to
fight for church/state separation and to educate the public about "freethinkers"—agnostics, atheists, and others
who, as copresident Dan Barker put it, "all disbelieve in
the same god." The FFRF has challenged a bunch of religious displays, and I wanted to get its leaders' thoughts on
why these displays might be harmful. I guess I count as a
"freethinker" myself, but I thought I should include some
voices of other atheists too, especially because I doubt that
I am typical of those who publicly identify as "freethinkers." For example, my own disbelief completely depresses
me, whereas when you look at the FFRF's Web site, you get
the feeling that these people couldn't care less that life has
no purpose and is just a bunch of random events leading
nowhere and how after you die you just become another
lump of dirt in a completely meaningless universe.

Freethought Hall is a modest, two-story sandstone
building in downtown Madison, two blocks west of the
capitol building. Although the group has over ten thousand members, many of whom have joined in recent years
(George W. Bush's "presidency" was good for the FFRF's

business), only a handful of people actually work at the building full-time. These include Barker and his copresident and wife, Annie Laurie Gaylor, whose mother started the organization in the late 1970s. When I arrived, Annie hadn't made it in yet, so Dan showed me around a little. It's a great, quirky place, and I felt perfectly comfortable there in a way I never could in a religious setting. Dan was indeed very cheery, despite just coming from some sort of medical procedure that involved getting a big needle shoved into his ear or something and left him woozy and wobbly on his feet. While we were chatting, ABC News called to discuss the possibility of sending a news crew over to interview him about Mother Teresa's recently discovered crisis of faith. Apparently Christopher Hitchens couldn't be reached, and Dan was the next most prominent heathen on ABC's Rolodex.

The walls of Freethought Hall are decorated with all sorts of funny signs and stickers and pictures and cartoons with atheist and separationist jokes on them. There is a bookshelf loaded up with books that the foundation sells, some of which it also publishes. When I got back to Boston, I ordered a few of these volumes. One of them is a little green illustrated gem called *Just Pretend: A Freethought Book for Children*, written by Barker himself, which introduces kids to the idea of atheism in the hope that they will "make their own decision" about religion. It raises lots of questions about God and religion and the Bible for kids to mull over. Of Noah, for example, it asks: "How could Noah get all those animals on the boat? Were there two of each kind of dinosaur? Two penguins? Two of each of millions of different kinds of beetles, cockroaches, rattlesnakes, vultures, and bedbugs? . . . Some animals eat other animals. How could Noah keep them from eating each other?" Of Jesus: "Most children think Jesus was a man of love. But he also told people to cut off their hands and pluck out their eyes. . . . Is that nice?" Of God himself: "There are billions of people in the world. To pay attention to everyone, God would have to listen to more than 10,000 prayers every second! Do you think anyone could really do that? Do you really think there is some big brain up in outer space that can do all that?"

After Dan got off the phone with ABC, we went upstairs to talk. We sat in a big, comfortable room with a kitchen off to the side and a piano in the middle. In addition to speaking and writing about atheism, Dan is a musician, and he has written and recorded "freethought music" that he also regularly performs. The foundation's Web site offers some of his music for sale, including the two-CD set, *Friendly Neighborhood Atheist*, which includes such ditties as the "Stay Away Pope Polka," "I Don't Need Jesus," and "You Can't Win with Original Sin." The Web site also has little MP3 links where you can listen to snippets of a few of the songs. My personal favorite is called the "Vatican Rag."

Annie arrived before too long, and the three of us discussed a smorgasbord of church/state issues. We talked, for example, about the differences between the FFRF and other separationist organizations, like Americans United for Separation of Church and State. Dan explained that though the two are "sister organizations," he is happy for the FFRF to be narrower and smaller because, unlike Americans United, part of its mission is to explicitly represent the interests of nonbelievers. I asked Dan whether he worries that having an organization and a building devoted to "freethought" feeds into the claim—not accepted by any court, by the way—that secularism or secular humanism or atheism or whatever is really itself a religion, which the state may not establish under the First Amendment. Barker said that he does worry about this a little, but then pointed out that "if atheism is a religion, then baldness is a hair color," which was good enough for me. Then we talked a bit about Dan's ongoing efforts to get himself invited to give a prayer on the floor of the House of Representatives. Dan and Annie pointed out the difficulty of finding a representative to sponsor an atheist to "pray" on the House floor. Apparently, exactly one member of the House has actually admitted to being an atheist. This was shocking to me. I had no idea there were so many!

I played devil's advocate on the religious displays issue. Come on, I insisted, surely these things aren't worth all the fuss. Who cares if the government puts up a baby Jesus on city property, especially if there's an elephant nearby? Annie said that the symbol cases might be even more important than other church/state cases, such as the ones about funding religious organizations. The symbols cases, she noted, are the ones that bring out death threats against plaintiffs. Did you get that? *Death threats!* She argued that it's the so-called little things, like the congressional chaplains and the "In God We Trust" motto, that make it so easy for people to claim we're a Christian nation. "Once these things get in people's heads, it's really hard to get them out." For his part, Dan said that although not all atheists feel strongly about symbols, "some feel very strongly. They pick a different route home from work to avoid the symbol. It's like if there were a KKK or a Nazi sign. It's the same thing with the nativity scenes. They like to say that it's just some nice fuzzy baby, but it's not. It's an insult to some of us to say that we're all so bad that we need a savior. It's not that our feelings are hurt. People who sign up as plaintiffs do so because they feel a real injury. The plaintiffs are brave."

Dan suggests that the government should not take any

position on religious truth. He said, for example, that he would also object if the government put up a display endorsing atheism, and this raises a point that is so important and so often misunderstood that I am going to start a whole new paragraph.

The opposite of endorsing religion is affirmatively denigrating religion, or affirmatively endorsing nonreligion, not remaining silent about religion. Would it be okay if I say that again, this time in italics? *The opposite of endorsing religion is affirmatively denigrating religion, or affirmatively endorsing nonreligion, not remaining silent about religion.* Lots of misguided people say that the courts are promoting secularism or atheism when they force the government to remove a religious symbol, as though saying nothing about religion either way is the opposite of endorsing it. The reason this seems like sort of a natural conclusion is that, as a practical matter in the United States, the government would never ever affirmatively denigrate religion by, for example, putting up a big granite monument etched with the words "God Is Dead" or "Jesus Was Not a Savior" or "Religious People Are Bananas." Lots of people believe these things, but if a government official ever suggested that "God Is Dead" be put on the dollar bill, he would be swiftly assassinated. Once you keep in mind that it's at least theoretically possible for the government to affirmatively denigrate religion, it's easy to see that saying nothing about religion is just the middle way between endorsing religion and denigrating it. The idea that stripping government property of religious symbols amounts to a promotion of atheism is just logically wrong.

Apart from the annual holiday brouhahas, most religious display fracases these days center around the Ten Commandments. Probably everybody remembers how a few years ago, Roy Moore, the chief justice of the Alabama Supreme Court, installed a five-thousand-pound granite monument of the commandments right in the middle of the courthouse rotunda. Why would he do such a thing? In this age of doublespeak and subterfuge, Justice Moore's candor was remarkable, if legally crackbrained. In a speech Moore made when he installed the monument, he said he put it there to remind judges, litigants, and visitors to the court that "in order to establish justice, we must invoke the favor and guidance of Almighty God." Then, at trial, Moore testified that he wanted the monument to acknowledge "God's overruling power over the affairs of men." These statements, along with the fact that the thing was the size of a large rhinoceros, made it easy for the Alabama federal courts to find that the monument unconstitutionally endorsed religion. In August 2003, five guys from out of state (nobody from Alabama would do it) came in with a jack and rolled the monument into a back room while protesters wearing "Satan Is a Nerd" T-shirts seethed, cried, and shouted creative slogans like "Bring the monument back! Bring the monument back!"

The Alabama case was so outrageous as to be legally uninteresting, but easy Ten Commandments cases like that are the exception rather than the norm. Two other cases that ultimately made it to the Supreme Court at the same time—one from Texas and one from Kentucky—are much more typical. The Texas case involved a six-by-three-foot granite monument that was donated to the state by the Fraternal Order of Eagles in 1961, possibly to help advertise Cecil B. DeMille's holiday epic starring Charlton Heston. The state placed the monument on its capitol grounds in Austin, right between the capitol itself and the Supreme Court. The Ten Commandments display is one of seventeen monuments on the grounds that are meant to commemorate the "people, ideals, and events that compose Texan identity." Other monuments honor the heroes of the Alamo and Texas schoolchildren. A lawyer named Thomas Van Orden, who had hit some hard times and was living in a tent, found himself passing the monument from time to time on his way to use the library at the Texas Supreme Court. Van Orden eventually sued the state to have the monument removed. The lower courts disagreed with him, so he asked Erwin Chemerinsky, a constitutional law giant who was teaching at Duke University School of Law, to take the case to the Supreme Court.

The Kentucky case was somewhat more complicated. In the summer of 1999, officials in a couple of counties there decided it would be a good idea to put up big, gold-framed copies of the Ten Commandments in their courthouses where everyone could see them. Their reasons for doing this were explicitly religious. After the ACLU sued, the two counties changed their displays to make them even more unconstitutional. The new displays included not only the Ten Commandments but also religious portions of eight other historical documents, such as the "endowed by their Creator" thing from the Declaration of Independence. A district court judge ordered the courthouses to remove the displays "IMMEDIATELY," after which the counties put up yet a third display, this time putting the Ten Commandments on the wall along with the full versions of eight other documents, including the Magna Carta and the lyrics to "The Star-Spangled Banner." The collection of documents was called "The Foundations of American Law and Government Display," and the Ten Commandments were included, according to a comment on the display itself, because they "provide the moral background of the Declaration of Independence and the foundation of our legal tradition." The lower federal courts held the display unconstitutional, and the Supreme Court heard arguments in the case on the same day as the Texas case. A couple of weeks before the arguments, I served as a judge on a moot court panel with maybe six other professors at Harvard Law School to help Chemerinsky and David Friedman, the ACLU lawyer who argued the Kentucky case, prepare for the arguments. Every single member of the panel predicted that the Court was going to strike down the Kentucky display and uphold the monument in Austin, and that's exactly what the Court did. The key thing about the Kentucky case was the history that led up to the final display. The majority of the Court thought it was clear from the first two attempts that the counties really wanted to endorse religion, and the justices didn't see anything in the final display to counteract that message. On the other hand, the Texas monument had been on the capitol grounds for forty years, was next to a bunch of other monuments that were all intended to celebrate Texan identity, and was donated by an organization (the Eagles) that had a real secular purpose in having the monument displayed (combating juvenile delinquency, and possibly increasing profits for Paramount Pictures). Justice Breyer contributed the deciding vote in the Texas case, and although his separate opinion is about as clear as a bowl of oatmeal, it seems that these factors played a deciding role in his enormous brain.

On my road trip, I visited two different Ten Commandments monuments. When I was talking to Dan and Annie at the Freedom from Religion Foundation, they told me about a monument they had successfully challenged (sort of) in La Crosse, Wisconsin, which is a great old city on the banks of the Mississippi River, right near the Minnesota border. Its downtown is filled with taverns and clothing stores and cool places to eat and sort of looks like a mini version of Chicago's North Side, which from me is a huge compliment, because Chicago is my favorite city in the world and also where I first met my wife on an alcohol-fueled blind date.

The situation in La Crosse is really odd. Right in the downtown area, between Fourth and Fifth streets going one way and King and Cass streets going the other, there's this tiny city park where people sit and eat their lunch and do whatever people do in little neighborhood parks. In the corner of the park there's one of these Fraternal Order of Eagles Ten Commandments monuments, surrounded by not one, but two fences, each of which has a sign on it. The sign on the inner fence says that the monument belongs to the Eagles, and the sign on the outer fence says that the city does not own or maintain the monument and does not endorse any religious message sent by the monument. It really says that. I'm not making it up.

What happened was that the FFRF sued over this display, and after the trial court sided with the FFRF and held that the monument was unconstitutional, the city sold the parcel of land on which the monument sits to the Eagles for a total of $2,640 (six dollars per square foot). So now there's like a tiny park within a park that belongs to a private party rather than the city, and so the appeals court said that the monument was okay.

When we went to La Crosse, Karen, Walter, and I were on a day trip and had other things to do, like dance around in a bunch of sprinklers because it was ninety-two degrees out, so I didn't spend too much time at the monument. But we did take some pictures, including one of Walter standing in front of the monstrosity and smiling. On my way to find a men's room in the food co-op across the street from the park, though, I walked by a *second* monument, this one lurking surreptitiously on the narrow strip of light-colored rocks that appears to separate the park itself from the Sara Lee baked goods factory right next to it. That monument is facing the first monument, like it's going to spring out and jump on it and strangle it to death, and it sports both a quote from the Book of Matthew and a statement that it was erected by people who think the country belongs to God. If I'm right that the strip of rocks belongs to Sara Lee rather than the city, then the display is certainly constitutional, but I still found it pretty creepy. I took a picture of it but then decided to hurry out of there before the guy on the bench who kept looking at me funny had the chance to come over and knock out my teeth.

One footnote to the La Crosse visit: Later in the day, while Walter was running around the sprinkler park getting wet and cooling off, I sat at a picnic table and talked about minor league baseball and the University of Wisconsin at La Crosse football team with a kind older gentleman. I asked him if he remembered the Ten Commandments controversy, and he said he did and that he couldn't see why there had been such a hullabaloo about it. He really said the word "hullabaloo," I swear. Then he said that he remembered something that a returning Vietnam veteran once said to him, which was that there are never any atheists in a foxhole. When people are in real danger of harm, he meant, they tend to pray, even if they would otherwise say they don't believe in God. I can testify that this can happen, because I myself came pretty close to praying the time I had to undergo an emergency MRI, complete with an iodine IV and a seriously uncomfortable barium enema, after a routine visit to the doctor revealed that my appendix was about to explode. I sort

of thought I knew where the man was going with the foxhole comment, but then I became puzzled when he said
that people can believe what they want to believe, but that
they shouldn't foist their beliefs on other people. Was he
saying that the atheists shouldn't have tried to force the
Ten Commandments out of the park, or that the believers
shouldn't have put them there in the first place? I figured
it was probably the former, but I really wasn't sure. Before
I could ask him to clarify, however, he changed the subject
to his son-in-law's new job as an elementary school principal, and that was that.

The grounds of the Texas capitol span twenty-two acres.
Because I've lived in cities my entire adult life and therefore have absolutely no idea how large an acre is, I had
assumed that walking around the entire capitol grounds
would require several days of hiking and overnight camp-
ing and that I'd have to use a telescope to see from one
monument to another. Alas, this is not the case. An acre,
it turns out, is big, but not too big. I showed up at the capitol at about eleven on a sizzling hot October morning. I
was hung over, because the night before at a bar in the
South Congress neighborhood of Austin, I kept drinking
beer after beer in the hopes that the stunning woman
two tables away really was Liz Phair, the Chicago indie
rock queen whom I've had a crush on for years and who I
thought might—well, I don't know what I thought, maybe
that she'd suddenly stand on the table and start giving me
a private concert or something. Anyway, thank goodness
whoever it was left before I drank myself into a real stupor
or said anything completely embarrassing or both. In any
event, as I walked around the grounds looking at all the
monuments, I had to take several rests on several benches

before finally arriving at the infamous Ten Commandments monument that sits fairly inconspicuously on the
capitol's northwest corner.

During the practice oral argument at Harvard three
years earlier, I had asked Erwin Chemerinsky whether it
was possible to see any other monument if you were standing right in front of the Ten Commandments monument.
The government had argued that it was possible to see a
number of the other monuments and that this fact argued
in favor of the monument's constitutionality. In its brief,
the government had included a photograph—taken from
a somewhat elevated perspective—that made it seem like
it would be possible to see other monuments. I pointed
out the picture to Chemerinsky, and he made fun of me,
saying something like, "Well, we don't dispute that if you
are hovering over the capitol grounds in a hot air balloon
or other floating dirigible, it would be possible to take in
a whole slew of monuments while gazing at the Ten Commandments." Everyone in the packed auditorium laughed.
Ha, ha, ha. Good one, Erwin, and a fair enough point. You
couldn't really tell anything decisive from the picture, and
his answer was really smooth, rhetorically speaking. Plus,
I'm used to being humiliated, so what do I care?

But what I learned from actually visiting the Texas
capitol is that in fact you *can* see all sorts of other monuments from right in front of the Ten Commandments. I
mean, maybe if you shove your face directly into the marble and look straight ahead you'll see only the Ten Commandments, but if you're a reasonable distance away and
you turn your head ninety degrees, you can totally see a
monument to the Statue of Liberty as well as side views
of two other monuments. If you stand right where you are
but turn around 180 degrees, you see the Thirty-sixth In-
fantry Monument. I don't know what that is, but you can

definitely see it. If you walk to the north for no more than twenty seconds, you see two other monuments. And if you walk in that direction for a minute at the most, you will arrive at a place where you can see four monuments up close. Unless you were to parachute onto the grounds, there's no way you could get to the Ten Commandments monument without walking by at least a couple of other monuments. In other words: my question was a good one after all, so put that in your pipe and smoke it, Chemerinsky.

I was interested to see how I would feel looking at the monument, so I stared at it for quite a while and tried to gauge my emotions. I looked at it up close, and then I sat on some steps and glared from a distance. I read the words, walked around the thing once or twice, even fondled the marble with my hot fingers. But try as I might, I really didn't feel much of anything. I wanted to feel indignation and atheist rage, but these emotions didn't come. Basically, I felt hot more than anything. And tired. Not enraged. The whole experience reminded me of the time some years ago when I stopped in Nagasaki while backpacking around Japan and stared for the longest time at some memorial sculpture of twisted bodies and melting faces and cursed myself for not shaking or crying or screaming to the heavens. I've since forgiven myself for that failure, because although I'm no psychologist, I sort of think that emotions are not always reliable; they can abandon you when you expect them the most and sneak up on you when you expect them the least.* On some other

---

*On the other hand, I still have not forgiven myself for what I did in Hiroshima during the same trip. I was standing in Peace Memorial Park staring at the "A-Bomb Dome," which is the famous skeletal remains of a building that was right near where the bomb hit, that bomb, of course, having killed seventy thousand people on impact as well as killing and maiming many thousands more over time. While

day, if I were in some other mood, and the sun wasn't making me feel like a fried egg, perhaps I would have bellowed with atheist rage. Instead, I just walked around the capitol one more time and then headed back to my hotel pool.

One good thing about Justice Breyer's opinion upholding the Texas Ten Commandments display was that it gave Thomas Van Orden and me a perfect place to meet to talk about his famous challenge to the monument. When I arrived back at the capitol on my second day in Austin, Van Orden was sitting on a bench near the monument waiting for me. During the case, the media had made a lot of the fact that Van Orden had hit hard times, was homeless, and survived on food stamps. I'm not sure you could tell this was the case from looking at him; the day we met, he was wearing a long-sleeved blue shirt, blue pants, and black shoes, and he seemed pretty together. He was really thin, it's true, and the smell of cigarettes around him was unmistakable, but that hardly screamed out "Living in a tent!" to anyone who would happen to look at him.

We shook hands and walked over to take a peek at his monument. Incredibly, someone had placed an orange right on the top of it, where the two tablets come together in a V. Van Orden took the orange off, as though he empathized with the monument and didn't want it defiled. "This monument and I have bonded," he told me as he

---

I was looking with awe at the memorial, a Japanese man came up to me and asked if I wanted my picture taken with the building behind me. Like an idiot, I agreed (I mean, I was startled and confused and kind of didn't really think about what was happening, not that this is any good excuse), and so now I have a picture of me smiling like some kind of brain-dead ape in front of a building that memorializes the greatest act of human destruction the world has ever seen.

tossed the fruit into a nearby trash can. "Like Andy Warhol and the soup can." He also pointed out, however, that this was the first time he had been back to see the monument since the case was decided. "These days I go around the capitol the other way," he said. "Too many memories." Later, he wondered aloud why he threw away the orange. "What am I doing throwing fruit away when I'm on food stamps?" he asked, to no one in particular.

We talked about the case for over two hours in a café in the basement of the capitol. I asked him why he brought the suit in the first place, and he said that it had not been an easy decision. He has nothing against the Ten Commandments, he pointed out, but he thinks that separation of church and state is important to the character of society. He made it quite clear that the case was not about promoting atheism. "I filed the suit over religious equality," he said. "I think that equality matters most for things that matter most, and religion is one of those things. There are twenty-seven different religions in Austin. For one sect to use its power with the government isn't right." Van Orden is a big believer that the endorsement test keeps the government honest. "Nobody should have to come to a state capitol and see a display for someone else's religion. If you put a sign up in your yard supporting someone for city council, you do it because you want that person to win the election. The state's not a bunch of idiots. Imagine if the state put up a Longhorn monument and claimed that it was a celebration of Texas football. The guys from A&M would throw it in a river by morning."

But bringing the case was difficult, and Van Orden was delighted when he was able to turn the case over to Chemerinsky as it went to the Supreme Court. For one thing, challenging a Ten Commandments monument is not a popular thing to do, even in a city like Austin that's known for being liberal and that sports the famous slogan, "Keep Austin weird." At times Van Orden felt in danger, and he certainly never publicly volunteered the location of his tent. More difficult than that, though, was the financial burden of bringing such a case. He recounted the awful feeling of putting in so much work on the case while worrying all the time that he wouldn't have enough money to print out and send all the copies of the briefs that the courts required him to file. "I wanted to send the court a disk, you print it out. You've got the national budget to work with. I'm on food stamps here." Nonetheless, every time a deadline approached, somehow Van Orden would find a way to file the necessary paperwork. He said he remembers having three dollars in his pocket one time after sending a set of briefs off to the Fifth Circuit Court of Appeals. The financial burdens of the case took a lot out of him. He kept waiting for someone with money to show up and help, but as he put it, Sandra Bullock (an Austin resident) "never showed up at my carrel in the library."

We talked a little bit about whether the government might have had some secular purpose in putting up the monument. Van Orden scoffed at the government's argument that the Ten Commandments are the basis for all of American law. He said that during the case he used to joke that if he won, he should get the monument and that if he got the monument, he would donate it to the law school at the University of Texas so that the professors there could use it as a teaching tool. When I asked if he thought the government could have gotten away with just putting up a disclaimer sign, like in La Crosse, Van Orden said it was an idea that he at first found untenable but later starting warming up to. After the La Crosse decision came down, he said that he offered to buy a ten-foot square around the monument so he could pitch his tent there (good security around the capitol building) and put up a sign that read, "My Monument, My Message. If You Don't Like It, Stick It."

Van Orden likes to joke, but he became very serious when I asked him what he thought of Justice Breyer's opinion in the case. "It infuriates me," he said. "I've always admired Supreme Court justices, so this was so disappointing." Justice Breyer writes a lot in his establishment clause opinions about whether a government practice or law or symbol is divisive, in which case he frowns upon it, or whether instead a court decision that would undo the practice or law or symbol would be more divisive, in which case he will tend to find for the government. In the Texas Ten Commandments case, he seemed to think that the monument itself had not been very divisive, but that a decision ordering its removal would be very divisive. Van Orden thinks that Breyer is just wrong in believing that the purpose of the establishment clause is to keep the peace. "Keeping the peace is an effect of separation, not the purpose," he told me. "If I wrote this on your constitutional law exam, you'd take off points. You'd write: *You're not getting it. You can't decide a civil rights case by counting noses.*"

More disturbing to Van Orden, though, was Breyer's suggestion in the opinion that the lack of any lawsuit challenging the monument for the forty years it sat on the capitol grounds is evidence that the monument does not endorse religion. The idea, according to Breyer, is that if the monument were really a problem, someone would have challenged it before. Van Orden thinks that when Breyer wrote this, he was knowingly and purposefully writing something that he knew was not true. Van Orden pointed out that the Freedom from Religion Foundation had filed a friend-of-the-court brief in the case recounting how plaintiffs in these types of cases are driven out of town and met with violence, even shot at. So Breyer knew that there are all sorts of reasons why nobody had previously sued to remove the monument. "His point here was dishonest," Van Orden said. "He turned the back of his hand to plaintiffs who endure so much in establishment clause cases." I'm not entirely sure that Breyer was being purposefully dishonest, but I agree with Van Orden that Breyer's argument on this score was very, very weak.

Talking to Van Orden was one of the highlights of my road trip. This is a guy who has met with a lot of misfortune in recent years, but still manages to remain engaged, courageous, reasonable, and sharp as hell. He makes the case against government endorsement of religion better than anyone I have ever met or any article I have ever read. And oh yeah, he's also really damned funny. As we were leaving the café, he told me that at one point during the case when his back was really bothering him, he told the assistant attorney general for the state, with whom he had become good friends, that if he died before the case ended, the state should bury him under the monument with a headstone that says, "Here lies the last guy who tried to challenge the Ten Commandments."

Keep Austin weird, dude.

5

SENATE PRAYER
SUSPICION

Destination the Nation's Capital

On the morning of July 12, 2007, the angry screeches of three protestors sitting in the public seats overlooking the floor of the United States Senate shattered the decorous morning proceedings and threw the ordinarily peaceful chamber into disarray. What were these protestors objecting to? They were all members of an antiabortion group, but they weren't protesting funding for family planning or making a point about *Roe v. Wade* or advancing insensible claims about how abortion is a mortal sin but the death penalty is somehow acceptable social policy. No, the screams of these three great Americans that day were aimed at a Hindu chaplain who was giving a guest prayer to start the day's legislative session. Rajan Zed was talking about togetherness and selflessness and peace when the protestors screamed, "This is an abomination!" and "No Lord but Jesus Christ!" and "There's only one true God!" A senator from Pennsylvania ordered the three removed from the chamber and arrested. Zed completed his prayer, albeit a bit nervously. In a press statement released later that day, the protestors' organization complained that "the Senate was opened with a Hindu prayer placing the false god of Hinduism on a level playing field with the One True God, Jesus Christ," and criticized the senators for not having "the backbone to stand as our Founding Fathers stood," presumably because people like Jefferson and Madison hated togetherness and selflessness and peace.

For many Americans, this news story was probably the first they had heard of this strange thing that happens almost every day in the United States. Whenever it's in session, the Senate starts its day with a prayer. Think about that for a second. Don't think too hard or overanalyze it yet; we'll do that in a minute. Just think about how weird it is that in a country founded on the principle of church/state separation, whatever that might exactly mean, the nation's most important lawmaking body starts every day by praying to God. Maybe you think that's okay, maybe you don't, but you've got to agree that it's frickin' weird.

The practice of Senate prayer is nothing new. Unlike many other constitutionally questionable practices, it was not instituted through executive order by George W. Bush. It wasn't the brainchild of Jerry Falwell. It predates the addition of "under God" to the Pledge of Allegiance, which admittedly isn't saying much, since that language was inserted by statute in 1954. More impressively, the practice of Senate prayer predates the First Amendment itself. The very first Congress elected a chaplain in April 1789 and passed a law authorizing payment of the chaplain on September 22 of that year, *three days before* reaching final agreement on the language of the Bill of Rights, which includes the establishment clause of the First Amendment. The Senate has begun its sessions with a prayer ever since.

Nor is the Senate the only government body that starts its proceedings with a prayer. Pretty much all of them do. The House of Representatives elected its chaplain only a few days after the Senate did back in 1789, and it continues to hold daily prayers today. Many, if not most, state legislatures also start their sessions off with prayers, as do all sorts of school boards and other deliberative bodies. The Vermont legislature, for instance, holds "devotional exercises," which in the past have included sessions of Buddhist drumming and Christian guitar playing. The Indiana House of Representatives once began its day with a prayer that transitioned to a group rendition of a ditty called "Just a Little Talk with Jesus," inspiring some legislators to clap and sing along and others to bolt for the exits. In this chapter, I take up the following question: if the government can't even put up a display that endorses religion, how can its main legislative body start every day with a prayer?

The Supreme Court has addressed the constitutionality of legislative prayer once, in a 1983 opinion called *Marsh v. Chambers*, which legal scholars generally agree Justice Burger wrote in about five minutes while sitting on the can. Burger put aside all the legal doctrine developed by the Court over the years, skipped over any consideration of the principles at stake, and simply concluded that historical practice justified the Nebraska legislature's practice of starting its sessions off with a prayer. "In light of the unambiguous and unbroken history of more than 200 years," he wrote, "there can be no doubt that the practice of opening legislative sessions with prayer has become part of the fabric of our society." Legislative prayer, far from being an establishment of religion, "is simply a tolerable acknowledgement of beliefs widely held among the people of this country."

The problem with Burger's opinion wasn't so much that it relied on historical practice to uphold legislative prayer—after all, it may be highly relevant that the establishment clause was written after the law authorizing congressional chaplains. The problem was that Burger failed to even consider any of the plausible counterarguments to relying solely on this history. These arguments, raised explicitly by the dissent, include the obvious possibility that the Constitution might not be "a static document whose meaning on every detail is fixed for all time by the life experience of the Framers." The dissent also raised a number of principled objections to legislative prayer, all of which went unanswered by the majority opinion. As Justice Brennan put it:

> Legislative prayer clearly violates the principles of neutrality and separation that are embedded within the Establishment Clause. . . . It intrudes on the right to conscience by forcing some legislators either to participate in a "prayer opportunity" with which they are in basic disagreement, or to make their disagreement a matter of public comment by declining to participate. It forces all residents of the State to support a religious exercise that may be contrary to their own beliefs. It requires the State to commit itself on fundamental theological issues. It has the potential for degrading religion by allowing a religious call to worship to be intermeshed with a secular call to order. And it injects religion into the political sphere by creating the potential that each and every selection of a chaplain, or consideration of a particular prayer, or even reconsideration

of the practice itself, will provoke a political battle along religious lines and ultimately alienate some religiously identified group of citizens.

Following the Court's decision in *Marsh*, there is little doubt that legislative prayer is generally constitutional. This doesn't mean, however, that anything goes. *Marsh* involved so-called "nonsectarian" prayers, which basically means prayers that don't seem like they come from any specific religious tradition. So a prayer to a generic "God" would be nonsectarian, while mentioning Jesus or the Cross or the Prophet Mohammed would not be. Of course, the idea that a prayer to a single god is somehow not sectarian is insane, since lots of religious people believe in more than one god or no god at all, but what*ever*, that's the distinction the courts have drawn. A few years ago, four citizens of Indiana sued the state's house of representatives for using its legislative prayers to promote Christianity. The judge held a trial and found that most of the house's prayers had been explicitly Christian. After all, this was the state where the legislators broke into a song and dance about Jesus. Another day, the prayer read: "And now, Lord, we ask this in Your Son's name, who is Lord of Lords, King of Kings, Jesus Christ, who gave us the most precious gift of all, to die on the cross for our sins. Thank you, Lord." Whatever "nonsectarian" means, it's not that. The court held that the state's practices violated the First Amendment, although an appeals court reversed the decision on unrelated procedural grounds.

A recent case from Georgia shows how wacky these prayer cases can get. In Cobb County, the board of commissioners and the planning commission both have traditions of starting their meetings with a prayer. The prayers are given by representatives of various religious organizations in the community, which administrators of the two commissions pick out of the Yellow Pages in a sort of random fashion. Some taxpayers sued, arguing that the process for selecting the prayer givers was not nearly random enough because, among other things, only large, established churches generally have it together enough to advertise in the Yellow Pages. The court rejected this claim, although it did find that the deputy clerk of the planning commission had acted illegally when she drew a vertical line through the "Churches—Islamic," "Churches—Jehovah's Witnesses," "Churches—Jewish," and "Churches—Latter Day Saints" sections of her 2003–2004 phone book (the same kind of line she drew through the "Chiropractors," "Cigar & Cigarette Accessories Dealers," and "Circuit Board Assembly Repair Persons" sections). The court ordered the county to pay only a nominal fine of one dollar, however, since it appeared that the deputy clerk had not drawn such a line in her 2005 volume (and had in fact contacted both a synagogue and a mosque during that year). The plaintiffs also argued that the prayers were illegal because they contained numerous sectarian references to things like Jesus and the Heavenly Father, but the court denied this claim because it thought that, overall, these occasional references were really not that big a deal.

I guess I always knew about legislative prayer in the back of my head, but I started thinking about it a lot a few years ago when Mike Newdow, the guy who sued to get rid of the phrase "under God" in the Pledge of Allegiance, also sued the U.S. Congress to make it stop praying every day. My interest has never been rooted in any desire to actually litigate the issue of congressional prayer's constitutionality. Newdow's case was dismissed on jurisdictional grounds that would probably bar just about any suit by a private party against congressional prayer, and in any event, the backlash from winning such a suit would probably undermine any of the benefits of winning it. After all, who really wants to win the case that finally gets enough people so sick of us ACLU types that they pass the "We are a Christian nation" constitutional amendment? Not me. I just became interested in the practice of Senate prayer because it's so bizarre.

My initial thought, since I'm an academic, and since I didn't have tenure at the time, was that I would write an academic article about Senate prayer. I did a little research on prayer itself and came across a piece in which a religion professor argued that there are three main aspects of prayer, what he called "prayer as text," "prayer as act," and "prayer as subject." What he meant is that it's possible to analyze a specific prayer or group of prayers in at least three different ways—by reading and analyzing the text of the prayer, by seeing how the prayer is actually read or performed, and by learning what people think and say about the prayer. I figured I would analyze Senate prayer in these three ways, with the goal of understanding it better and maybe shedding some light on whether it should be considered constitutional. I figured I would read lots of the prayers and maybe visit the Senate so I could see what happens there.

I may still write that academic article someday, but when I hit on this road trip idea, I figured I'd shelve the more formal project and add the Senate to the trip, even though there's never been a case involving Senate prayer at the Supreme Court—or anywhere else, really. Are you pissed? Do you feel like you've been ripped off? I totally understand. You thought you were buying a book about places where Supreme Court cases came from, and now you've got this whole chapter that has nothing to do with the Supreme Court. I won't be offended if you decide to throw the book away or even (gasp) return it (please don't), but I hope you'll stick with me, because what I found in D.C. was pretty fascinating.

Assuming you're still reading, I'll now explain that the current Senate chaplain is Dr. Barry C. Black, a Seventh-day Adventist who was appointed in the summer of 2003, making him the sixty-second chaplain in the country's history. Here is a graph representing the diversity of religious affiliations that has marked the office since its inception:

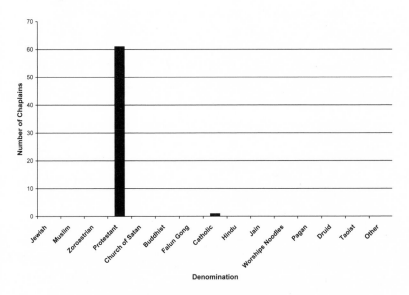

In case you can't quite see it clearly, a Catholic did serve as the Senate chaplain once, for exactly one year, between 1832 and 1833. Incidentally, back in 2000, the House of Representatives erupted in controversy when GOP leaders appointed a Protestant over the recommendation of a selection panel that had urged appointment of a popular Catholic priest. When opponents raised charges of anti-Catholic bias, it became clear that the Protestant's appointment was doomed, and the appointee withdrew. To put an end to the controversy, House leaders then appointed the Reverend Daniel Coughlin to be the first Catholic chaplain in the House's history. Despite this one ugly incident, however, the congressional chaplain offices have not generally contributed to interdenominational strife, unless of course you include in your idea of "strife" the helpless feeling of exclusion that anyone who isn't a Christian feels when they think about whether they might one day become a congressional chaplain.*

The first thing I did to prepare for my trip to Washington was to print out six months' worth of recent prayers—spanning January through June 2007—so I could read them and see what they said. I have to admit that one reason I am fascinated by legislative prayers is that most of the prayers I've read seem, on paper anyway, to be incredibly banal, which to me just adds to their weirdness. I think it's mostly because the idea of invoking the sacred in a chamber full of folks known primarily for blathering, filibustering, and logrolling just seems out of place. I actually like Chaplain Black's prayers better than most of the others I've read, but even his suffer, in my view, from the fact that he has to direct them to a bunch of politicians. Consider, for example, this excerpt, from March 29:

> Eternal Spirit . . . May the Members of this body build with You a world without dividing walls and

---

*Yes, yes, there's a "guest chaplain" program, under which a guest speaker—like Rajan Zed, the heckled Hindu—can give the morning prayer, if a senator agrees to sponsor the guest. But this happens fairly infrequently, and even these guests are predominantly Christian. For example, in the first six months of 2007, guest chaplains gave the opening prayer eleven times. Of these eleven guests, only one—a rabbi—represented a minority faith. Not much solace for the non-Christian in the guest program, then, it would seem.

partisan strife. Empower our Senators to set country above party and place Your will above all else. Keep them faithful in their efforts to unite our world. Strengthen them to work together for the common good as You place Your peace that passes all understanding in their hearts. Bless them abundantly beyond all that they can imagine.

Or maybe this one, from the previous day:

Eternal Spirit . . . Liberate our lawmakers from deceptions that distort and misrepresent facts. Teach them the fine art of conciliation, and inspire them to choose rational roads instead of emotional dead ends. May they commit their time, effort, and resources in formulating policy which is in accordance with Your will. Lord, lift them above partisan rancor, and give them the power to walk in Your light.

Or this one, from January 4, the opening day of the new Congress:

Eternal Spirit, whom to find is life and whom to miss is death, from age to age you provide hope to those who trust you. In a changing world, you are changeless. Lord, you have given us the gift of a new year, with all of its possibilities and promises. Empower the Members of this new 110th Congress to use this season of opportunity for Your glory. As they labor with You, help them to place our country's needs ahead of perceived political advantages. Lead them from mistrust to trust. Use them to help bring peace to our world. Show them the priorities that best honor You and inspire them to act promptly. May they strive to achieve and maintain ethical and moral fitness. When they feel discouragement, remind them that You are working for the good of those who love You. As a challenging and promising future beckons, guide their steps and supply their needs. Lead the new leaders of our legislative branch with Your sure hand. May they follow You without hesitation. We pray in Your Sovereign Name. Amen.

And finally, from January 25:

Eternal Lord God, in whose life we find our life, today hold our Senators within Your providential hand. Guide them when they feel perplexed and strengthen them to meet every challenge. Infuse them with courage and keep them close to You. As they seek to represent You, fill them with Your peace. Do for them what they cannot accomplish in their own strength. Give them a new delight for matters of drudgery, a new patience with difficult people, and a new zest for unfinished details. Let Your spirit rule in their lives. We pray in Your sacred Name. Amen.

"A new delight for matters of drudgery"? "A new zest for unfinished details"? Isn't this stuff weird? It's not just because I'm a heathen atheist Jew that this seems weird, is it? Is it?

In addition to the just plain weirdness, I came away from reading the six-month set of prayers with two primary impressions. The first is that these prayers, as a whole, come pretty close to being sectarian. It's true that Chaplain Black rarely refers to Jesus expressly by name. None of his prayers from the first half of 2007 mention Jesus, although his prayer on July 17 did end with, "With respect for other faiths, I pray in Jesus's name. Amen." But despite not mentioning Jesus, lots of his prayers contain Christian references like "cross," "Redeemer," "crown," "Lord of Hosts," and "Prince of Peace." No prayers mention the Tao or the Buddha's eightfold path. On a couple of occasions, moreover, Chaplain Black's chief of staff offered a prayer on the floor; one of his prayers referred to the "Savior" and the "King." And since guest chaplains can apparently say whatever they want, their prayers often contain explicit references to Jesus and the New Testament. All in all, one gets the impression that the Senate is a pretty Christian place.

My major impression, though, was that I just didn't get the point of having these prayers. They seemed kind of pointless, even silly, and I didn't see why anyone would feel the need to start off a legislative session with one. At the same time, as a nonbeliever I found them mildly irritating, and I wished they didn't exist. In short, I found the prayers to be an excellent example of what lots of people call "ceremonial deism," a phrase that refers to the relatively minor but offensively ubiquitous references to God that government is able to get away with—things like the national motto, official days of prayer, and maybe the Pledge of Allegiance. The idea is that these references are so minor and such an ingrained part of our culture that courts shouldn't bother with them. Personally, I agree that they are kind of minor, but I agree too with other separationists who would like to see them gone, so that as a nonbeliever I don't always feel like the government views me as a complete dope. As Mike Newdow likes to say, our society wouldn't stand for "ceremonial racism" (although team names like the Washington Redskins suggest that sometimes we do), so why should we allow the government to practice ceremonial deism?

Anyway, this was my mindset when I went to D.C. to see a few of these opening prayers and talk with Chaplain Black himself. I can honestly say that my week in Washington really changed my mind about Senate prayers and the chaplain's office generally. It turns out that they are far more dangerous to our constitutional system of church/state separation than I had ever thought.

Visitors are allowed to sit in the gallery overlooking the Senate floor anytime the Senate is in session, but unless you go there as part of an excruciatingly long staff-led tour of the entire Capitol building, it's not exactly easy to figure out how to get in there. In the weeks leading up to my trip, I called the offices of both of my senators and got different advice. Both said I had to come to their offices to get a pass, but Senator Kerry's office said the pass was good only for a day, while Senator Kennedy's office said the pass was good for the entire year. Neither office was willing to send me any passes through the mail.*

I decided to ask my friend and ex-student Stacy for help. Stacy has worked in the Senate legislative office for several years, but even she didn't know how you get into

---

*Neither senator responded to my requests for an interview to discuss his views on Senate prayer, even though I said I would take only five minutes of their time and even though I worked stuffing envelopes and making ridiculous cold-call phone calls to voters in Iowa for Senator Kerry's presidential campaign in the summer of 2003, which I'd just like to emphasize was not the summer of 2004, when he already had the nomination, but *2003*, when everybody and his grandmother assumed that Howard Dean was going to get the nomination and nobody but me and three college kids making ridiculous cold-call phone calls to voters in Iowa had faith that Kerry, with that incredible hair, was going to get the nod.

the gallery. Her first e-mail had me wondering whether I could get a refund from U.S. Airways. "I'm nearly 100 percent certain that you have to have a staff member with you to be in the gallery," she wrote. "You might have to take the tour every time. Eeek." Eeek indeed! The idea of taking five tours of the Capitol just to see five thirty-second prayers did not sound too inviting, especially because the prayers usually go on around ten in the morning, so unless I got a really early tour, there was a good chance I'd miss them anyway. Luckily, though, Stacy's next e-mail kicked off with "HOLD THE SHOW," and I exhaled with relief when she explained that in fact you don't need a staff member to go with you into the gallery, as long as you have a pass. And within a week, she sent me a stack of passes skillfully obtained from the office of Senator Kennedy.

Another great thing that Stacy did for me was put me in touch with Meg Saunders, who at the time was the communications director for the chaplain's office. Stacy told me that Meg was well known around the Capitol for being about the nicest and most helpful person in Washington, and this turned out to be the case. I asked Meg if there was any chance I could talk with the chaplain, and even though I'm sure everybody would have been happier if they could have dissuaded the creepy little liberal Boston academic from visiting, Meg was incredibly helpful in setting up the appointment and giving me advice on getting around the Capitol and everything else I needed to know.

My family and I arrived in Washington on a Sunday in late July for a week's stay, and my hope was to see a bunch of opening prayers before returning home the next weekend. For my first visit I wore my suit (no beach hat), because Meg told me that the nicer you dress, the better the security guards treat you. I can see how this might be the case. Most of the people milling about the Capitol building were wearing sandals and shorts and T-shirts with not-very-funny slogans on them, so wearing a suit made me seem like I actually had some business in the building. This was my first trip back to Capitol Hill since I had lived there in a rat-infested apartment on Constitution and Second around the turn of the millennium. That was before 9/11, and compared with how the Capitol grounds were back then, these days the area is much more closed off. It used to be that you could just wander anywhere you wanted—the steps, the lawn, the front, the side, the lovely white marble terraces with their sweeping views of Pennsylvania Avenue and the Mall, wherever. Now you can't. You can walk up the grand stairs on the west side of the building, but not all the way to the top. They don't let you on the terraces without a pass. There are all these new walls everywhere that block your sight lines, and there are so many cops it feels more like Tiananmen Square than Washington, D.C. Not that these measures aren't justified or anything, but still, it's pretty depressing.

My pass in hand, I approached the little makeshift security building on the Capitol's east side. A couple of cops were standing outside, so I went up to them. Here's an approximation of our conversation:

> *Me:* Hello. Can you please tell me how to get to the Senate gallery?
> *Cop 1:* What time do they convene today?
> *Me:* Ten o'clock.
> *Cop 2:* (*to Cop 1*) Why are you asking him? Shouldn't you know?
> *Cop 1:* I do know.
> *Me:* (*to myself*) Was he testing me? Boy, that's strange.

I was told to go through a metal detector inside the security building and then to walk around the north terrace to the west side of the Capitol, where I would have to wait in a line near a blue flag. The line had about thirty people in it. At about nine thirty, the security guards let us into the building. Everyone in front of me was ushered up some stairs directly in front of us, but when I came in, a guard told me to go around the staircase to the right. I figured that the people in front of me were going to one gallery and that everyone behind them was being sent to a different gallery because the first one was filled already, but that wasn't the case. I ended up all by myself with no idea where to go. In front of me was a huge circular room with statues and pillars and about a thousand tourists; this didn't look like it could be the right way to go, but I didn't really have any other option, so I went in. I saw a tiny sign that said "Senate Gallery," but the arrow on the sign was pointing to some painting. It was like one of the traffic signs we have in Boston that seem deliberately intended to confuse visitors.

I started to worry, because if I couldn't make my way to the gallery by the time the session started, the day would have been wasted. I started sweating like a pig in my wool suit. Also, there were all these fluorescent lights that made me feel like I was having a stroke. I walked down a random flight of stairs and asked a couple of security people how to get to the Senate gallery. They kind of shrugged, and one said she thought it was on the third floor maybe. Thanks a lot. It wasn't like I could just go find an elevator somewhere and press "3" and get out at the gallery. More sweat. The smell of toast. Finally, I took a deep breath and found a real cop, who told me what to do. I indeed had to follow the little arrow, just a hair to the left of the painting, and that took me in a circuitous route to a desk where I was asked to stow all my anthrax and electronic equipment. A minute later I found myself all alone in a quiet, empty staircase going up two floors to the gallery, where apparently nobody ever goes just to take in the morning prayer.

As the first person to arrive in the gallery, I was ushered to the front row by a nice lady and reminded not to put any items on the railing in front of me where they might accidentally fall down on a senator's head. There are a lot of rules about sitting in the gallery, most of which are printed on the back of the pass. Nobody under the age of six is allowed inside. The following items are not permitted: "packages, bundles, cameras, suitcases, calculators, aerosol/non-aerosol sprays,* pointed objects, electronic instruments, food, beverages, or briefcases." These activities are prohibited: "Standing or sitting in the doorways and aisles, smoking, applauding, reading, taking notes, taking photographs, and the wearing of hats by men, except for religious purposes." Now, I wasn't really hoping to do any long division on my handheld calculator while having a smoke during my time there, but these restrictions did seem to be a little much. And weird. As Stacy pointed out, the prohibition on "bundles" is particularly odd. *Bundles of what?* Anyway, the one prohibition that did make it kind of hard on me was the "no taking notes" rule. I had hoped to make notations about what was happening on a little notebook, and I was perfectly happy to use a dull crayon rather than a dangerously pointy pencil, but the rules wouldn't allow it, so I just had to try to remember everything I saw. Therefore, it's quite possible that all the stuff I say later on about what happened during the prayers is totally inaccurate.

Figuring out where to go was a lot easier the next few days. By Thursday, I was a Senate Gallery Superstar, zip-

---

*Really, why not just "sprays"?

ping around the crowds, taking the scary empty staircase two steps at a time, not bringing any questionable chemicals along to hold me up at the checking station. The staff started recognizing me too. On Thursday, the woman at the second metal detector said, "Weren't you here yesterday?" That same day, the usher joked "Don't you have a home?" when she saw me, and then patted me on the arm and asked "Are you going home now?" when I left. I miss that kind lady.

Pretty much the same thing happened on the floor each day. I tried to arrive about fifteen minutes before the prayer started. At that point, the only people on the floor were generally fresh-faced pages, high school or college kids I'd guess, all dressed in identical blue suits, gaining valuable experience and sweet lines for their résumés. It was pretty interesting how relaxed they seemed; they were all lounging around the stairs that lead up to the main dais, doing crosswords or working Sudoku puzzles or giggling with each other like it was recess at the local elementary school. As the time for the session to start approached, some clerk-like people would take their seats at various tables and look over documents, and a few staffers would shuffle in holding files and papers. By the time the "opening ceremony" (that's what the ushers called it) started up, there were generally about thirty or forty people on the floor, mostly pagers and staffers and generally only two or three actual senators. Also, usually about ten people had made their way into the galleries to watch. So the attendance at the prayers was usually about fifty people altogether, although on one of the four days I was there, for some unknown reason, I'd say there were double this number of people.

The chaplain tended to show up about ten minutes before he was scheduled to go on, dressed each day in a beautiful suit and holding a small dark portfolio from which he read the prayer. He usually made his way over to the pages first to chat, and then he would stand to the side of the main dais, often looking over the prayer he was about to read. At the appointed time, the ushers would tell everyone in the gallery to rise, and the presiding senator would announce from the top of the dais that the chaplain "will lead the Senate in prayer," at which time the chaplain would ascend to the top of the dais and the senator would take one step down to the chaplain's left. The chaplain would then read the prayer, which would take something like one minute. After the prayer, the chaplain would step down and stand on the gallery floor while the presiding senator took his place at the top of the dais and asked everyone present to "please join me in reciting the Pledge of Allegiance." After the Pledge, everyone would sit down, and the Senate would begin its official business.

There are a few things about this ceremony that make it a lot more powerful and meaningful to watch than the prayers seem when you just read them on a piece of paper. For one thing, the prayer completely transforms the atmosphere in the chamber. Before the prayer, everyone is acting casually, but when the ceremony starts, everything changes. The pages stop flirting with each other and stand still by the doors on each side of the dais. The staffers stop talking about last night's episode of *Two and a Half Men* and stand quietly. The senators stop looking over their recently proposed pork-barrel legislation and put their heads down in solemn contemplation. When the ceremony is over, the chamber remains serious and formal as the Senate begins its work.

The second thing about the prayer that makes it different is the setting of the chamber itself, which lends its own grandiloquence to the religious ceremony. The chamber is an impressive place. It's all mahogany and marble and velvet and gold. I bet it costs a fortune to dust. The chaplain stands between the U.S. flag and the Senate flag in front of a snazzy blue drapery. Right above the chaplain's head is the old national motto, "E Pluribus Unum," and across the chamber is the new motto, "In God We Trust." This is the place where laws get made, and when you're in the chamber, you can feel its power. Finally, Chaplain Black has a truly beautiful voice. It is strong and deep, and he reads slowly and powerfully, with real passion. It makes you take notice. You can't ignore it. Even I looked forward to hearing it each day, and I believe that there's a god up in heaven about as much as I believe that a potato created the planets. In short, this guy is good. And that's what really worries me.

On the Wednesday of my week in Washington, I left the gallery right after the prayer, because I was scheduled to meet with the chaplain. Even though the spectators empty out basically right in front of the chaplain's chambers, the security officers made me go down two flights to the "appointments desk" so someone at the desk could call up to the chaplain's chambers for Meg Saunders to come down two flights and then accompany me back up two flights so I could visit the chaplain's chambers. It was nice meeting Meg, because, as I already mentioned, she's the nicest person in Washington. She led me into the actual chambers, which really consist of only two offices, one for the chaplain himself and one for the three other people who work for him. The best part of this office is definitely the giant round window that looks directly out toward the Washington Monument and, incredibly, opens. Meg opened it to show me how it actually opens.

Meg accompanied me into the chaplain's own office, a small but lovely room with endless books lining the walls, a picture of the Ten Commandments hanging on a nail, a sitting area with a couple of nice chairs and a small couch, and a little nook where the chaplain was working on his computer. Meg introduced us, and we retired to the sitting area to talk. The chaplain spoke very slowly and deliberately, with that same deep voice from the Senate floor, peppering his sentences with all sorts of biblical references from both the Old and New Testaments. I'll admit to being pretty nervous. What the hell did I know about interviewing the chaplain of the United States Senate, much less this guy, with his umpteen advanced degrees, twenty-seven years of experience as a Navy chaplain, and an incredibly impressive life story? (As he explains in his book *From the Hood to the Hill*, Chaplain Black came a long way from the Baltimore ghettos where he grew up.) Luckily for me, Meg had asked me before I came to write up a list of questions. This was intended for them, so they would have some idea of the things I wanted to talk about, but it turned out to be much more helpful for me, because it saved me from having to think too much during our conversation.

I was interested in how the chaplain goes about drafting the prayers and how he decides what to talk about, so I asked him, and his answer was a little surprising. I guess I sort of thought that he would just sit down and knock a few lines out at his computer—that the drafting would be basically a solitary affair—but that apparently is not the case. Instead, Chaplain Black explained that to a large degree, each day's prayer is a culmination of the interactions he has with the senators and the seven thousand other people who work at the Senate. He said that he has pastoral contact with the members and the staff throughout the day, both at various Bible study sessions and just through informal talking with people, and that through these interactions, he gets a sense of the needs of his community and what it is concerned about. He then builds on what he's learned to draft a prayer that will have an impact on the community. He said that all his prayers have some combination of the typical prayer components—adoration, confession, supplication, thanksgiving—but that he moves the pieces around based on the needs of the listeners. This idea that the prayer is not just this thing that pops up in the chaplain's head each morning, but rather grows out of the chaplain's ongoing relationship with the community he serves, made me think that the morning prayer is a far more meaningful event than I had figured before I came to D.C.

I asked Chaplain Black about his views on including sectarian references in the prayers, and he emphasized that he tries to make his prayers inclusive, because he wants "as many people as possible to be able to give a heartfelt 'Amen' to the prayer." He generally thinks it's not necessary to mention Jesus by name. He pointed out that various scriptural models, like the Psalms, do not mention Jesus. "To pray in the name of Jesus," he said, "does not require mention of Jesus." He said that he gets positive feedback from the 10 or 15 percent of senators who are Jewish and that he thinks the common themes among traditions make it easier to communicate with a religiously diverse community.

One thing I didn't realize before I came to Washington is just how big a deal the Bible study sessions are. According to Chaplain Black, he holds five sessions a week, and a lot of people regularly attend. The chaplain runs a separate session for the senators themselves, at which chitchat about various important issues facing the body will often ease into talk about the Bible itself. On the subject of his relationship with the senators, Chaplain Black said that through his interactions with them, he has the opportunity to touch their lives, to help them through difficult challenges when they need someone to talk to. He realized soon after getting the job that he can have a real behind-the-scenes impact by reflecting with the senators about what is theologically and ethically the correct thing to do in a given situation. His relationships give him a "significant opportunity to change minds and shape opinions." When I asked whether the chaplain needs to be religious, or whether (as someone else has suggested) the poet laureate could do the job just as well, Chaplain Black thought about it for a bit before answering. He said that if the primary responsibility were just the invocation, then maybe the poet laureate could handle it. But the job is more about being a pastor than giving the invocation, and for the spiritual counseling part of the job, the chaplain needs a spiritual orientation. How is the poet laureate going to answer a theological question without knowing anything about theology?

I wasn't there to engage in a debate about the constitutionality of the chaplain's office, but I was curious about what Chaplain Black thought about it, so I asked him. He seemed to think the issue was an easy one, given the timing of the establishment clause. He thought it clear that the framers of the Constitution intended there to be spiritual representation in the legislative branch. When I asked about the incident with Rajan Zed, the Hindu speaker who had been heckled a couple of weeks earlier, the chaplain said that based on the calls and e-mails his office received in the days leading up to the prayer, the interruption could have been a lot more serious. One e-mailer claimed that the framers would be spinning in their graves to learn that a Hindu was giving the invocation. But Chaplain Black disagreed with this view of the framers. Zed should have the right to pray, he said. "The founders did not intend only Christians to pray on the floor."

After a half hour or so, I left the chaplain to his work, but I was able to talk some more with Meg out in the hallway about the chaplain's role in the Senate community. Her main point, which she made in several different ways, was that the Senate community needs the spiritual dimension provided by the chaplain's office. Over and over, she said, she has seen how people working at the Senate need something more in their lives, something higher and mysterious, especially in times of great need, and the chaplain's office provides that. She explained that she came to the office by happenstance after working for a couple of representatives and had been working at the chaplain's office for seven years, first for the previous chaplain (for whom she clearly has a great deal of affection) and then for Chaplain Black. She said that at first she wasn't sure whether the office was good for the country, but seven years later, she is sure that it is. The office brings the community together, she explained, and she hopes it never stops being a tradition. She wanted to make sure I got the following quote down just right: "Inviting God to be part of the process is a very important piece in decision making and our international image."

So why did I say earlier that the Senate chaplain is more dangerous than I had originally thought? Am I just some sort of Grinch-like figure, out to deprive the hardworking staff members of the U.S. Senate of their spiritual guide during times of need? I mean, if there were no Senate chaplain, what would these poor people do if they had to face some sort of personal tragedy? Oh, wait. They'd do what every single other person in the country has to do: *go see their own clergy member!* Government-sponsored chaplains in the armed forces or in prisons are okay—perhaps even necessary—because people in the military and in prisons are not free to go see their priests or sages or abbots or nihilist gurus whenever they want. But people in civilian jobs don't have this problem. Sure, Senate work is hard, and it might not always be easy to get away any particular minute. Same is true with data entry. And teaching six-year-olds. But that doesn't mean the government can provide a paid Christian chaplain whenever it might be difficult for a government worker to get away and see his or her rabbi. And if this truly is a problem, the answer is simply to pass a law allowing employees a certain amount of leave to go seek the spiritual counseling of their choice, not to install an in-house chaplain of a particular faith right there in the building.

All of this, however, is just to say that the chaplain is not necessary. It doesn't explain why his office might be a bad thing. After all, I'm quite sure that Meg Saunders is right and that the chaplain's office has brought people together and made a lot of people happier than they otherwise would have been. All else being equal, these are good things. The problem is that when the government puts a chaplain into a workplace, it inevitably promotes a particular religious faith within the institution. Now, Chaplain Black claims to be very familiar with non-Christian faith traditions and quite able to talk with members of those traditions in helpful ways, and I do not doubt for a minute that he's right about his abilities. As I said before, this guy is good. But no matter how much he knows about all sorts of beliefs and nonbeliefs, the fact remains that this chaplain, like all others before him, is a Christian who believes in a specific foundational text and embraces particular theological positions. Inevitably, discourse with a Christian chaplain will tend to be Christian in character. The fact that Chaplain Black's prayers are peppered with Christian imagery and not Taoist ones, and the way the chaplain invoked biblical passages in our conversation as opposed to passages from the *Bhagavad Gita* or *Infinite Jest*, are testimony to this truth. I don't fault the chaplain for being more conversant with Christian images and teachings than with those of other traditions; that's what anyone would expect from a professional Christian. The fault lies with the system that allows him, and him alone, to administer to the spiritual needs of the Senate community.

The fact that the chaplain is probably very good at what he does makes the problem worse, not better. Imagine that I were a Senate staffer. Of course, I think the Bible is as authoritative as *The Collected Tales of Mother Goose*. But if I were working at the Senate and something terrible happened to me or my family, I might very well be tempted to go see Chaplain Black to talk with him about it. He would realize that I'm an atheist, but I bet that a lot of what he would say to me would come from a Christian perspective, not because he would be seeking to convert me, but because he is a deeply believing Christian. It would be inevitable. And then, who knows, maybe I would be inclined to go pick up a Bible or see the world slightly more religiously. If it wasn't hardheaded me who went to see the chaplain, but a more unsure, on-the-fence kind of guy, that guy might very well change his religious views because of his interaction with the charismatic chaplain. Should the government really be in the business of actively influencing people's religious choices, one person at a time, in the quiet office of a powerful Christian officer?

Then, of course, you have to remember that some of the people whom the chaplain is counseling are United States senators, whose problems include things like "Should I vote for this bill that will profoundly affect every single American?" and "Should I authorize the use of force in Iraq and stick the U.S. military into a quagmire the likes of which we haven't seen since the Vietnam War?" In other words, by virtue of his institutional position, the chaplain can use religion to influence public policy. Now, again, I'm not saying that the chaplain would do this intentionally or consciously. But imagine this hypothetical situation. A non-Christian senator is trying to figure out what to do on the aforementioned use-of-force question. Maybe the senator is a Buddhist or a Jew or not really religious at all, even though surely she would have had to say she's religious and thinks about God every second of the day to get elected. Maybe that senator is unsure about how to vote and wants to seek guidance from somebody who is not involved in the legislative process. If there were a Buddhist abbot or a rabbi or a poet laureate hanging around the Senate, she might go visit him to seek counsel. But of course there are no such people around. The only independent person around is Chaplain Black, who is really charismatic and really smart and totally Christian. So she goes to see him, and maybe he tells her about Christian just-war theory. Maybe he labels it as Christian, or maybe he doesn't. The senator is impressed with her discussion with the chaplain and ruminates about it back in her office. After much thought, she decides that in light of the just-war theory she's learned, this particular use of force is legitimate. As such, she votes to authorize the use of force. Presto: Christian policy!

I should say that I actually think it's kind of a nice thing, at least in theory, for there to be some independent,

thoughtful people around the Capitol to whom the senators can talk in confidence about their obviously stressful
jobs. The problem is that there is only one such person,
who is by definition religious and whose religious affili-
ation is inevitably Christian. Maybe if there were a whole
cadre of chaplains or chaplain-like people working at the
Senate, all of whom had different backgrounds and governing philosophies and whatnot—sort of an Office of
Thoughtful Advisors Who Come at Life from Different
Angles, Some of Whom Are Religious and Some of Whom
Are Not—then it would be okay if a lot of these people were
religious and some of them were Christian. Then the senators could choose which one they wanted to talk to, and
if they felt like it, they could talk to more than one. They
could compare the advice they got on the pending health
insurance bill from the priest, the Falun Gong practitio-
ner, and the hippie philosopher before deciding how to
vote. The various advisors would take turns giving the
opening prayer, which would go a long way toward remov-
ing the symbolic endorsement of religion that exists under the current practice. Of course, such a solution is not
without its own flaws. For instance, there would always
be debates about whether the group of advisors was broad
enough. Is it okay that of the ten people in the office, none
are Buddhists? Or that there's a Theravada Buddhist but
no Mahayana Buddhist? Or that only one of the advisors is
an avowed Satanist?

Moreover, an additional problem with the proposal is
that it's totally crazy and therefore not worth considering
for a single additional second. I'm afraid to say that even
in the United States—where the state is allegedly not allowed to establish any religion—Senate prayer, led by a
single Christian chaplain, is here to stay.

6

FUNDING RELIGION FRACAS

Destination Cleveland

Although I said a little about it in the last chapter, you might have noticed that for a book about the First Amendment, I haven't said much about what the framers of the Constitution thought about what the amendment was supposed to mean. There are a number of reasons for this, among them that I am not a so-called "originalist." I don't, in other words, believe that our current understanding of the Constitution should directly reflect the meaning ascribed to the document by those who actually wrote it. A related point is that many of the church/state questions we face now are radically different from the ones the framers had in mind. For instance, I would guess that the issue of whether the government can put up a Christmas tree on public property was about as far from the minds of those who wrote the First Amendment as whether to drive a hybrid car, outlaw stem-cell research, or subscribe to *Maxim*.

Unlike the problem of religious displays, the question of funding religion was very important to some of the

Constitution's framers. The most famous historical document on the issue is James Madison's 1785 "Memorial and
Remonstrance against Religious Assessments," in which
Madison remonstrated like you wouldn't believe against
a proposed bill that would have required every citizen of
Virginia to give money to the Christian group of his choice
in order to support Christian teachers. Madison's "Memorial," which ultimately defeated the bill, reads like a laun-
dry list of all the reasons government should not fund
religion: it is unnecessary; funding some religions but not
others can lead to divisiveness and violence; funding promotes inequality among religions; providing economic
support harms religion itself by making it complacent
and reliant on the state; and on and on. Interestingly, one
of Madison's points is that even small breaches of the no-
funding principle are bad, because once the principle has
been sacrificed, what will stop the government from providing greater and more substantial amounts of funding
in the future? As he wrote, "Who does not see that . . . the
same authority which can force a citizen to contribute
three pence only of his property for the support of any one
establishment, may force him to conform to any other establishment in all cases whatsoever?"

Madison's "Memorial" is certainly instructive when
thinking about whether government should fund religion,
but I think it's worth noting that the Virginia scheme was,
in fact, quite different from anything we see these days.
Even today, in the pro-funding world of faith-based initia-
tives, nobody would seriously suggest that the government
could choose to fund only Christian teachers. Or even just
religious teachers. The key question of the modern era is
whether government can fund religious recipients *alongside* other similarly situated recipients. So for example, if
the government funds all teachers in some way, the ques-

tion is whether it can include religious teachers in the set of teachers that it funds. On this type of question, the answer used to be sometimes yes, sometimes no; nowadays, the answer is almost always yes.

Trying to explain how this area of law developed in any sort of a comprehensive way is kind of hopeless, because there are just too many cases, most of which are about as short and clear as some of Pynchon's or Hegel's more ambitious works. The best I can do is give you some idea of what the law used to look like before the modern-day Supreme Court basically decided to throw its collective hands up in the air and say "ehhh, whatever." Then I'll explain in somewhat more detail what I mean when I say that the Court threw its collective hands up in the air and said "ehhh, whatever." And somewhere in there, I promise to tell you about the week I spent in Cleveland.

Between the mid-1940s and the mid-1990s, the Court issued a series of completely confusing, but also weirdly fun, decisions as it struggled to balance the harms of funding religion with the practical fact that it's impossible to completely separate religion and public money. You can see this tension clearly in *Everson v. Board of Education*, the first case that the Court ever decided on the issue. The question was whether a New Jersey town could reimburse parents for the money they spent to send their kids to and from school on public buses. The program reimbursed the parents regardless of whether their kids went to public or religious schools. Challengers said that the funding was unconstitutional because it paid for kids to go to religious school and thus advanced religion. The majority of the Court spent most of its opinion explaining why it is so important to keep public money out of religion's hands. It talked about the "wall of separation between Church and State," lauded Madison's "Memorial and Remonstrance" to the rooftops, and stated unequivocally that "no tax in any amount, large or small, can be levied to support any religious activities or institutions, whatever they may be called, or whatever form they may adopt to teach or practice religion." The Court then upheld the town's funding program.

Huh? What? Hello?

The Court recognized that the town's program helped kids get to religious schools. It even conceded that in some marginal cases, parents might not have sent their kids to religious schools if it hadn't been for the reimbursement. But the Court wondered whether this assistance was really any different from the incidental benefits the government already gave religious schools every day. The town provided police and fire protection to the schools, kept the sidewalks safe so the kids could get to the schools, and picked up the trash so the kids didn't have to learn their religious lessons in buildings full of filth and vermin. Nobody would claim that a town violates the First Amendment when it takes away the school's garbage, or that it would be unconstitutional for the fire department to put out a blaze in the rectory. Why should a bit of transportation funding be any different? If a town is going to help out parents who send their kids to public schools, shouldn't it also be able to help the kids who go to religious institutions? Hopefully, you see the problem. Once you concede that the state has to be able to give some incidental financial support to religion, it becomes kind of difficult to say how much support is too much. Where, in other words, should the Court draw the line?

In 1977 the Court decided where to draw the line: field trips! The case was called *Wolman v. Walter,* and it involved six different funding programs in Ohio, some of which the Court upheld and others of which it struck down. One of the programs that the Court struck down would have reimbursed private schools, including religious schools, for the costs of transporting their students on field trips. The lower court thought this was the same kind of thing as in *Everson*, and so it upheld the program. The Supreme Court, on the other hand, thought the situations were very different. For one thing, the public money was going right to the religious schools instead of to the parents. More important, though, was the special nature of field trips. Unlike the bus transportation to and from school in *Everson*, which was "unrelated to any aspect of the curriculum," field trips "are an integral part of the educational experience." As such, the Court said, transportation for religious field trips could not be funded with public money.

This distinction was just one of the dicey ones the Court drew during this period as it tried to make sense of this incredibly complicated area of law. Teaching these cases turns out to be pretty enjoyable, because you can act really cocky when you talk about them. "Ooooh, ha, ha, ha, look at that silly Supreme Court," you can say, "they are soooooo silly with their silly distinctions. Busing to school is okay, but busing for field trips is not okay. Lending books to religious schools is okay, but lending filmstrips is not. The state can give religious schools money to administer state-prepared tests, but not to administer tests prepared by the religious teachers themselves. The state can't send public school teachers into religious schools to teach regular courses like math or history, but it can send in teachers to provide speech, hearing, and psychological services. The state can give money to religious colleges to construct buildings, but only if those buildings are not used for religious purposes." And so on and so on.

You probably won't be surprised to hear that I don't think these cases were crazy at all. Just like when they apply the endorsement test to evaluate religious symbols and displays, the justices in these funding cases were simply using their best judgment to sort out which kinds of funding programs went too far in supporting religion and which ones were okay. What's wrong, I've always wondered, with judges exercising *judgment*? It's true that when the Court issues decisions that turn on very specific facts and circumstances, it becomes harder for lower courts and everyone else to know what is legal and what is not, but so what? I think it's better for the Court to issue thoughtful decisions that are difficult for lower court judges and litigants to follow than for the Court to issue crystal clear opinions that make no sense.

Weary of being mocked by law professors (not really), the Court in the 1990s started cleaning up its jurisprudence by settling on a couple of very broad and clear principles that are easy to follow and for the most part ignore the harms posed by funding religion. The first principle is this: if a government program gives money to private individuals who then choose to give that money to religious institutions, the program will be upheld if the set of potential recipients of the money is neutral with respect to religion, that is, it includes both religious and nonreligious potential recipients. Take school voucher programs, for example: the government wants to make it possible for lower-income parents to send their kids to private schools, so it says that anyone who qualifies can have a certain amount of money to go to the private school of his or her choice. So long as the money goes to the parents first, rather than directly to the schools, and so long as the parents can theoretically choose to spend their money at either a private religious school or a private nonreligious school, then the program is basically fine. Again, the key points are that (1) the money has to go to the private individual, who then chooses what institution to give the money to, and (2) the set of institutions from which the individual can choose must include both religious and nonreligious institutions.

The Court actually cemented this principle in a 2002 case involving the Cleveland school voucher program, which I will talk about in some depth in a minute, but it started invoking the idea a lot earlier. In 1986, for instance, the Court said that a blind student who wanted to attend a Christian college could take advantage of a state program that gave money to visually disabled students to assist them in their studies. Even though the money ended up benefiting the religious school, it did so "only as a result of the genuinely independent and private choice" of the student who chose to attend the religious school. In 1993 the Court said that a school district could provide a deaf student with a sign language interpreter to help him in the Catholic school he chose to attend, for the same reason.

These cases involved relatively small amounts of money, so it was not clear what the Court might do with a program that involved a whole lot more clams. Would the Court go back to its zany ways and distinguish small programs from big ones? Or would it extend the principle from these smaller cases and uphold any funding program, no matter how gargantuan, so long as the money is funneled to religion through the private choices of individuals?

Enter the Cleveland voucher case. By the late 1990s, the Cleveland public schools were in such a bad state that an auditor declared they were suffering a "crisis . . . perhaps unprecedented in the history of American education."

Only one in ten Cleveland ninth graders were able to pass the state's proficiency examination, which, believe me, is no MENSA admissions test. The "citizenship" portion of the October 2005 exam, for instance, asked students to identify which letter corresponded to Washington, D.C., on a map; the wrong answers represented cities in Pennsylvania, Illinois, and Iowa. Another multiple-choice question reproduced a map of Ohio with its major cities and asked students, "In what direction would you be traveling if you were going from Cincinnati to Cleveland?" This question would probably have been easy enough even if the test writers hadn't put a compass in the corner of the map.

After a federal court placed the failing school district under state control, Ohio enacted a school voucher program to give inner-city kids some chance of getting out of the Cleveland public schools. The details of the program were complicated, but basically the idea was to provide particularly poor parents (we're talking those with incomes way below the poverty line) with a voucher of about $2,200, which they could use in any private school that chose to participate in the program. Both religious and nonreligious schools could join the program, so long as they agreed not to discriminate against anyone on the basis of race or religion or to "advocate or foster unlawful behavior or teach hatred of any person or group on the basis of race . . . or religion." In the year under review, 82 percent of the fifty-six schools in the program were religious; 96 percent of the about 3,700 students who got a voucher used it in a religious school. Remarkably, about two-thirds of the parents who sent their kids to religious schools chose a school of a different religion than their own.

The Court held the Cleveland program constitutional by a 5–4 margin. The four dissenters thought that underwriting religion with a vast amount of public funds was incredibly dangerous. One problem was that the program violated the conscience of nonbelievers. Why should a Jew have to pay taxes to support Catholicism, or an atheist have to contribute to the growth of Islam? Second, some justices were concerned that funding religious schools might harm the religious mission of those schools because the state can always attach conditions to the funding. This is the so-called "strings" issue. A religious school that becomes dependent on government aid might find itself agreeing to a condition that is inconsistent with its religious mission if doing so is necessary to keep itself afloat. For example, the Cleveland system forbids participating schools from discriminating on the basis of religion. Does that mean a conservative Christian school might have to hire an atheist to teach an ethics class or lose its public funding? Is that a choice we really want to put to religious institutions? Finally, the dissenters worried about social strife and divisiveness. They were concerned that religious groups in Cleveland might start fighting to get the most cash from the program, thus starting a "struggle of sect against sect." Justice Breyer, who thinks a main purpose of the establishment clause is to create civil peace on issues of religion, was particularly concerned about this possibility.

The dissenters also found problems with some of the specifics of the Cleveland program. For example, they thought the size of the voucher encouraged parents to send their kids to religious schools. They argued that $2,200 is not enough to send anyone to the generally expensive secular private schools, but is perfectly suited for paying Catholic school tuition, which runs (lo and behold!) about $2,200. The dissenters also felt queasy about the fact that such a large percentage of the money was going to religious schools; if the program is truly neutral, they wondered, why are 82 percent of the schools religious and 96 percent of the money going to them? The majority, however, was not impressed. In typically terse fashion, Chief Justice Rehnquist paid little attention to these concerns and concluded that the program was fine because it relied on private choice and included both religious and nonreligious schools. Of course, all sorts of *policy* arguments can be advanced against school vouchers, not least of which is that they destroy what's left of the public schools by sucking away money and the top students, but the Court's decision in the Cleveland case means that from a *constitutional* perspective, they are generally fine.

Spending a week in Cleveland to learn about the voucher program was unlike any of the other trips I'd taken thus far. Since I was trying to get some handle on how the case had affected an entire city, there was no obvious specific place to visit or people to meet. Also, Cleveland is big. I realized pretty quickly that I was going to have to come up with some targeted questions to investigate if I was going to learn anything useful in the limited amount of time I had, particularly because the Red Sox–Indians American League Championship Series had just moved to Cleveland, and I had bought tickets online for two of the games at an enormous cost that, quite frankly, is going to make it hard for Walter to attend college (sorry, kid).

I decided to focus on three questions. First, I wanted to know how minority religious traditions felt about the voucher program. Were they happy to be able to share in the public funds, or did they resent the program, since it would probably benefit bigger religions more than themselves? Second, I wondered whether any minority religious groups had managed to make use of the voucher money, and if so, how. Finally, I was curious as to whether either minority or majority religious groups were worried about the "strings" issue—in other words, were they concerned that at some point, either now or in the future, they might have to sacrifice some of their religious beliefs to continue receiving government funds. By focusing on these questions, I decided not to inquire too much into how people felt about the policy issues raised by voucher programs or into the thorny issue of whether a program that delivers tons of money to religious schools violates the conscience of nonbelievers.

I hadn't looked into any of the great Asian religions on my trips so far, so I contacted a couple of Buddhist temples around the city to see if anyone would talk to me. It took a while to hear back, but while I was in Cincinnati staring open-mouthed at animatronic biblical characters at the Creation Museum (see chapter 8), I got an e-mail from an abbot at a small temple, who said that if I could come to their service the next morning, I might be able to talk to some people with thoughts about school vouchers. So after a leisurely day of learning about creationist astronomy and the Fall of Man, I drove the four hours to Cleveland and got in just in time to watch the Red Sox blow Game 2 of the ALCS on my hotel television sometime after one in the morning. I was therefore completely exhausted when my alarm buzzer went off five hours later and I went in search of the CloudWater Zendo Buddhist temple, way out somewhere on Cleveland's west side.

From the outside, the CloudWater Zendo Buddhist temple looks a lot like the Suds-n-Dogs restaurant next door or the accounting storefront offices across the street. It's a tiny, nondescript, tan and hunter green building with a little parking lot in the back—a far cry from, say,

Tibet's Potala Palace. Inside, however, CloudWater Zendo was comfortable and welcoming and smelled of incense. This was not the first time I had attended a Buddhist service. A few years back, Karen and I were traveling around Japan and stayed for a couple of nights at a Buddhist monastery, which was lovely and pleasant despite the fact that about two hundred seven-year-olds had camped out there on a field trip, screaming nonstop like they had happened upon an all-day Hannah Montana concert. The kids were asleep, though, for the 6:00 a.m. service, which was truly beautiful and moving and involved all sorts of drumming and chanting and bell ringing and delightful colors and smells that to this day relax me if I think about them.

The room where the service was held at CloudWater Zendo was a lot like the room where we saw the service in Japan. The incense was even stronger than in the entry room, and an entire wall had been transformed into a Buddhist shrine, with lots of small statues and oranges and flowers and incense holders surrounding one big fat smiling Buddha in the middle. I love looking at these peaceful, plump guys with their casual postures and enlightened grins, and I was immediately glad that I had made the early morning trip out, even if I didn't end up getting to talk to anyone about vouchers. As in other Buddhist places I've been to, the colors were rich and warm, mostly reds and browns and oranges. A thick burgundy rug covered the floor. Two female monks were sitting to either side of the abbot himself, a tall white man with a shaved head wearing a red and orange robe. All three had bowls next to them, which they used during the service to make gongs and boops and bings and other sounds to calm the spirit and honor the Buddhas.

I took a seat at the edge of the rug and looked around. I was one of six people who were sitting cross-legged, waiting for the service to begin. Among the others in the room, all of whom had clearly been there before, probably many times, there were three women and two men, one African American and one Ukrainian, most a little on the youngish side of middle age. Of all the people in the room, I was definitely the one whose hamstrings were making the loudest creaking noises. Squished between the floor and the entire weight of my upper body, my knees groaned in pain, to say nothing of my prostate. Even sitting on a round pillow, I was sure that if the service lasted more than about seven seconds, I was going to die. I silently implored the smiling Buddhas to deliver me serenity and relief.

I guess the Buddhas heard my prayers, because about three minutes into the service, my lower body went completely numb, thus allowing me to focus on the proceedings instead of my impending paraplegia. We had all been given a handout with Sanskrit or Chinese words transliterated into English syllables, and from time to time we would chant along with the monks, although I have no idea what we were saying.

After the service, we moved to the other half of the room for some meditation. This part of the room was much like the other part, except that the lighting was softer and I think there were somewhat fewer Buddhas. Squashy pillows were set around the room in a horseshoe, and since I had no idea what was going on, I stood back and watched to see what everyone was going to do. It turned out that the thing to do was to sit cross-legged on the pillows and face the wall, but I also noticed that at least one person was using a little stool-like thing to sit on, and since I thought my body had taken enough abuse for one morning, I opted for that. The stool-like thing was harder to negotiate than I thought, however, and when it became clear that I was about to break both of my feet, one of the monks kindly came over and showed me how it worked.

The idea with the meditation was to stay completely silent for twenty-five minutes. If you've never tried it, let me tell you that this is a ridiculously difficult thing to do. The room was perfectly quiet, save for the gurgling of coffee and bagels in the stomach of the guy next to me. I knew that I was supposed to empty my mind of all conscious thought, so that's what I tried to do. It worked for about eleven seconds. After that, I devoted some time to working out possible strategies for the Middle East situation and global warming. I thought up a new recipe for beef wellington. I made some headway on an epic poem I've been meaning to start on. I mentally sketched out (rather roughly, I'm afraid) an idea for an alternative proof of Fermat's last theorem. With about fifteen minutes left in the session, I made a concerted effort to stop thinking of such things and to once again empty my mind of all conscious thought. But then my ear started to itch, which of course made me think of the hammer, anvil, and stirrup, my three favorite parts of the human body, which in turn made me think of the islets of Langerhans, and so on, until the abbot gonged the gong that signaled the end of the meditation, at which point I realized I had kept my mind quiet from all conscious thoughts for about twenty-eight seconds total.

After some fun and surprisingly not too awkward prostrating of ourselves before the room's lone Buddha, the nine of us retired back into the casual waiting room of the temple for some tea and conversation. The abbot gave what is called a dharma talk, in which one explains some aspect of Buddhist thought and then opens up the floor for discussion. The topic that day was the three aspects of the Three Jewels (Buddha, Dharma, Sangha), for which the abbot drew a perplexing nine-box graph on the temple's whiteboard. I understood about 4 percent of what he said. After a little conversation on this topic, the abbot introduced me and mentioned my interest in the voucher program. I was a little surprised, because I didn't know I was going to be an official part of the morning's proceedings, but there it was.

We talked as a group about public education, charter schools, and vouchers for close to an hour. Most of the conversation was about vouchers and education in general rather than on the religious aspects of the program. One guy, for example, talked at length about his terrible experience running a charter school for a company that cares only about making money and hates teachers, which, it turns out, is not a recipe for educational success. I tried whenever possible to move the question back to how Buddhists in particular might feel about the voucher program, and I got some interesting responses. One nice lady said that the program has contributed to the ghettoization of the public school system, which she thought was bad from a Buddhist perspective, since Buddhists want all people to prosper. The abbot worried that the program is a cash grab for evangelical Christianity, which is already the "top dog" that informs the policies of the country.

One woman, who was visibly bristling at most of the conversation, finally broke in with an objection. She said that we were ignoring an important philosophical difference between Western and Eastern religions. Since Western religions tend to take a "we're right, you're wrong" attitude, it's not surprising that they want support for their schools to train their kids in the "right" views, so the kids don't end up going to hell. Eastern religions, however, are different, according to this Buddhist woman. Since Buddhists don't care much about dogma, there's little reason for them to seek state support for their religion. "It's about making a personal journey, and it's inclusive. If you want to come at it from a Christian perspective, or a Jewish perspective, then rock on with your bad self." I'm not sure that all Buddhists think everyone should just rock on with their bad selves, but it was a provocative thought, and also I enjoyed saying "rock on with your bad self" about a thousand times over the next two weeks, until Karen exasperatedly erected an official and permanent household ban on the phrase.

One argument against vouchers is that only certain religions have the inclination and, more importantly, the ability to start their own schools, and therefore even a "neutral" program (in the sense that any religion can theoretically participate) is not really neutral at all. In an ideal world, a parent could use a voucher to send his or her child to schools representing a huge range of religious beliefs—not just Catholic and Protestant, but Jewish, Confucian, Buddhist, Hindu, and all sorts of others as well. Otherwise, what are parents who belong to a minority tradition that has no school in the program supposed to do if they want their kid to go to a private school? Maybe they could send their child to a nonreligious private school, but if those schools are too expensive or undesirable for some other reason (say they are run by people who hate teachers), then the parents might have no choice but to send their child to a Christian school. How is that neutral?

With this in mind, I asked whether it would make any sense to talk about setting up a Buddhist school in Cleveland, and the consensus was no. The abbot described the Cleveland Buddhist community: there's a large Japanese temple outside the city limits, a Vietnamese community where the kids go to public school and excel, and some other smaller groups, including themselves and one that the abbot for some reason called the "Tina Turner Buddhists," I guess because they've figured out the secret to eternal youth and have a great set of thighs. In any event, the various subcommunities are all small, and they are all very different. There is no way they could start a school. "We can't even get together for a meeting or a picnic, much less a school," was how I think the abbot put it.

In other words, *neutral shmeutral.*

Perhaps you're a Christian reading this book and wondering: What is all this fuss about minority religions? How hard is it really, you're wondering, to be a minority surrounded by people who disagree with your views on important matters? If this describes your situation, I propose you do the following: become a Boston Red Sox fan, travel to Cleveland for the championship series, don a Red Sox cap, and go sit in the bleachers of Jacobs Field while the Indians trounce the Red Sox 7–3 to go up 3–1 in the series. I guarantee that sitting there in the midst of forty-five thousand maniacal Cleveland Indians fans screaming "Boston sucks" after about thirty beers each, whooping and hollering like Chief Wahoo himself while John the Drummer beats a warpath drum in the stadium's back row, will give you a whole new appreciation for the plight of minorities, especially if you have to sit near a certain creepy, hammered asshole who will haunt your dreams for the rest of your life.

No book about religion in the United States can be complete without some account of Islam, so while I was in Cleveland, I tried to learn what I could about the Muslims in the city and how they felt about the voucher program. It turns out that there is a small Muslim elementary school within city limits that receives vouchers; as far as I could tell, it was the only non-Christian religious school getting voucher funds.* I wanted to look around the school if I could, but I was too chicken to just call up the principal and ask if I could visit, so instead I went trolling around online to find people who might have some connection with the school. This led me in circuitous ways that I can't possibly reconstruct to two incredibly helpful members of the Cleveland Muslim community, who generously agreed to meet and explain their faith to me. Since I shamefully know very little about Islam, this was no easy task for them.

I met Suna at the Grand Mosque in the town of Parma, right outside the Cleveland city limits. The mosque is the largest of about a dozen or so around town, and it is the home of the Islamic Center of Cleveland (ICC). The word "grand" definitely describes the building; it's gigantic and capped with an impressively huge gold dome and the half-moon crescent symbol of Islam. Suna is a short woman, born into the faith; she grew up in Michigan and, after living for a year in Jerusalem, moved to Cleveland, where she got married and had kids. Since she was wearing a head scarf, I couldn't really tell how old she was. I guessed she was somewhere between twenty-five and forty-five, give

---

*A note regarding the Cleveland Jewish population. There really isn't any, at least within the city limits. There are no Jewish schools in the city, much less ones that receive voucher funds. There is, however, a large Jewish population in the surrounding suburbs. I contacted several prominent members of this Jewish community to talk about the voucher program, and their unwillingness to speak about the issue suggested they thought it about as suitable for public discussion as, say, what position they prefer during sexual intercourse. The one person who was nice enough to speak to me did so off the record, and so I can't tell you anything that he or she said or did not say, if indeed he or she said or did not say anything to me, which I can neither confirm nor deny.

or take a few years on either side. Carrying her cute little one-year-old son, she greeted me at the entrance of the mosque, where there was a round fountain-like structure that looked just like a fountain, except that there was no fountain anymore. Suna explained that about a week after 9/11, a twenty-nine-year-old guy drove his Mustang into the mosque going eighty miles an hour. The car flew six feet in the air, up three steps, and through two sets of doors and some pillars, landing right on the fountain that understandably is no longer a fountain. He caused at least forty thousand dollars' worth of damage. Suna explained that he then sat in his car for fifteen minutes before calling for help. According to a news account, the guy, whose brother was in the military, had been conducting a candlelight vigil when his girlfriend blew out the candle and told him to settle down. He assaulted her and then got in the Mustang and drove through the mosque. He broke bones in his back and feet; pleaded guilty to ethnic intimidation, burglary, and vandalism; and was sentenced to five years in prison.

Since I had never been in a mosque, I found Suna's tour of the place incredibly interesting. The most dramatic part is the enormous open space under the dome, where the community prays. For someone far more accustomed to temples and churches, being in a massive, open room under maybe a forty-foot ceiling, with no chairs or pews or tables of any kind on the floor, is pretty striking. Suna explained that although the mosque has an official membership of only about three hundred, more than a thousand people come in for the regular Friday service, and maybe four thousand show up to pray during the holidays. I tried to imagine the room packed with people praying on the light purplish-blue carpet, and I have to say that it must be quite impressive. There are two pulpits high on the front wall, a large Arabic word "Allah" in a circle near them, and the Islamic testimony of faith in a rectangle slightly below. There are pillars everywhere, but Suna explained that they are for holding up the ceiling, not for representing the pillars of Islam. Indeed, she told me that symbols are not really part of the faith at all.

On one of the walls were shelves of huge volumes of the Qur'an, and Suna told me that there are people, one just eight years old, who have memorized the whole thing. I was impressed, particularly since I can't even seem to remember all the words to "I've Been Working on the Railroad," which pisses my son off to no end. I asked Suna about the different schools of Islam and whether they mattered for worship at the mosque. She said that the mosque is very diverse and attracts both Shia and Sunni worshippers. Although most of the other mosques around the city are primarily Sunni, the different schools don't really create much controversy. "You wouldn't be able to tell who is what," she said. "People in Cleveland are just trying to survive. The economy is bad. Crime is bad. This is a place where people can come and get respite."

Although a branch of the Al Ihsan School rents space in the mosque, Suna didn't know all that much about the voucher program. This wasn't surprising, because the mosque is outside the Cleveland city limits, and thus the branch cannot accept vouchers. She did mention that some Muslims think that admitting voucher students into the Cleveland branch of the school has kept back that part of the school academically and that this was one of the reasons the school opened a branch in Parma. I looked around, and at the entrance of the area leased by the school, there was a poster titled "Al Ihsan School ICC Campus, Teachers' Wish List," which had pictures of all sorts of things that the teachers wanted for the school, including alphabet blocks from Toys "R" Us and a collection of books by Dr. Seuss.

I asked Suna about Muslim views on church/state relations generally. She said that the Muslims she knows generally agree with keeping church and state separate, but that they don't think religion should be kept out of public life. Believers should enjoy free exercise rights, she said, and indeed the Cleveland schools have been pretty good about giving Muslim children the time and space to pray and have been mostly supportive of their dress obligations as well. Then Suna told me something that I found incredibly surprising. She said that a lot of Muslims, including herself, have chosen to send their high-school-age kids to Catholic schools. I told her I found this odd, and she explained that since there are no Islamic high schools in Cleveland, Muslims often send their older kids to the Catholic schools so that they can be in a religious environment, even if it's not their own religion. This is true even though the Catholic schools in Cleveland require students to partake in Catholic ceremonies and say Catholic prayers. Suna said that her daughter went to a Catholic school and figured out how to pray in a Muslim way even when Catholic prayer was mandatory.

It took me a while to figure out why this seemed so bizarre to me, and I finally concluded that it's because I just can't imagine any Jewish parents, regardless of how secular and reformed and liberal they might be, sending their kids to a Christian school of any type if the kids were going to have to participate in a Christian ritual of any kind. I say this having gone to a Catholic high school myself, where I was one of eight Jews (in an incredible triumph of creativity, we called ourselves "the Jew Crew") who were excused from rituals and religion class and everything else that was specifically Catholic. My parents had been on the fence about sending me to St. John's Prep in the first place (and probably wouldn't have if my hometown's school system wasn't the kind of place that made national headlines when a bus driver diverted her bus to a police station after realizing that the students were smoking dope on board), and when I suggested one day that I might enroll in religion class instead of taking Technical Theater for the third time, they came pretty close to killing me dead.

Later in the week, I met Shamsuddin Waheed at, of all places, a Starbucks near Case Western Reserve University. Brother Waheed had for a while been an imam of a small, local, mostly African American mosque but had recently stepped down to pursue other activities, such as moderating an online forum about Islam that is in part intended to spread knowledge about Islam and dispel stereotypes of Muslims. Waheed and I were actually both sitting in the Starbucks at the same time for maybe ten minutes without speaking to each other. I guess I was looking for someone older and more elaborately dressed or something; at first I hadn't taken the casually dressed young guy surrounded by books and looking at his cell phone to be an imam. But if there's one thing I've learned on this road trip, it's that you can never guess what someone is going to look like just by knowing his or her religion, and when I took a peek and saw that all the books on the table were about Islam, I introduced myself in the hopes that this was Waheed, and it was.

We talked about vouchers and the Al Ihsan school a little bit (he put me in touch with a board member, who put me in touch with the school itself), but since Waheed is not affiliated with the school, we quickly moved on to talk more generally about the plight of Muslims in a post-

9/11 world and his own views on church/state relations. I asked him why he set up his online forum, and he said that he wanted to explain that Islam is a rational faith that is about spirituality rather than confrontation and violence. He thinks that Muslims have become too insular after 9/11 and that they should come out of their shell. Specifically, he told me that with his forum, he wants to show the world that Muslims are "not monsters waiting to devour your brains like in a movie."

Although Waheed concedes that this insularity is somewhat responsible for the tense relations between Muslims and non-Muslims in the United States, he placed most of the blame for this state of affairs on the government and media. He thinks that the government views Islam as the enemy, and that Muslims therefore view the government with great suspicion. On a global scale, he pointed to President Bush's war in Iraq and attitude toward Iran as possible evidence that official government policy might be driven by anti-Muslim feeling. Closer to home, he raised the relatively recent deportation of the imam at the Grand Mosque in Parma for lying on immigration documents. According to Waheed, the imam was actively promoting interfaith relations, but got "caught up in the atmosphere of fear and hate that 9/11 produced." Waheed thinks the authorities were unjustified in deporting the imam, and he was clearly quite upset about the incident.

I wondered whether this suspicion that Waheed was talking about leads Muslims to see government sponsorship of Christianity as a problem. As with Suna's point about Muslims sending their kids to Catholic schools, Waheed's answer surprised me. He said he thinks most Muslims would agree with his view that this sponsorship is not a problem. "We're a minority," he said. "It's to be expected that the government would sponsor religious symbols like the Ten Commandments." When I pressed him a little on the issue, he said simply, "I don't even think about it." Then I wondered whether this attitude might have something to do with the close relationship between Islam and the state in a number of countries, which might make the close identification of Christianity and the U.S. government seem more natural. Waheed agreed that there are a lot of Islamic countries that fit this profile, but he did not think that Muslims have, for the most part, brought that attitude to the United States.

I took my leave of Brother Waheed, because it was about time for Game 5 of the ALCS. I would like to just stress that going to a playoff game on the road is a lot more fun when (1) you are sitting in the expensive box seats, where the other patrons might make fun of you (and Manny Ramirez) a little bit, but generally aren't drunk, or at least aren't "the bad guy in *Sling Blade*" drunk, and so do not seem highly mean or unpredictable or threatening in any way; (2) the opposing team's management makes the boneheaded move of inviting Josh Beckett's ex-girlfriend to sing the national anthem; and therefore (3) your suddenly revitalized favorite team remembers how to play baseball and kicks the crap out of the home team, making all their fans, especially that one odious hammered guy, sad.

The original branch of the Al Ihsan school on Cleveland's west side is the only Muslim school that participates in the city's voucher program and must be one of only a very few Muslim schools to receive public money in the entire United States. It is located in a small, brown brick, two-story building that seems to be directly in the flight path of every plane that takes off from Cleveland's Hopkins Airport. When I arrived, Sister Julia was outside shepherding a bunch of skipping and chattering children back inside the building following a routine fire drill. I said hello, and she showed me in to see Sister Sara Syed, the school's exceedingly sweet and very tiny principal. Syed seemed fairly young, although again, it was hard to tell because she was wearing a black head scarf. She told me that she had applied for a teaching job at the school and had been offered the principal's job instead. A former science teacher at a local nondenominational charter school, Syed told me that she prefers being in the classroom to managing paperwork, but that she shares the school board's vision to make the curriculum more academically rigorous and thereby increase enrollment in the older grades. About eighty students attend the K–6 school, but most of them are very young. Only three kids were enrolled in the sixth grade at the time I visited.

The school has apparently had a bit of a rocky history. It was established in 2003, and according to a letter I spied on the wall from a city employee, the school has made big improvements as of late in response to some "horror stories" from prior years involving a "lack of discipline, respect, and education." Syed told me that a good percentage of the students are there on vouchers. She showed me a list of all the students in the school, with voucher recipients highlighted in yellow; it looked to me like maybe two-fifths or even half of the students were receiving public funds. The curriculum involves both core academic classes, like science, math, and social studies, and religious classes, which include Islamic studies, Arabic, and Koran. About two hours in the day are devoted to the religious part of the curriculum, although Syed said she hopes to place more emphasis on the core classes in the future.

The core classes, she pointed out, also include religious perspectives on whatever the students are learning. Girls and boys are taught together in the classroom, but they are separated for recess and lunch, for religious as well as disciplinary reasons. I asked Syed about the "strings" issue—whether she or anyone else was concerned that the school might become dependent on government money and thus subject to manipulation by the state. She said there was no such concern whatsoever.*

The principal generously gave me a tour of the school and even let me look in on a couple of classes. The fifth and sixth graders, who are the only students in different grades grouped together in a single classroom, were in science class learning something about the exchange of gases. The fourth graders were in math doing multiplication tables; my heart started palpitating as I recalled doing the same thing back when I was a kid. The younger children were in classrooms learning Arabic and the Koran. Some other kids were upstairs sitting on the floor in a semicircle around an imam, who was giving them lessons in Islamic studies. Another class was reading from a book called *I Love Islam: Level 2*.

The school was a fascinating combination of tradi-

---

*I actually asked a number of Muslims who were familiar with the school the same question, and without exception, they voiced no concern whatsoever about the potential danger of government funding. For the most part, the issue was so far from people's minds that I had to do some real explaining to make the issue clear. The same thing was true with the representatives of the Catholic diocese that I met with. One would think that since the majority of voucher schools are Catholic schools, this might have been a real worry for the diocese, but neither of the people I spoke to seemed worried or even, frankly, familiar with the issue. Whether this means that the issue is not a real one, of course, is an entirely different matter.

tional academic stuff and religious stuff. On the walls were posters kids made about things like "The Life Cycle of Spiders" and "Frogs" ("some people eat frogs legs, yuck!"), but also construction-paper crescent moons with "I want to help the poor" and "Praise Allah" on them. There were Dora and Transformer backpacks, but also glitter posters that read "There's no God but Allah" in English and Arabic. There was a box of soccer balls underneath a colorful sign that said "I Love Mohammed." A picture with "TEAM: Together Everyone Achieves More" was on the wall right next to a quotation from the Koran reading "God . . . has willed to spread his Light in all its fullness, however hateful this may be to all who deny the truth." In the corner of one otherwise empty classroom with maps on the wall, a teacher was quietly prostrating herself on a prayer mat in the direction of Mecca.

I said earlier that the Supreme Court had come up with two broad principles for deciding cases involving aid to religion. Here is the second: the government may aid religious organizations directly (as opposed to indirectly, through the choices of private individuals, as in the voucher situation) only if it aids them as part of a neutral set of recipients that includes religious and secular organizations, and only if the aid is not actually diverted by the religious organizations to religious uses. It's the last part of this principle that is the most important. If the government gives aid to religious organizations directly as part of a program of giving direct aid to both religious and nonreligious organizations, the religious organization cannot use the aid to promote its religious mission. In other words, indirect aid can be used by the religion for religious purposes, but direct aid cannot. The reason I keep annoyingly using the word "aid" here instead of "money" is that the Court has suggested it might treat money differently from in-kind aid, like computers or books or the like, although I doubt very much that if it came down to it, the Court would treat the two kinds of aid any differently.

This, anyway, is the rule right now. It wasn't always the rule, and it might not be the rule for long, but for today, under the rationale of a case from 2000 called *Mitchell v. Helms*, it's the rule. That case involved a Louisiana program that gave computers and other instructional materials directly to schools, both public and private. Challengers said the program was unconstitutional because religious schools were among the recipients of the aid and would inevitably use the equipment for religious purposes, even though a condition of receiving the computers was that they could not be used to further religion. The Court, in a 6–3 decision involving three separate opinions, upheld the program. Four justices who voted to uphold the program said that it didn't matter whether the religious schools used the computers to promote religion. On the other hand, the three dissenters agreed with the challengers and thought that since the religious schools *might* divert the computers for religious purposes, the program should be invalidated. This left Justices O'Connor and Breyer, whose separate concurrence took a middle-ground approach and said that the program was okay because there was no evidence that the schools were actually using the instructional materials for religious purposes. Importantly, the concurrence said that if the schools had actually used the computers for religious purposes, the program would have been unconstitutional.

This rule—that direct aid cannot be used for religious purposes—was the main limitation on the Bush administration's so-called "faith-based initiative." That thing is kind of hard to explain, but it basically referred to the administration's concerted efforts, through institutional reforms and some other stuff, to make sure that religious groups got their fair share (or, depending on who you ask, a larger than fair share) of public money for various social services like substance abuse, mental health assistance, and welfare-to-work programs. The initiative resulted in a massive increase in public funding of religious organizations, but under current law, a group receiving such funding cannot use the money for promoting religious activities, religious education, proselytizing, or other parts of its religious mission. Opponents, of course, thought the administration did not monitor the use of the funds closely enough and brought all kinds of lawsuits challenging specific funding arrangements, like the time an abstinence-until-marriage organization called "The Silver Ring Thing" used federal funds to promote Christianity, Jesus, and the Bible alongside its view of human sexuality.

Of course, in 2005, Sandra Day O'Connor retired and was replaced by Samuel Alito. If the issue comes up again, Alito is likely to side with the four justices in *Mitchell v. Helms* who said that religious groups should be able to use direct public funding to promote religion. If this happens, there will be pretty much nothing stopping the government from providing massive direct assistance to Christian groups to promote Christianity any way they want. Talk about the founding fathers rolling over in their graves!

7

BALL-FIELD
PRAYER BROUHAHA

Destination East Texas

The last chapter concerned the limits that the First Amendment places on government funding of private religious schools. But what about the public schools? What limits apply there?

Let's start with a seemingly simple question: can kids pray in the public schools? This may be a surprise to you, but the answer is absolutely yes. Although a lot of people think that the Supreme Court has banned all forms of prayer in the public schools, the fact is that as long as school personnel are not themselves involved with the prayer, public school students may pray all they want, to whomever they want, willy-nilly, before school, after school, during recess, between classes, and during moments of silence. They can pray by themselves or together with other students. They can pray, in other words, like praying is going out of style.

What the Supreme Court has said, and what has pissed people off for almost fifty years now, is that the school itself cannot be actively involved with the prayer. School personnel cannot lead the kids in prayer, pick out which prayers the kids will say, draft a little prayer for them, invite someone to give a prayer at the school graduation, or set up a policy to pick which kid will get to deliver the prayer before a football game. At the moment, for some reason, teachers *can* pressure their students to declare that there is one God and that this God is intimately related to the well-being of the United States of America; but other than the Pledge of Allegiance, school-led religious exercises are generally not allowed.

I am not sure why there is such a misconception out there that the Supreme Court has banned school prayer. It's not like the Court itself hasn't tried to explain that there is a difference between government-sponsored religious exercises, which are not okay, and privately initiated religious exercises, which are protected. The Supreme Court has said this over and over again. Several times, for example, it has repeated the following sentence: "There is a crucial difference between government speech endorsing religion, which the Establishment Clause forbids, and private speech endorsing religion, which the Free Speech and Free Exercise Clauses protect." And although there are cases where it's not entirely clear whether the government is sponsoring the prayer, the distinction is generally not all that hard to understand. Somehow the Court's message just hasn't come across clearly, maybe because the justices don't always write readable English sentences, or maybe because the media doesn't always report the Court's decisions accurately, or maybe because the Court's detractors have successfully confused everyone with their inaccurate characterizations of the Court's decisions.

I've often thought that the Court should hire a public relations firm. With so many people out there trying to distort the Court's decisions to promote a political agenda, how else can a court that speaks through unintelligible legal gobbledygook hope to get its message across? Certainly not through the media, which has an incentive to overdramatize the Court's decisions, and definitely not through law professors, who make their living by pointing out how stupid they think the Court is.* I would probably stop short of urging the Court to hire celebrities to sell the Court's opinions to the public, but I don't see how it would hurt to have some slick Madison Avenue types talking up the Court and packaging its opinions in an understandable and palatable light, perhaps even with bullet points and posters with puppies on them.

Anyway, the Supreme Court first got involved in the school prayer issue back in the early 1960s, when it held in two cases that public schools cannot lead religious exercises in the classroom. In *Engel v. Vitale*, a public school in Long Island drafted this inspiring gem of a prayer, which it then required its students to recite every morning: "Almighty God, we acknowledge our dependence upon Thee, and we beg Thy blessings upon us, our parents, our teachers, and our country. Amen." The Supreme Court said this clearly promoted religion and was therefore unconstitutional. In *Abington School District v. Schempp*, a Unitarian challenged a Pennsylvania law that required the reading of ten Bible passages every morning in the public schools. The Court said the law was unconstitutional, in an 8–1 decision that nonetheless went out of its way to explain that it would be not only okay, but also a really good idea for schools to teach *objectively* about the Bible and other religions in the classroom, a point that the Court's critics usually don't mention. It is often said that these decisions are two of the most unpopular ones in Supreme Court history,

---

*No law professor, for example, has ever gotten tenure for writing an article titled "The Supreme Court: What a Lovely Court!"

and although I understand why, the fact is that they are among the most obvious and straightforward applications of the First Amendment you are ever going to find. The harder questions arise when the prayers move outside the classroom, and those questions (as well as what happened when I went to east Texas) are the subject of this chapter.

One of the most interesting and difficult cases the Supreme Court has ever decided in the church/state area involved a graduation prayer given by a rabbi at a middle school graduation in Providence, Rhode Island. The school had a practice of inviting clergy to give one of those so-called "nondenominational" prayers at the beginning of the ceremony to solemnize the occasion or something. One year the school invited Rabbi Les Gutterman, an extremely popular and prominent rabbi in the community, to give the opening prayer and benediction. A family sued. In *Lee v. Weisman*, the Court ruled that the school's practice of inviting someone to give a graduation prayer violated the First Amendment. The majority opinion was written by Justice Kennedy. Justice Scalia, of course, wrote the dissent.

Justice Kennedy and Justice Scalia are very different kinds of judges. Justice Kennedy is always hemming and hawing and wringing his hands and rubbing his temples and changing his mind and struggling mightily to come up with the right answer to whatever question he's wondering about, while Justice Scalia seems to, well, not do these things. To judge from his written decisions, public speeches, and questions at oral argument, Justice Scalia appears incredibly sure of himself and his views. I don't know for sure, but I imagine their different styles must drive each other nuts. Perhaps it's evidence for this that some of Justice Scalia's most vitriolic dissents, including the one in the graduation prayer case, have come in cases where Justice Kennedy has written the majority opinion for a closely divided Court.

Whenever there's a case where Kennedy has written the majority and Scalia has penned the dissent, I like to think of how they might have talked about the case, if indeed they had discussed the matter personally. Additionally, I like to imagine that this conversation takes place on the golf course after the boys have finished a hard day at the office. And so, in lieu of just describing what the two opinions actually said, I present to you instead a short excerpt of what I think a conversation between Justices Kennedy and Scalia on the subject of *Lee v. Weisman* might have sounded like, with direct quotes from the opinion placed in quotation marks.

KENNEDY: Hmmmm, 156 yards to the hole. I guess I should use the old five iron. Well, I don't know, the wind's moving right to left, and the green slopes upward. Perhaps this is a job for the trusty four iron. On the other hand, I have been working out at the Supreme Court gym. (*He makes a muscle and squeezes it with giddy pleasure.*) Perhaps I could get away with the six iron. Or should I use the eight wood . . . ?

SCALIA: Oh, for goodness' sake already, Kennedy, just pick a club.

KENNEDY: Geez. Okay, take a chill pill, Nino. I'll use the six iron.

Justice Kennedy takes the club and approaches the ball. He takes fourteen practice swings, then bounces the ball about three and a half feet on the ground.

KENNEDY: Dagnabbit!

SCALIA: All right, it's my turn. My ball is right over here. Get out of my way.

Justice Scalia picks a four iron out of his bag, steps directly up to the ball, and smacks it two hundred yards over the green.

SCALIA: Stupid liberal golf club companies! (*bites golf club in half*)

KENNEDY: Hey, Nino, what do you think about the *Lee v. Weisman* case? I know I originally thought the prayer was constitutional, but I've changed my mind.

SCALIA: What?! Are you nuts?

KENNEDY: Here's my thinking. First, this is a state-sponsored prayer. The state is really involved in the whole thing. It chose that there would be a prayer and then chose who would give the prayer. It told the rabbi he had to give a nonsectarian prayer and even gave him a pamphlet explaining what that meant. Second . . .

SCALIA: Hold on there. That's nothing. The school didn't draft the prayer. It didn't review the prayer or edit the prayer. School officials didn't lead the prayer. The rabbi wasn't a mouthpiece of the state. Your conclusion is "difficult to fathom."

KENNEDY: Well, I guess we'll just have to agree to disagree on that one, huh, Nino?

SCALIA: I've never agreed to disagree with anyone on anything. That would constitute too much agreement. I'm too disagreeable to agree to disagree!

KENNEDY: Anyways, the second thing is that by sponsoring the prayer, the state has "in effect required participation in a religious exercise." Obviously, if a student agrees with the prayer and wants to participate in it, he or she will stand up and remain silent. But what about a "reasonable dissenter"? Won't that person feel peer pressure to also stand or remain silent? And won't that make the dissenting student feel like he or she is participating in the prayer? That's coercion. I've read an article from a 1963 volume of the *American Sociological Review*, and it supports my view that "adolescents are often susceptible to pressure from their peers toward conformity." What do you think about that, Nino? Nino? Hey, you should get off the ground and stop pounding your fists. You're getting your Speedo and fedora dirty.*

SCALIA: (*getting up and adjusting his fedora*) I can't believe this. Your views are all wrong. I don't even know where to start. For one thing, we've had state-sponsored nonsectarian prayers at public functions since the beginning of the republic! We can't just "lay waste a tradition" that has a long history in our republic.

KENNEDY: You mean like racially segregated schools?

SCALIA: Grrrrr.

KENNEDY: Sorry. You were saying?

SCALIA: And this psychocoercion thing, what is up with that? This makes no sense to those of us "who have made a career of reading the disciples of Blackstone rather than of Freud." If the state uses force to coerce someone into

---

*Did I mention that when I imagine the two justices arguing on the golf course, they are wearing only Speedos and fedoras?

participating in a religious exercise, that's a problem, yes. But just peer pressure? Come on. I mean, this is "incoherent." It makes our endorsement test look like a "rock-hard science." In any event, the idea that a nonbeliever who stands in respectful silence is actually participating in the prayer is crazy. Everyone knows that person isn't signaling his or her approval of the prayer. He's just "maintaining respect for the religious observances of others," which is a "fundamental civic virtue that government can and should cultivate." I mean, you can't write this stuff in an opinion. It would be a "jurisprudential disaster." (*jumping up and down*) Your views are "ludicrous," "absurd," "unsupported," and "senseless."

KENNEDY: You scare me.

The End

Anyway, this doesn't summarize all of the arguments made by the two justices (and the thing about racially segregated schools wasn't actually in the opinion, though it could have been), but it should give you a pretty good idea of where they were coming from. My own view is that the prayer was unconstitutional, but not for the reasons Justice Kennedy gives. The prayers are unconstitutional, from my perspective, because they are a state endorsement of religion, just like a crèche on public property. Justice Kennedy, however, doesn't believe in the endorsement test, so he had to convince himself that there was coercion going on before he would find the prayer unconstitutional. Although it's kind of hard to tell through his venomous rage, Scalia makes a pretty good point that a nonbeliever who respectfully stands or remains silent during the prayer probably does not feel like he or she is participating in the prayer. I haven't read the *American Sociological Review* article or either of the two other ancient articles Kennedy cited in his opinion on the peer pressure point, but I did, as you well know by now, spend four years as a nonbelieving Jew in a Catholic high school, and while I stayed respectfully silent during many an Our Father, I never felt like I was participating in the prayer or that anyone thought I was participating in the prayer. I always felt like the school was endorsing God and Christianity, of course, but since it was a private Catholic school, I fully understood the school's interest in making such an endorsement and its right to do so. A public school, however, like the one in *Lee v. Weisman*, has no such right.

When I drove down to Providence in early January to talk with Rabbi Gutterman at Temple Beth-El, where he'd been officiating for the past thirty-seven years, I was determined to finally get the yarmulke thing right. I still didn't own a yarmulke myself, but I knew, based on my Hebrew school experience, that the temple would have a box of generic yarmulkes somewhere near the front door, and so I planned to pick one up there. It wasn't an ideal solution, because the little black polyester scraps that temples like to pass off as yarmulkes are not really designed to fit any normal human head. Anybody who wears one ends up looking like a Conehead from the early days of *Saturday Night Live*. Also, the yarmulkes never get washed, so they are inevitably covered with a thin film of grime congealed from the greasy hair ooze of hundreds of unwashed boys who are forced to wear them inside the temple walls. I wanted to be respectful, though, and I knew that anything would be better than wearing that salty beach hat again, so this was my plan.

Imagine my surprise, then, when Rabbi Gutterman arrived to meet me in his office wearing no yarmulke at all. *What the hell,* I thought, *do I know nothing about religious headgear?* To make things worse, after a while talking about the case, the rabbi asked me what temple I attended, and I was forced to admit that I'm not religious, which confused him because, as he explained, he had assumed I was religious since I was wearing a yarmulke. I told him I was wearing it out of respect, which he seemed to think was very nice of me but not necessary because, as the rabbi of a Reform temple, "hat or no hat," it didn't matter to him. At that point, I was faced with much the same conundrum I had faced back in Joel Petlin's office six months earlier: do I take the yarmulke off and make a show of how I'd rather not be wearing it, or do I keep it on and feel pointy-headed and self-conscious and need to take another shower when I get home, all in the name of showing respect, which the rabbi had just indicated was unnecessary (but nice)? I had no idea what to do, and so of course took the path that required me to take the least action. I kept the yarmulke on for the entire interview and just tried not to think about it again.

Luckily for me, Rabbi Gutterman is an incredibly great guy, so I'm sure it didn't matter to him what I did. We started our conversation by talking a little about Rhode Island, which I've always thought would be a great place to live, because it gets the same representative power in the Senate (and in the Miss America pageant) as California, which has about thirty-five times more people in it. The rabbi confirmed my feelings about the Ocean State by pointing out that he had been lucky enough to be invited to give prayers on the floors of both the U.S. House of Representatives and the U.S. Senate, indicating that "Rhode Island has its benefits." Benefits, indeed. More to the point, though, Rabbi Gutterman told me a little about the religious history of Rhode Island, which was founded by the great religious dissenter and separationist Roger Williams. The rabbi said that even though Rhode Island is a very religious state, with Catholics making up about 70 percent of its population, the legacy of Williams has been one of great respect for other religions, which (and this is my point, not the rabbi's) might explain why the Pawtucket crèche display included a clown and an elephant in addition to the baby Jesus.

I asked Rabbi Gutterman why he agreed to give the graduation prayer that brought about the famous case. He said that in Rhode Island, there is a tradition of having a prayer at big civic events, and he agreed to do it as a favor to the school. Although he said that he wouldn't "die unfulfilled" if he never gave another public prayer, he thinks that sometimes these prayers can move an event "up to a higher level." He was somewhat surprised to learn that his giving the prayer was going to be controversial, and he said that he gave it a lot of thought and consulted people he respected about what to do. Ultimately he decided that praying at a graduation ceremony is not really the same as praying in a classroom, where the students are a real captive audience, and so he went ahead with the prayer. But he made a serious effort to draft a prayer that would be inclusive and make everyone feel comfortable, regardless of his or her religious beliefs. He certainly had no intention of proselytizing for his faith, or faith in general, or anything else. Rabbi Gutterman is a really smart guy, and he completely understood what was at stake with his prayer; he simply came down slightly closer to the Scalia side than the Kennedy side of a very close issue.

As for the case itself, Rabbi Gutterman said that, although he followed it, he was not particularly invested in the result, and he didn't think it was "a big loss" that the decision came out the way it did. He did think it was a fascinating episode, mostly because of the emotions that the case engendered on all sides. In the anteroom to his office, he has put up framed copies of a couple of articles about the case from the time, including one from *U.S. News & World Report.* One of the articles refers to him as the "people's rabbi," and from our short and extremely pleasant conversation, I can certainly see why he has earned that nickname.

In case you were wondering, I did succeed in ignoring the yarmulke again during my conversation with the rabbi. Indeed, I didn't even remember that I was still wearing it until I was in my car heading back to Boston, at which point it was too late to turn around. Yes, that's right, do the math: I stole the temple's yarmulke. Once again, if you want to stop reading the book at this point, I totally understand.

The most recent chapter of the school prayer saga took place in a small east Texas town called Santa Fe, which is different from Providence, Rhode Island, in just about every way imaginable. It's smaller, hotter, sandier, more Protestant, less politically powerful on a per-capita basis, and it contains a somewhat greater number of tumbleweeds. Anyone who is a sports fan, or knows anything about Texas, or watches TV, or isn't dead, knows that the state of Texas lives for high school football. What happens on the field under the "Friday night lights" is about as religious as what happens in church on Sunday morning. Indeed, in lots of places in Texas it's impossible to tell where football stops and religion begins. For example, like many Texas high schools, Santa Fe High School used to have a practice of allowing a student to deliver a prayer prior to the beginning of each football game. A Mormon (not, as many people assume, a secularist ACLU type) sued to have the practice invalidated.

Once again, the Supreme Court defied expectations and sided against the prayer. The city tried to distinguish its case from *Lee v. Weisman* in a bunch of different ways, but the Court didn't buy any of them. For example, the city said that football games are different from graduation ceremonies because students don't really have to go to football games in the same way they have to attend graduation events. Who knows what the Court would have said if the case had come from a different state, but the argument was clearly frivolous with regard to Texas; indeed, the plaintiffs probably could have argued that students in east Texas are *more* likely to go to a football game than to a graduation ceremony. The city also said that its case was different because it was a student praying, not a member of the clergy. It's true that if the case was just about a student praying voluntarily, or a group of students likewise praying on their own volition, it would have been different. But the Court rightly recognized that this prayer, though drafted and uttered by a student, was authorized, organized, and directed by the school itself, which had created a policy by which one student would be elected by the student body to deliver a prayer over the school's public address system at each home game for the whole season. Probably, the Court realized, a religious minority was not going to win such an election.

Moreover, the Court thought the entire setting of the prayer would lead to the perception that the school had endorsed its religious message. I guess Justice Stevens must have season tickets to the Washington Redskins or something, because his description of what he figures the pregame ceremony probably looked like is so evocative, I can hardly wait to get some buddies together and throw around the old pigskin:

> Once the student speaker is selected and the message composed, the invocation is then delivered to a large audience assembled as part of a regularly scheduled, school-sponsored function conducted on school property. The message is broadcast over the school's public address system, which remains subject to the control of school officials. It is fair to assume that the pregame ceremony is clothed in the traditional indicia of school sporting events, which generally include not just the team, but also cheerleaders and band members dressed in uniforms sporting the school name and mascot. The school's name is likely written in large print across the field and on banners and flags. The crowd will certainly include many who display the school colors and insignia on their school T-shirts, jackets, or hats and who may also be waving signs displaying the school name.

As a lifelong football fan and a former second-and-a-half-string center for my own high school freshman football team (don't ask), I just had to go see this for myself.

I couldn't seem to find any hotel rooms online in Santa Fe, so I booked one at a place in Texas City that was notable only because it was within walking distance of both the Mall of the Mainland and an enormous dog-racing track. The Santa Fe Indians were set to play the Texas City Stings the following evening, and I felt kind of like a

traitor staying in Texas City, because I had begun fancy-
ing myself a fanatical Santa Fe supporter. I'm not exactly
sure why I wanted to root for a team with an offensive
name and a history of sponsoring unconstitutional religious practices, but I guess it was because Santa Fe was
a huge underdog coming into the game. I had been following the Indians' season from afar with some degree
of regularity, checking on their progress by reading the
online version of the *Galveston County Daily News* and
its associated sports blog. The team was having a rough
season. They were coming off a dismal 2006 campaign. A
brand new coach had installed a complicated new offensive system. The squad was 1–3 when I arrived, having lost
to rival Friendswood 56–6 the previous week. The starting quarterback had just quit the team. Moreover, Santa
Fe is a pretty small town, with a population of about ten
thousand, and it plays in a league with much bigger towns
like Texas City, which has four times as many people in
it. The Texas City High School football team is a perennial
east Texas powerhouse that has sent numerous players
to the NFL. I am a total sucker for an underdog, so I had
enthusiastically adopted Santa Fe as my absolute favorite high school football team in Texas, at least among the
seven squads in Class 4A, Division II.

The first thing I had to do was get a ticket. It would have
sucked to come all this way to see a high school game and
not be able to get in. I took Farm Road 2004 to Route 6 to
the high school, which is big and new and resembles just
about every other high school I've ever seen. In the front
office, I learned that the athletic department secretary was
busy faxing, so I took a look at the various bulletin boards
on the office walls. The "Weekly Bulletin" announced the
following under the heading "Additional Notes and Instructions to faculty and staff":

> Just REMINDER [*sic*], the Pledge and Moment (Minute) of silence ARE NOT OPTIONAL. Please ensure the students respect this state legislation obligation.

I thought that was pretty interesting, but the next bit was even better:

> Teachers, please be aware of your students' activities in class. No sleeping is allowed.

No sleeping allowed? I sort of figured that schools down south would be tough on their students, but come on!

When the athletic department lady was finished faxing, we took a long walk together to her office, during which she basically talked nonstop about the game and the students and the game and also the game. She was what I would call *peppy*. In the office, I picked out what I thought was a nice seat: Row 21, Seat A, right on the aisle so I would be able to go buy a hot dog without bothering anyone. I paid my six dollars and told her how excited I was to finally be seeing a "Friday night lights" game. She warned me that Santa Fe was probably going to lose and that they needed all the support they could get. I told her I was happy to help out any way I could, with clapping or hooting or whatever. Then she asked me if I was new in town, and I had to decide right then and there whether I was going to tell her the real reason for my visit.

I should have told her. If I had, we would have talked about the prayer issue, and given how peppy she was, I'm sure she would have said some really interesting stuff that I could have written about here. But I didn't tell her, and I'm almost too embarrassed to explain why. I was suddenly struck with the fear that if I admitted I was there to see whether anyone still prayed before the game, somehow I would never know whether the pregame ceremony I got to see was the typical ceremony or whether the school had changed it by deleting any religious aspect so that I wouldn't be able to see it. I think it might be hard to express how narcissistic this fear was. Just to be clear: I thought the school might change its entire pregame ceremony *just for me*. I can imagine how this would have worked: I leave the building, and the athletic department lady immediately calls the principal and tells him that some law professor is here to see if they still pray, and the principal sends an emergency message to every school employee: *No Prayer, No Prayer. Repeat, Cancel the Prayer. Liberal, Atheist, Northeastern Law Professor Coming to Game. No Prayer at Football Game Tomorrow.* Then the next day, everyone watches me take my seat (because the principal has informed the community what I look like) and giggles as I write down in my notebook, "No prayer tonight," while they all secretly plot to have an even bigger prayer next week. Yes, that's exactly what I thought was going to happen!

To my credit, I realized the absurdity of my fear only seconds after I told the athletic department lady that I was in town on business for a couple of days.* But of course, by then it was too late.

The next twenty-four hours passed like cold sludge. There's not much to do in Santa Fe and Texas City when you're not watching high school football. I walked around the mall, hoping to see some football-crazy kids whooping it up in anticipation of the game, but the place was almost com-

---

*Thank goodness she didn't ask me what business I was doing. "Shoes. Selling shoes. Oil wells. Rare cats?"

pletely empty. On the way back to my hotel, I saw a bird running along the road; I assumed, safely I think, that it was a roadrunner.

I got to the field around an hour before game time so I wouldn't miss any surreptitious prayers or crucifixion reenactments or anything. A lot of people were already there. Because my wife is a teacher, I've been to a good number of high school football games in my adult life, and I have to say that the atmosphere didn't seem much different from the games I've seen in California or Virginia or even Massachusetts. Maybe the stands held a few more people, and maybe everything was a little bit more hyped up—the teams did enter the field through silly inflatable tunnels with fake smoke coming out of them—but mostly it would have been hard to guess that this was Texas and not some other state if you didn't already know. Justice Stevens surmised correctly that many people would be wearing Santa Fe T-shirts, jackets, and hats and holding Santa Fe signs, but he missed the boat with his prediction that the team name would be printed in large letters across the center of the field. There were a few cheerleaders and two mascots—a boy wearing a big feather headdress and a girl dressed like Pocahontas. A little tepee was sitting on the side of the field, but I didn't notice if the two mascots ever disappeared inside it.

At last it was time for the moment I had been waiting for. Following an introduction of the senior band members, the PA guy announced that everyone should rise for the Pledge of Allegiance and a "minute of silence." No prayer, oh well. I hadn't really expected the school to violate the Court's ruling, but still, some part of me hoped that I could uncover some dastardly doings as part of all this research. Everyone in the stands (including me) stood up and took off his or her hat and said the Pledge. But then instead of offering a minute of silence, the PA announcer went right into introducing the cheerleading squad. It was actually quite weird. One big guy sitting a few rows ahead of me jokingly yelled something like "What about the minute of silence?" Then a little guy in back of him screeched, "More like a second of silence."

The game itself wasn't that great. For one thing, my beloved Indians got completely crushed. Texas City was just too much for them. It was 21–0 before I even blinked, and by halftime it was up to 31–0. Moreover, sometime during the second quarter it started to rain like crazy. It rained cats and dogs, whatever that means. An ark would have been nice. Before the rain started, though, I was lucky enough to have a conversation with the guy sitting in Row 21, Seat B. I asked whether he had a son on the team. He told me that he himself used to play for Santa Fe and that he had kids in the band and the dancing squad. Then he asked me what I was doing there, and this time I didn't hesitate to mention the book. He definitely remembered the controversy, and he didn't think much of the Court's decision. Without any provocation from me, he went into a bit of a mini-lecture about constitutional law, and he urged me to take the whole thing down in my little notebook. I can't guarantee I got every word exactly right, but it was pretty much like this: "The Constitution doesn't say separation of church and state; it says we can't make a law regarding the free practice of religion. Well, now we've got a law that is about the free practice of religion, and it's perverted. We don't have law, we have judges who are interpreting law, and that's wrong. One of the framers of the Constitution thought that justices shouldn't be lawyers, because they should just go with the plain language, but now we've got all lawyers with their interpretations as judges."

I wondered whether to point out how nothing he was

saying made any sense to me, but I had a couple of reasons for keeping my mouth shut. For one thing, I viewed my role at the game as being pretty much an objective observer, and I didn't think it was appropriate or helpful to my project to start playing law professor in the stands of a football game. More importantly, when the guy wasn't talking about constitutional law, he was telling me about how many fights he had gotten in during his life. I swear that in a conversation that lasted fifteen minutes at most, this guy talked about fighting at least three times, including how, when he lived in a different state for three months, he had gotten into a fight every single day. Also, he mentioned that he was a "gun nut," and declared that "trying to stop crime by regulating gun ownership is like pulling the dog's teeth because the coyote ate the chickens." Once again I had no idea what he was talking about, but one of the tenets I live my life by is to not challenge guys in Texas who like to fight and shoot guns. I decided to let the heterodox constitutional theory—and gun control policy simile—stand without comment.

I spent most of the rest of the game hiding under the bleachers, trying not to get too wet. At one point I tried to strike up a conversation with a woman who was wearing a shirt that said "assistant principal." I said, "I think this is going to blow over soon." She looked at me like I was an idiot. "Right," she said, and then turned away. Sometime during the fourth quarter, I ventured out into the rain and watched the end of the game from the fence next to the field. Texas City continued to play strongly, though not as well as it did in the first half. Santa Fe's offense did just about nothing, although its defense did manage a late-game safety. The contest ended with a series of running plays going nowhere in the deep mud and pounding rain. Final score: Texas City 44, Santa Fe 2.

They never had a prayer.

As I hope I have made clear over the course of this book, the First Amendment raises a lot of hard issues. Whether the current version of the Pledge of Allegiance is constitutional, however, is not one of them. It is clearly unconstitutional. When Francis Bellamy first wrote the Pledge in 1892, the oath contained no reference to religion at all. It wasn't until 1954 that the U.S. Congress passed, and President Eisenhower signed, a bill adding the words "under God" to the Pledge. The purpose of the amendment was to assert the unique religious character of our great country and to distinguish us from the damned atheist communists with whom we were struggling for world dominion. Ever since, little kids in the public schools have started their day by declaring that there is a single god who enjoys a cozy relationship with the United States of America. It's true that the Supreme Court has said schools cannot force students to say the Pledge, but I venture to guess that it will be the rare eight-year-old who will be willing to risk the wedgie or noogie or wedgie-noogie-punch-in-the-mouth combo that inevitably follows any public demand to leave the room during the recitation of the Pledge.

When Mike Newdow, an atheist emergency room doctor with a law degree who lives in Sacramento, first challenged the "under God" part of the Pledge in federal court, nobody gave him much of a chance. The Pledge is one of those things, like having a religious motto on our money or starting every Senate session with a prayer, that has always been assumed to be somehow okay. Certainly the Supreme Court has assumed that the Pledge is okay; in opinion after opinion, it has kind of noted in passing that of course public schools can start their day by saying the Pledge. But Newdow—silly him—read the Court's church/state opinions and realized that, if you fairly apply the

Court's tests for determining what practices violate the establishment clause, the Pledge was clearly unconstitutional for three independent reasons. Not only is it obviously a government endorsement of religion, and not only was the purpose of adding "under God" to the Pledge manifestly religious, but leading a group of students in the Pledge also clearly violates the noncoercion principle of the Court's school prayer cases.

I think when most people hear about Newdow and his mission, they must assume that he's just a nut job who hates religion and wants to eradicate it from the public square to please his own atheist sensibilities. Not true. I've met Newdow a couple of times. The first time was at a conference at the University of North Carolina at Chapel Hill, where he gave a talk about the Pledge and I spoke about intelligent design. During the Q&A session after I gave my paper, all of a sudden Newdow starting haranguing me that some position I had taken was too hostile to religion. In my typical fashion, I stuttered and croaked out some dumb answer. He kept pushing me, and I kept stuttering. One reason I couldn't really answer him was because he had made a decent point, and I don't think fast on my feet, but the other reason was that I kept thinking, "Holy crap, Mike Newdow is lambasting me for being hostile to religion, wow!" The second time we met was at Boston University, where I was lucky enough to get him to speak to a packed room of students about his experiences. The event passed without incident, although Newdow did manage to knock a jar of apple juice all over himself during his speech. He also kindly gave me a free CD of his very own hilarious atheist songs that he wrote and performed, including my favorite, "God Is in My Soul," in which Newdow intersperses his own lyrics with bits and pieces of inane, cruel, and obscene answering-machine messages that he has received from religious people who hate his guts and want him to rot in hell. If you are an atheist like me, I highly recommend picking yourself up a copy of the CD.

Newdow may be a little quirky, but he is absolutely not a nut job. For one thing, he's brilliant. Did I mention that he was practicing emergency room medicine during the time he was bringing his famous lawsuit? Against all odds, Newdow actually won his case in the Ninth Circuit Court of Appeals, and then he argued the case himself at the Supreme Court. I'm sorry, did you get that? *He argued his own case at the Supreme Court.* Moreover, by all accounts, his argument there was spectacular. Court watchers called it "stellar" and gave it "five stars." At one point the courtroom burst into applause—which is something that never, never, never happens—and the chief justice threatened to clear the Court.

In addition to being smart, though, Newdow is also actually quite reasonable. He doesn't want to turn the United States into an atheist country or stop people from practicing their religion. He just wants the government to stop telling him his beliefs are wrong and making his daughter declare a set of beliefs that are completely different from his own. He says that, from the perspective of an atheist, the government's statement that his nation is "under God" is infuriatingly offensive to him. Just as a religious person probably wouldn't want a Pledge that said "under no God" or a Christian wouldn't want a Pledge that said "under Confucius," he too doesn't want the Pledge to affirm something that he does not believe in. All he wants is for the government to respect atheism as a legitimate perspective and treat him like it treats everyone else. Indeed, he's so reasonable about this that the two times I've heard him talk, I can't believe anyone actually disagrees with him.

But of course nearly everyone in the United States disagrees with him, and when he won his case in the Ninth Circuit, the nation pretty much lost bladder control. Tom Daschle said the decision was "just nuts." George W. Bush said it was "ridiculous." And in a totally pathetic display of pure patheticness, almost the entire House of Representatives took time to protest the decision by standing on the Capitol steps and holding hands and reciting the Pledge and singing "God Bless America" and (at least in my head) dancing the Macarena. The nation cheered mildly when the Supreme Court ultimately reversed the lower court's decision on technical grounds that had nothing to do with the merits of Newdow's case, and at the time of this writing, the case is back in the lower courts awaiting a decision.

One of the major differences between my wife and me is that while she is totally focused on what's happening in the present, I am obsessed with thinking about the future and the past. For this reason, it's really good to have Karen around, particularly when I'm doing something like driving a car, which is not a very safe thing to do when you're trying to reenact some embarrassing episode from nursery school or mentally planning your own funeral. I used to think more about the future than the past, but since I'm getting old now, and therefore don't really have much of a future left, I find myself thinking more and more about the past.

In the course of researching this chapter, I spent a lot of time trying to remember how often I was required to say the Pledge of Allegiance during elementary school. I generally pride myself on my clear memory of my youth. I'm fairly sure, for example, that I could name every single person in my fourth grade class, and I know I could tell you in great detail about the time in seventh grade that I got caught in the girl's bathroom at a school dance making out with a girl whose cigarette breath smelled like salami. My memories about the Pledge, however, are unfortunately really fuzzy. I do clearly remember having to stay after school for singing the national anthem in a falsetto voice, and (more to the point) I vividly remember staying quiet during the "under God" part of the Pledge at least once. My guess is that I stayed silent a lot, but I'm not sure about that. Moreover, the thing I can't remember, and the thing I most wish I could remember, is whether at some point I started saying "under God" again, and why. I bet I did start saying the phrase again, and I bet the reason I started saying it was because, as a little kid, I didn't feel comfortable (or safe) being the only person in the class to not say it.

I wish I could confirm that I had felt peer pressure to start publicly declaring belief in God, because then I would have some anecdotal evidence to support what I think is an obvious point, which is that when an entire class recites the Pledge in unison, even those little kids who don't want to affirm a belief in a single god will feel pressure to say "under God." This, of course, is important as a legal matter, because in *Lee v. Weisman* the Court held that it's unconstitutional for a school to make a student feel peer pressure to participate in a religious exercise. It seems to me quite evident that if a teenager would feel pressure to participate in a religious exercise when a single clergyman says a prayer one time at a giant graduation ceremony (I don't know if this is true, but that's what the Court has said), then an even younger student would be even more likely to feel pressure to join in when the religious exercise takes place every single day in a small classroom while everyone around her is participating in the exercise.

I'm not the only one who thinks this, by the way. Another person who thinks it is Justice Clarence Thomas, who is about the most conservative person in the world and who has almost never seen a church/state arrangement that he doesn't want to put on his lap and cuddle like a teddy bear. Thomas wrote a separate opinion in the *Newdow* case in which he said that under *Lee v. Weisman*, the Pledge of Allegiance cannot be said in schools. "Adherence to *Lee*," Thomas wrote, "would require us to strike down the Pledge policy, which, in most respects, poses more serious difficulties than the prayer at issue in *Lee*." Now, this didn't matter to Justice Thomas, who believes that *Lee* was wrongly decided and (insanely) thinks the Supreme Court should rethink the entire establishment clause to find that its only purpose is to prevent the federal government from interfering with state establishment of religion. But as my good friend and general legal genius Trevor Morrison of Columbia Law School has explained, it's pretty fascinating to linger over the implications of Justice Thomas's opinion. If lower courts are required to faithfully apply Supreme Court precedent (they are), and if the most conservative member of the Court thinks the Pledge of Allegiance is unconstitutional under that precedent (he does), than it's kind of hard to see why the Ninth Circuit's decision was "nuts" or "ridiculous" or would call for a public singing of "God Bless America" on the Capitol steps. Indeed, it would seem that the Ninth Circuit had *no other choice* than to invalidate the Pledge.

Supporters of the Pledge assert that saying the Pledge is not a religious exercise at all and therefore should not be analyzed under the Court's school prayer decisions. The Pledge, it is suggested, is a *political* exercise, not a *religious* one. It is undoubtedly true that, as a whole, the Pledge is primarily political rather than religious. But people who challenge the Pledge under the establishment clause aren't talking about the whole Pledge; they're just concerned with the "under God" part. And while it's also true that saying "under God" isn't exactly like a prayer— saying the phrase is not an act of worship or devotion, for example—uttering the phrase does amount to an assertion of a theological position that lots of people do not believe in, namely that there is one god. If saying this is not a religious act, I don't know what is. Substitute "Allah" or "many gods" or "no god" into the Pledge if you don't agree with me, and see if you change your mind.

Some people will grant that the Pledge contains some minimal religious content but suggest that since the rest of the Pledge is political, the overall effect of the statement must be considered political rather than religious. I fail to see, though, how linking the existence of a single god with the identity of the nation makes the Pledge any better from the perspective of the First Amendment; it seems to me to make it much worse. Finally, it is often argued that the Pledge simply acknowledges the fact that historically, many people in the United States have believed in a single god. That's an indisputable historical fact, of course, and if the question were whether that fact can be taught in public schools, the answer would obviously be yes. Perhaps students could even be made to say a daily pledge like "I pledge allegiance to the flag of the United States of America, which was founded by a lot of people who believed in God." But this is a far cry from pressuring students into making a *personal affirmation* that God exists.

Ultimately, though, I don't think it should matter whether the Pledge is a religious exercise exactly like a prayer or not. I think *Lee v. Weisman* was wrongly reasoned. The coercion rationale for striking down school prayers and the Pledge seems to me to be the weakest of all the rationales.

When a public school drafts or leads or organizes a prayer, it promotes and endorses religion; that should be enough to make it unconstitutional. The same thing holds true for the Pledge of Allegiance. When a teacher (or a Senate chaplain or a PA announcer at a school football game) says that our nation is "under God," that person sends an official government message that to believe otherwise is wrong. To make everyone feel like they're full and valued citizens of the United States, regardless of their religious beliefs, we should just get rid of the "under God" part of the Pledge. Would it really be so bad if we went back to the pre-1954 version: "I pledge allegiance to the flag of the United States of America, and to the republic for which it stands, one nation indivisible, with liberty and justice for all"? I mean, we won the Cold War, didn't we?

Amen.

CREATIONISM COMMOTION

Destination Kentucky

Although I find the school prayer issue really interesting, the church/state issue that has always fascinated me the most is the controversy over teaching evolution in the public schools. One thing I like to do from time to time is to read the comment threads connected to news articles about the topic to see what people are thinking. I find that reading these comment threads not only keeps me up to date, but also reminds me of the sophisticated level of discourse that we Americans enjoy when talking about our most contentious issues involving religion. For example, after the Florida Department of Education decided in February 2008 to require, for the first time, that schools teach the "scientific theory of evolution," readers of the *Orlando Sentinel* wrote these words of wisdom:

> Well, one more battle won by the devil. The atheists and agnostics are taking over the world and no one seems to care. But God will win in the end. America will continue to throw God out until such a time comes that people will be begging God for mercy and he will not be there for them. Judgment is coming to America!!

Why don't we give equal credit to the theory of Intelligent Descent, which has supporting evidence in the bible verses about Jesus walking on water? I mean, come on, gravity is only a THEORY too, right? Religious nutcases will be the downfall of the nation. Look what happened to the Asian subcontinent.

WAKE UP people. This is the 21st century . . . put your silly myths away. Or at least, keep them to yourselves in your churches and homes. Don't try foisting this crap on the rest of us.

I personally love the idea that all of humanity came from two people who sprouted out of the ground like a couple of tomatoes, then encouraged their descendents to engage in incest to produce the 6 billion people that are on the planet today. That's classic! No wonder the world is in the shape it's in now . . . we're all a bunch of genetic retards. Imagine how smart Adam and Eve must have been . . . oh wait . . . they did screw us all didn't they . . . DAMN

OK . . . So now can all you religious zombies back off??

The controversy over evolution, as you can see, does not bring out the best in people. There are millions of examples, some of which are far more serious than saying a few mean things on a blog. One of the worst comes from Texas, where in late 2007 the science curriculum director of the state's education agency was basically forced to resign for circulating a brief "FYI" e-mail announcing an upcoming talk by an opponent of intelligent design. But overreaction and obstinacy are by no means the sole property of the religious right. Scientists, too, can be completely hardheaded and unreasonable. A few years ago I was invited by a student group at Harvard Law School to debate the constitutionality of teaching intelligent design with a professor from Baylor University. I was eager to debate this guy, because in one of his books he had called my arguments "patently unreasonable," "philosophically irrelevant," and "wide of the mark" (can you imagine?). I accepted the invitation and did the debate.

It turned out that although I disagreed with the guy's positions, I found him to be really interesting and pretty thoughtful. We got along great. And although I totally kicked his ass halfway to Sunday in the debate, our discussion was, in fact, quite civil. Not so the question and answer period. The first person to "ask" a "question" identified himself as an MIT scientist named Steve and then spent fifteen minutes badgering my opponent with accusations and ad hominem attacks. The room was filled with people who wanted to ask questions, but the guy just would not shut up, even long after it was clear to everyone in the room that things had gotten out of hand. My opponent was gracious and answered all the guy's claims, but the scientist *still kept talking*. For defenders of evolution, the episode was completely embarrassing. As an observer, also named Steve, put it on a blog the next day, "I attended the debate. Although I am completely opposed to creationism and ID [intelligent design], I found your questions, comments, and general demeanor to be rude, irritating, as well as off-point. . . . It was clear that the majority of the audience agreed with me about your behavior. In fact, you so attempted to monopolize the limited question-and-answer session, it seemed that you were a step away from being asked to leave. If you are the best our side can muster, then I fear that ID will soon be taught in schools across the country. At the least, you were an embarrassment to Steves everywhere."

I have always thought that if we're going to make any

progress on this issue at all, everyone needs to settle down a little. Both sides have valid claims. Scientists are right that evolution should be taught in biology classes and that alternatives to evolution that have enjoyed no success at all in scientific journals should not be (and indeed cannot be, under the First Amendment). But some critics of evolution do reasonably argue that the typical public school curriculum wrongly ignores religion. How can schools claim to turn out educated citizens if they teach their students nothing about religion? In this chapter, I'll try to explain why a curricular compromise is needed. I'll suggest that schools should continue to teach evolution, and only evolution, in biology classes, but should also start teaching students more about religion. And in the meantime, I'll also tell you about my trip to a museum where people roam the earth with dinosaurs.

In the United States, we've been battling over evolution in the courts for nearly a hundred years. Everyone's heard of the infamous Scopes trial, which took place in Dayton, Tennessee, in 1925. Tennessee had a law prohibiting teachers from talking about evolution, and Scopes agreed to be a guinea pig in a case organized by the ACLU to challenge the law. What I love most about the case is that part of the trial was held outside on the courthouse lawn. Wouldn't it be great if more trials were held outside? The state could sell tickets and use the money to hire competent defense lawyers for defendants facing the death penalty. Anyway, Scopes lost. In fact, it took the jury something like nine minutes to convict him, and most of this time was spent getting to and from the jury room. It wasn't really until the play *Inherit the Wind* came around thirty years later, with its depiction of the William Jennings Bryan character as a buffoon, that the case started being seen as a big victory for science over religion, which it never really was.

Apart from *Scopes*, the courts have been incredibly friendly to evolution. Two Supreme Court cases have struck down state laws that were trying to undermine it. In the sixties, the Court struck down a *Scopes*-like law from Arkansas, and in the eighties, the Court struck down a Louisiana law that said if a school teaches evolution, it has to give equal time to "creation science," which is basically creationism except with a few graphs thrown in. In both cases, the Court said that the laws were completely motivated by religion, although I'm sure that if they had explicitly considered the question, the majority of the justices would have said that the programs also endorsed religion in violation of the First Amendment.

Foes of evolution think these cases are a real pain in the ass, but they certainly haven't stopped trying to find a way around them. One of the most recent strategies has been to promote "intelligent design" (ID), a purportedly scientific theory that allegedly proves an intelligent designer created the world. Supporters of ID never say that the intelligent designer they have in mind is God— indeed, sometimes they say that aliens from another planet might have created the world, or (my favorite) that human beings traveled back in time to do it. Basically, the idea behind ID is that there are scientific methods for distinguishing between things that happen randomly and things that are designed by some intelligent being. It's possible, ID proponents say, to use these methods for determining, for example, whether a watch that you find on the beach was created by an intelligent being or just came about randomly. If you can do this for a watch (or a structure happened upon during an archaeological dig, or a suspicious scene happened upon during a crime investigation), then you can surely do the same thing for the origins of the universe.

Proponents of ID spent a good decade developing a frighteningly well-organized strategy to get their pet theory into public school science classrooms as an alternative to evolution. Their work finally paid off when a school district in central Pennsylvania implemented, over the objections of science teachers, a policy to introduce students to ID and to refer them to an ID textbook in the library for more information. Fourteen seconds after the policy went into effect, the ACLU sued. The case was assigned to federal district judge John E. Jones III, an appointee of George W. Bush, and Judge Jones held a trial that lasted over a month. The trial involved all sorts of testimony about blood clotting and bacterial flagella and the scientific method and how one of the school board members had said, "Two thousand years ago someone died on a cross, can't someone stand up for him now?" (oops) and all sorts of other stuff, like how when the ID textbook was written, the authors used an existing textbook that had phrases like "scientific creationism" and just crossed out those phrases everywhere they showed up and replaced them with "intelligent design" (double oops). Also, the defendants were caught lying under oath about where they got the money to buy the ID textbooks (they raised the cash in church—triple oops). At the end of the trial, evolution supporters were pretty sure they were going to win, but they had no idea exactly how far the judge was going to go.

As it turned out, Judge Jones totally obliterated ID. It was like he took ID outside, set it down on a long, smooth stone, stepped into a pair of Doc Martens, put Metallica's Black Album on his CD player, and then jumped up and down on ID with both feet for two straight hours while screaming like a banshee. In an opinion that went on for 139 pages, the judge found the school's policy unconstitutional for at least three or four different reasons. He said the policy endorsed religion and was motivated by a religious purpose. He said that ID is not "science." He excoriated the defendants for lying and described the school's policy as "breathtaking inanity." The decision was more than anything any evolution supporter could have hoped for or predicted. And although the decision was not appealed (by the time it came down, the original school board had been replaced by a pro-evolution board) and officially applies only in a small area in central Pennsylvania, most people think the decision effectively sounded the death knell for intelligent design.

The bottom line of Judge Jones's opinion is right: teaching ID in public schools violates the First Amendment. In my view, the reason for this is that it endorses religion. Why? It's a complicated argument that I've droned on and on about in academic journals, but the basic point is that because opposition to evolution has historically always been inextricably linked to religion, and because credible scientists reject ID overwhelmingly, and because ID "theorists" have failed to get their papers published in peer-reviewed scientific journals, and because the idea that the world was designed by a single creator is essentially a religious belief, any decision to teach ID sends the message: *Our science curriculum is determined by religion.*

Thus I agree with Judge Jones that the Pennsylvania policy endorsed religion, and I also agree that under the specific circumstances of this particular case (the guy who said the thing about Jesus, for example), the school board's purpose was religious. The only thing I don't agree with is the judge's finding that ID is not science. It's not that I think ID *is* science. I think at best it's probably really sucky science. But since I'm not a philosopher of science, I have no idea what distinguishes science from nonscience. I do know that philosophers of science have argued a lot about what is and is not science and that some of them think it's fruitless to even try to distinguish science from nonscience, so I'd be pretty surprised if a lawyer without training in the philosophy of science sitting behind a bench in the middle of Pennsylvania would suddenly be able to come up with the definitive answer on the question. I think the judge should have just left the science/nonscience question alone. Whether ID counts as science in some technical or philosophical sense doesn't actually matter at all to the constitutional question. The Constitution doesn't prohibit schools from teaching nonscience (or bad science) in science classes; it simply forbids schools from endorsing religion. Since it's quite obvious that teaching ID endorses religion, even if it happened to be scientific in some sense, there was no need for the judge to decide whether ID is or is not science.* Anyway, it's not a big point in the whole scheme of things. Despite the fact that intelligent design supporters like to point to the ar-

----

*Saying that it matters whether ID is science or not is actually dangerous for supporters of evolution. What would happen if another judge hearing an ID case were to read some philosophy of science and decide that what distinguishes science from nonscience is whether a theory is "falsifiable," one of the factors that philosophers of science have always mentioned as maybe being a key characteristic of science? Since opponents of ID like to argue that lots of things about the world appear not to be intelligently designed (the human appendix, for example, or the fact that pandas can't really digest bamboo too well), and that therefore ID is in fact false, might ID proponents credibly argue that ID is in fact falsifiable? Would this make ID science? Would teaching ID then become constitutional? Yikes!

ticle I wrote on this issue as evidence that even ID critics disagree with Judge Jones, the fact is that his opinion is mostly A-OK with me.

A lot of the confusion about the issue of teaching evolution stems from two fundamental misconceptions that many people share, one of which is generally held by evolution supporters and the other of which is embraced by evolution opponents. Let's take the one held by evolution opponents first. More times than I can count, I have heard something resembling the following argument: Schools must teach alternatives to evolution in science classes in order to remain neutral with regard to the religious beliefs of the students and their parents. Since many people believe that God created the world in its present form and that human beings did not come about through evolution, teaching evolution in the public schools is not neutral from the perspective of those religious believers. Sometimes this argument is phrased in constitutional terms (schools that teach only evolution violate the First Amendment), and sometimes it's just put forward as a policy argument (good and/or fair education requires schools to teach all sides of the evolution issue). Either way, though, the argument, as we say in the academy, totally blows.

Of course, government neutrality toward religion sounds like a good goal. Why should the government intentionally take a position that is harmful or offensive to religious belief or practice? Why should a public school be able to send a message that is at odds with someone's sincere religious beliefs? If you look a little closer, though, it becomes obvious that it is impossible for government, including public schools, to be truly neutral toward religion. The key to understanding this point is to recognize both the numerous ways in which government takes positions in public life and the countless viewpoints embraced by the numerous religious groups (and students) that populate the United States.

The government affirms specific positions in all sorts of ways in its everyday operations, through everything from the speeches of public officials to the funding of certain groups and viewpoints to the monuments it puts up on public property to the criminal laws it passes to the curricula adopted by public schools. Because the country is so religiously diverse, these government positions inevitably conflict with somebody's religious viewpoint. For example, some Quakers are pacifists; some Christian Scientists do not believe in conventional medicine; some religious people believe in polygamy, while others preach violence against blacks and Jews; some people believe that the Bible shows that the earth is flat; the Church of Satan believes in indulgence, vengeance, and engaging in sins for purposes of gratification; Raelians believe that aliens created the human race thousands of years ago; some practitioners of Voodoo religions believe that dead people can be revived after being buried; some Wiccans believe they can communicate with the dead through séances; some Jains believe it is wrong to kill any living thing at all, including bugs and vegetables; and some adherents of Falun Gong believe they can harness their life force to cure illnesses, see into other worlds, move objects by telekinesis, walk through walls, and fly.

Does anyone really think that the government, in the actions it takes and messages it sends, must be neutral with regard to all of these religious beliefs? Of course not. The state can take the position that racial intolerance and violence are wrong, that eating vegetables is not a sin, that the world is round, that people ought not to be vengeful, that war is sometimes justified, that it is wrong to marry more than one person, that conventional medicine works, and that it is impossible to walk through walls and fly, no matter how well one manages his or her life force. The government can punish hate crimes, run public service ads urging citizens to eat their vegetables, employ navigation systems that assume a spherical earth, preach kindness and tolerance toward others, engage in war, make polygamy illegal, fund conventional medicine, and teach in its schools that people cannot fly (and even give detention to students who try).

So although it might seem like a nice idea for the government to try to be neutral toward religion, it's impossible. It is certainly not required by the First Amendment. Teaching evolution may not be neutral from the perspective of those who don't believe in it, but that doesn't mean anything for what the schools should teach about it. The argument that the public school curriculum should be viewpoint-neutral with regard to religion is totally unworkable, ignores the fact that there are many religions rather than just one, and misapprehends the nature of public schooling, which takes all sorts of positions on all types of important issues in almost everything it does. If the argument were true, schools would have to teach racial hatred, flat earth theory, and flying, in addition to ID, to make sure they were being neutral with respect to people who happen to believe in these things. They would also have to teach that the universe was created by a turtle, a raven, and a spider woman, since some people believe these things as well. And what about the jackasses who say the Holocaust didn't really happen? Some people surely hold that view as part of their religious beliefs. Does that mean that public schools should have to teach "alternatives" to the "theory" that the Holocaust actually occurred?

Here's the second misconception, the one you hear a

lot from those who support teaching evolution: Ever since Darwin wrote *The Origin of Species*, millions and millions of religious people have been able to reconcile their religious beliefs with evolution by believing that God in fact guides evolution. Even some of those who believe that the Bible is the ultimate authority have been able to reconcile the biblical account of creation with evolutionary theory by, for example, interpreting each "day" of God's creation in *Genesis* with an era or epoch of evolutionary history. For Christ's sake, even the Pope believes in evolution! So, the argument goes, if it's possible for religious people to reconcile religion and evolution, then there's no problem teaching evolution. Schools can teach evolution and not worry about how religious people feel about it because those people can always, if they want, decide that religion and evolution are compatible.

This argument has a number of problems. For one thing, it is completely wrong. Sure, it's theoretically possible for those who believe in a literal reading of the Bible to abandon the view that six days in fact means six actual twenty-four-hour periods and that therefore evolution is completely incompatible with their religious beliefs, but that doesn't mean they're going to do it. Lots of things are possible. Scientists might decide to bag the scientific method. My son might decide to eat bluefish. I might decide to open a zoo with only black-and-white animals (pandas, zebras, penguins, and so on). But this doesn't mean that any of these things are going to happen. The fact is that a lot, lot, lot of people believe things because of their religion that are simply incompatible with evolution. If we really want to, evolution supporters can say *well, screw them*, but we cannot in good faith say that teaching evolution doesn't hurt anyone because creationists can simply change their views. If you have any doubt about how fervently people believe things that are totally irreconcilable with evolution, then I suggest you take a trip to Petersburg, Kentucky, throw down twenty bucks, and have a look around the 65,000-square-foot Creation Museum, where (as the promotional materials put it) the "Bible Comes to Life."

When I was thinking about where to go on my road trip for this chapter, I obviously had a lot of places to choose from. I could have gone to Dayton, Tennessee, where the Scopes trial took place, but come on, every law and religion professor and his grandma goes to Dayton, Tennessee. I wanted to do something different. I could have visited Dover, Pennsylvania, where the recent ID trial happened, but again, there have already been at least four "on location" books written about that trial, and I saw no need to provide yet another account of how the townspeople reacted to the goofballs they elected to the school board. I really wasn't sure what to do. But then I came across a news story about how some creationists in the Cincinnati area had spent $27 million to build a museum that was outfitted with animatronic dinosaurs *and* biblical characters. How could I possibly resist?

I pulled into the parking lot of the museum about noon on an unseasonably warm October day. I expected maybe a smattering of cars and people; why would anyone who is not writing a book about his church/state road trip want to spend such a beautiful day indoors, I figured. Wrong! The parking lot was packed like Paul Brown Stadium when the Steelers are in town. I had to park on a grass extension of the parking lot, which appeared to actually be in somebody's backyard. I couldn't believe how many people were there. Countless church groups and student groups and old people and young people and families and people in wheelchairs and people dressed in Amish or Mennonite garb and people wearing "Lost? Use GPS, God's Plan of Salvation" T-shirts were flocking toward the entrance doors. Almost everyone there looked like they were on some sort of pilgrimage. I would hazard a guess that other than me, very few (if any) people were there because they thought the place was super-duper weird.

It took me a half an hour just to get a ticket. Waiting in the curvy-snaky admissions line, I pondered the meaning of the rhinoceros and dinosaur statues that flank the museum entrance. At first I had no idea at all what the point of such a juxtaposition could be, but thinking about it later, I figured it must have to do with how rhinoceroses sort of look like dinosaurs. There are a lot of references to rhinoceroses and statues of rhinoceroses throughout the museum, and I guess the idea is to say to visitors, *hey, look, rhinoceroses look like dinosaurs.* I'm still not sure why it matters, but anyway, that's what I think the point was. I tried to listen in on the conversations of the people around me in the line, but I didn't hear anything too interesting. Someone was talking about her dead pet alligator, and a bunch of oxygen-toting old people were comparing their walkers, but that was about it.

For the record, I'd like to note that a girl in front of me was wearing a green T-shirt with a clover on it that said, "I'm Not Lucky, I'm Saved." Someone else in line had a red sweatshirt that read, "He Died 4 Me."

I got my ticket and entered another long line to get into the main exhibit of the museum. Luckily, I was able to entertain myself by watching a couple of huge animatronic dinosaurs that wouldn't have been out of place in a theme park (indeed, some of the exhibits were created by the guy who made the *Jaws* exhibit at Universal Studios Florida).

One of the dinosaurs was happily munching some leaves and wagging its tail. I smiled. What a cute dinosaur, I thought. But wait, I wondered, what was that next to the dinosaur? Could it be? Yes! It was a *person*. A *person* was standing next to the *dinosaur*. The person was holding a carrot and smiling and nodding her head. It looked like she was going to feed the carrot to an animatronic *squirrel*. Wow, what a place. For the first time in my life, I thought: I love young earth creationism!

I have to give the place credit. As a kind of monument to biblical literalism, the museum is unbelievably fascinating, and if you put aside the actual content of the exhibits, it is really well done. I usually find museums to be supremely boring, but I never lost interest in this one. The designers successfully integrated all sorts of stuff—from still photography to video to animatronics to a kind of Disney-like set design—in order to convey their message in an incredibly effective and entertaining fashion. Of course, I personally think the message is pretty nutso, but you've got to hand it to the people who made the museum for doing an extraordinary job at what they set out to do.

When you're in the main exhibit, you follow the people ahead of you through a series of rooms. As the brochure you get when you enter says, the museum experience is "a walk through time portraying significant, life-altering events from the past, illuminating the effects of biblical history on our present and future world." From the very beginning, the museum makes clear what it thinks about evolution and the Bible. On the way in, you walk by a display that says that according to the fossil records, a massive flood 4,350 years ago caused the death and burial of massive piles of animals and plants. This, of course, was Noah's flood. The first two stops once you're inside the actual exhibit build on this theme, pointing out that since "fossils don't come with tags on them," it is possible for different scientists with different "starting points" to come to different conclusions about how old they are. Whether you believe in "human reason" or "God's word" will determine whether you think the fossils were caused by one massive flood that occurred 4,350 years ago or not. At the end of these exhibits, visitors are met by sculptures of a boy and a girl with funny speech bubbles coming out of their mouths. "Come on, let me show you the rest," says the boy. The girl responds, "I never heard this before in school." At this point, I overheard a woman talking to her friend about the "human reason"–based theory that the universe is fourteen billion years old. "I can't fathom fourteen billion," she said. "That's a long time. How can they do it?"

In case you're wondering why we ought to believe in God's word over human reason, the next exhibit kindly offers a couple of reasons: because it offers hope, for one thing, and also because it's true. Citing various scrolls and archaeological discoveries, the signs explain that hundreds of biblical prophecies have been fulfilled. One sign announces, "Linguists/paleontologists/geologists confirm the biblical truth." At this stop, where it suddenly got quite congested and uncomfortably hot, lots of people paused to have their pictures taken in front of a three-dimensional display of Isaiah, Moses, and David. I, however, was more interested (repulsed?) by the picture of the Buddha with the caption "New religions have come and gone since Babel." Come on, creationists. That's not very nice!

For the record: signs throughout the museum say "Thou Shalt Not Touch." They are, admittedly, kind of funny.

After a little movie about how the Supreme Court has kicked the Ten Commandments out of the public square (wrong) and forced prayer out of the schools (also wrong), things start getting really cool. In the so-called "graffiti corridor," visitors are forced to smush together and inch their way through a dark, reddish, narrow hallway with scary lighting, which is meant to resemble an abandoned area of an inner city, complete with a little mouse sitting precariously up on one of the walls. The exhibit actually reminded me a lot of the dicey alleyway in back of the Boston building where I live, only with fewer prostitutes. On the walls are posted all sorts of newspaper headlines and magazine articles and the like proclaiming all of the terrible things that are happening in the modern world, like pornography, school shootings, mothers killing their babies in microwave ovens, and (ohmigod!) gay teens. Signs make it clear that all of these awful things have occurred because our culture has abandoned scripture. Wow, who would have guessed that this was the cause of all those microwavings spreading like wildfire over our national landscape?!

Perhaps my favorite part of the museum is the next area, called "Culture in Crisis," which consists of various little televisions inset into the walls, each playing a short movie depicting some relatively minor thing that has gone wrong because we have disregarded the Bible. In one movie, a teenage girl sitting on a round chair talks on the phone to a friend about how she thinks she's pregnant. In the next, a boy wearing a shirt that says "☹ + Beer = ☺" ignores his little brother's warnings and rolls a joint. A third movie shows a fat guy sitting on a couch drinking beer, watching football, and eating popcorn while in the foreground his wife and another woman gossip about some friend of theirs. I have no idea how the museum designers got into my apartment to film this one. The last movie focuses on a mother and her two sons sitting in church listening to a Christian minister give a sermon about how it's not necessary to interpret the words of the Bible literally; as the sermon drones on, the older son sits there bored, popping Tic Tacs, listening to his iPod, and checking his cell phone as his mother angrily urges him to pay attention. The camera never leaves the family or shows the minister, and it goes on for a pretty long time. I stood transfixed watching this last piece of postmodern cinema; it's maybe one of the weirdest things I have ever seen in my life.

Beginning with an uncharacteristically boring four-minute movie in the "Six Days of Creation Theater" involving a dramatic reading of Genesis, the rest of the main exhibit takes visitors through the so-called "7 C's of History"—"Creation, Corruption, Catastrophe, Confusion, Christ, ~~Chickpeas,~~ Cross, and Consummation." This is where the animatronics really start kicking in. Visitors are treated to a little speech by Noah about his ark, which is displayed in various stages of being built, and (even better) one by Methuselah, Noah's grandfather, who apparently lived to be 969 years old and looked like Yoda, the shriveled little Jedi Master from *Star Wars*. After the big "M" gave his little spiel about his famous grandson, I overheard an old woman say to a young man, "Isn't that something, we'll see him one of these days," to which the man nodded his vigorous assent.

I learned a lot in this part of the museum. For example, although I sort of knew that Adam and Eve's original God-ignoring, snake-believing, apple-eating sin was supposedly the beginning of all suffering, it hadn't occurred to me how broad the effects of the sin were. Did you know, for example, that neither venom nor scavengers existed before the Fall? Or weeds? Do you get that? Before Adam and Eve's blunder, *there were no weeds*. Damn you,

Adam and Eve! Were you responsible for every little bad thing? Smudges? Awkward silences? Anyway, in addition to being informative, the exhibits were also entertaining. I particularly enjoyed watching a couple pose for a picture in front of a 3-D dinosaur that was eating the dead body of another dinosaur (part of the scavengery exhibit).

The most striking exhibit in this part of the museum, however, is the "Cave of Sorrows." After you get through with Adam and Eve, you pass through a dark corridor with a scary snake and then enter a horrifying gray passageway where the walls are covered with huge black-and-white photographs of all sorts of bad things—rows of skulls, a wolf eating an animal, an atomic bomb, a guy getting ready to shoot heroin, a woman in labor. On the far wall, a grainy film of war images, heavy on Hitler and the Holocaust, plays in a constant loop, and the loud, angry soundtrack, along with the flashing effect of the quickly changing scenes, makes the whole exhibit radically disorienting and more than a little bit nauseating. Even though it wasn't very pleasant, I stepped out of the sea of people so that I could stay in the room a little longer and hear what people were saying. Listening to parents try to explain this stuff to their little kids was in turn depressing and comical. "That's drugs," one mother barked, pointing at the guy with the needle, while her kids stared wide-eyed at the picture. "This is because of sin," another grownup said. "Yucky things." I watched as two teenage girls tried to figure out what the picture of the woman in labor was supposed to represent. One proferred, "I think she's dying." (Might these children have been "excused" from sex ed class?) Their mother joined them and explained what was going on in the picture, but she said she had no idea what the picture of the heroin-shooting guy was all about. Maybe she thought he was illustrating the dangers of self-vaccination? Or maybe she just didn't want to let her kids know that some people use drugs. She and her kids shuffled off to take a look at the concentration camp images and then moved on.

One thing I found surprising about the museum is that until the very end of the main exhibit, there is no mention of Jesus. The son of God finally makes his appearance in the twenty-minute film in the "Last Adam Theater" that tells the story of the crucifixion. The movie was well done, and I kind of enjoyed it. I don't believe in any of the Christ narrative, but I've always found it incredibly fascinating. Maybe I'm just irretrievably jaded against Judaism by my Hebrew school experience, but I find the Christian story to be much more subtle, sophisticated, and interesting than the Jewish one. God sacrifices his son on a cross to atone for the sins of humankind? Are you kidding? To me, it is so counterintuitive and strange that I can't help but find it somewhat compelling. If I believed any of it, I might actually become a Christian. Of course, I don't, and so as soon as the lights came up and the usher urged everyone in the audience to convert and be done with their sins, I left the theater shaking my head like any other nonbelieving heathen. Still, kudos to the guys who came up with this stuff.

In addition to the main exhibits, there are a handful of other things to see and do in the museum. You can buy creationist literature and stuffed dinosaurs in the bookstore, or you can head over to Noah's Café for a salad and hotdogosaurus for lunch. There is a tiny "first century synagogue" that is supposed to be a chapel where people can "come in and enjoy a time of meditation and reflection," but it was the only place in the museum not completely packed with people (indeed, nobody was in it at all). A very popular planetarium show turned out to be extremely boring. The point of the show is to explain how the vastness of the universe reflects God's majesty, but the only thing I found interesting about it was its occasional critiques of "secular astronomy," and that was only because I had no idea there was such a thing.

My favorite non-main-exhibit part of the museum turned out to be the "Dragon Theater," a pretty grand name, but actually sort of a misnomer, because it was just a room with some folding chairs and a television in it. I sat down along with a couple of other people and watched the short movie that runs over and over again all day. The movie argues that dinosaurs existed four thousand years ago and were known in literature and elsewhere as "dragons." As a Harvard PhD guy explains in the film, dinosaurs had limited food and were thus a threat to human beings, who killed them off to stay safe and to "show off." The movie closes by posing the provocative (but ludicrous) possibility that perhaps "the dragons of our myths were really dinosaurs." For me, the film served as a perfect exclamation point for the whole museum, which I found to be—to borrow a word from Judge Jones—breathtakingly bizarre.

Now, I know my description of the Creation Museum is a little snarky, and I probably went too far when I called it "nutso," and for this I apologize, because even though I do think it's pretty nutso, I should really keep that to myself, and anyway my only point in going there and describing it here is to underline the obvious point that many people do not believe in evolution. I know it seems weird, and almost impossible to believe for many of us, *but it is true.* How else could someone get $27 million together to build a museum devoted to that very point? Hundreds of thousands of people have visited the museum, and I promise you that most of them believe that a great deal of what they saw was true.

Of course, a lot of people find the Creation Museum to be far more sinister than I do. If you go online and do some searching, you will learn that a lot of people think bringing kids to the museum constitutes child abuse. In the course of my road trip, I wanted to get some prominent scientist's opinion of the museum. Luckily for me, one of the most famous scientists in the world lives on the top floor of my building and agreed to talk to me. Steven Pinker, who teaches at Harvard and has written lots of important books and has wild hair and was recently ranked in one poll as the world's twenty-sixth most prominent public intellectual, lives in a loft that is so huge and beautiful that I almost passed out when I saw it. We talked for a while about the nature of science and the relationship of both science and religion to morality and a little about my view that Judge Jones shouldn't have ruled that ID is not science, but for fear of misstating his sophisticated and subtle views, I'll just report his response to the question of whether taking your kids to the Creation Museum is child abuse: "No. It's not child abuse. We need to maintain a distinction between something that is a little bad and something that is a lot bad. It's sad. It's a sheer waste of money. The falsehoods it spreads are stupendous. But no, it's not child abuse."

The real question is how those of us who believe in evolution should deal with the fact that so many people don't believe in it. One possibility would be to simply say that since half of the country believes in creationism, we should let those beliefs have as much influence on our public policy (education, funding for scientific research, and so on) as evolution does. I would guess that close to zero evolutionists would take this position. I certainly don't. Alternatively, we could simply dismiss these millions of people as ridiculous fools who have no claim whatsoever on our attention. We could, like some of the people writing to the Orlando newspaper, reject them as nutcases or zombies and then do whatever we want, without any regard to how this massive part of our national population feels about it. Call me "overly reasonable" or "too nice a guy" if you want, but I just don't feel that dismissing a massive portion of our national population as insane or unworthy of our attention is a very healthy way to act in a democracy.

Instead, what I think we should do is treat creationists with some teasing that occasionally creeps over to snarkiness, work as hard as we can to stop creationism from influencing our public policy (sweet lord, I do not want "creation scientists" determining how public money should be spent on medical or scientific research), but ultimately recognize that those who reject evolution are citizens just like us who are entitled to our respect, even if we disagree fundamentally with what they believe. And if there is anything we can do within the realm of public policy that can signal this respect without causing tangible harm, we should do that too, if for no other reason than it might go some way toward promoting civic peace.

This is partially why I have argued for a long time that public schools should teach students more about religion. For a variety of reasons, schools teach very little about religion. They rarely offer comparative religion as a separate subject, and often they don't even talk about religion in history class or English class or current events class or anywhere else that religion would seem to be a self-evidently important thing to talk about. Part of the reason for this is that schools misunderstand the Supreme Court's holdings on religion (while schools cannot teach that religion is true, they can teach *about* religion) and also reasonably fear being sued by those who want schools to be completely free of religion. It is also the case that not many teachers have been trained to teach about religion and that materials for teaching about religion have traditionally not been that great either. But whatever the reason, one of the effects of excluding religion from the curriculum is that it sends a message to religious believers that the state thinks religion is completely unimportant. It's no wonder so many deeply religious people hate public education, push for school voucher programs, and move money away from the desperately needy public schools and into private religious education.

The case for teaching about religion, however, goes far beyond this concern and in fact is fully justified by completely secular reasons. Whether you are religious or not, you've got to concede that over the course of history, religion has played an unbelievably important role in every aspect of human affairs, from art to literature to politics to economics to science and beyond. Moreover, religion is probably as important today as it has ever been. From terrorism to bioethics to *The Da Vinci Code*, religion plays a central role in our current world. How can we say we are educating our kids if we teach them nothing about religion? How can we expect our graduates to participate intelligently and effectively in our democratic system if they don't understand anything about one of the most important characteristics of the human race?

Of course, I fully realize that teaching about religion will not be easy, uncomplicated, or a panacea. The line between teaching objectively about religion on the one hand and promoting religion or proselytizing for it on the other can get pretty fuzzy, particularly in the messy context of the school classroom. Can teachers explain their own views, or must they talk only about the views of others? What should a teacher do if a student asks whether some other student's religion is right or wrong? How should the teacher present issues that are disputed within religious communities? Which religions should the school teach, and which should it leave out? These details aren't the only problems. For example, some groups will inevitably try to use the "teaching about religion" label to smuggle in promotion of religion. And of course, many deeply religious people who dislike the public schools will not be satisfied by this relatively minor reform. For some, the problems in public schooling run too deep for it to be salvaged by a comparative religion course. Others will view teaching about religion as being even worse than the current state of affairs. They might object to a nonbeliever teaching about their religion, or to teaching about religions other than their own, or to the suggestion that religion can even be talked about objectively at all. Still, I am confident that teaching about religion more in the schools would do far more good than harm, and I think that is why an increasing number of people in recent years have started embracing the idea.

One person who has embraced the idea that schools should teach about religion is my colleague Stephen Prothero, who is chair of the religion department at Boston University (go Terriers!). Prothero is a brilliant and creative scholar who has written several important books about religion in the United States. A couple of years ago, Prothero wrote a book called *Religious Literacy: What Every American Needs to Know—and Doesn't,* in which he pointed out that although the United States is probably the most religious country in the world, most Americans know very little about religion. Prothero finds this ironic, but he also thinks it is dangerous, because so many of our public disputes center around religion. As examples of how religious illiteracy can lead to disaster, he cites an incident involving the murder of a Sikh, who was mistaken for a Muslim because of his turban in the wake of 9/11, as well as to the Branch Davidian debacle in Waco, which he suggests was exacerbated by religious ignorance (had authorities understood David Koresh's "end times theology," things might have turned out differently). As part of the solution to this dangerous religious ignorance, Prothero argues that schools should start teaching students more about religion. Specifically, he says that schools should teach at least one course in world religions and one course on the Bible.

Prothero wrote his book for a popular audience, and he stuck in a lot of clever stuff to appeal to readers. The book includes a "Religious Literacy Quiz" so that readers can see how much they know about religion. The quiz has questions like "Name the Four Noble Truths of Buddhism" and "What is Ramadan? In what religion is it celebrated?" The book also has an eighty-five-page dictionary of religious literacy in case a reader needs to brush up on Christianity or Taoism. Finally, it relates some sadly hilarious anecdotes about how Americans are real dolts when it comes to religion. Lots of high school seniors in the United States think that Sodom and Gomorrah were married. Ten percent of Americans think that Joan of Arc was Noah's wife. Only one-third of those asked could identify Jesus as the source of the Sermon on the Mount. And so on.

Now, I've also written about religious literacy (though admittedly in a law review article read by maybe seventeen law professors rather than a best-selling book), and while Prothero and I have very similar views, we differ on a few details. For example, as Prothero explains in his book, he disagrees with my argument that promoting tolerance should be part of the justification for teaching about religion. In his view, improving knowledge, rather than tolerance, is the only justification we need for teaching about religion. I agree that promoting knowledge is a sufficient justification for schools to start teaching more about religion, but I also suspect, as at least one recent study has demonstrated, that when people learn more about other religions, they are more likely to respect those who are different. And I also think that teaching about religion will go a long way toward making a lot of deeply religious people feel more comfortable with public education. In my view, these are important justifications for making such a significant change in educational policy.

I also am not sure about Prothero's emphasis on how people need to know specific facts (such as names and doctrines) about religion, as opposed to learning general themes and characteristics of religious beliefs and practices. I think the literacy dictionary and the literacy test and the anecdotes about how people are dolts when it comes to religion are shrewd hooks for getting people to think about the problem of teaching about religion, but I don't think that the real issue with religious literacy is that people don't know specifics. After all, are adults really supposed to remember all the stuff they learned in school? For example, I'm sitting here unsuccessfully trying to recall the different stages of meiosis. I know I learned them in Brother Tim Paul's biology class back in ninth grade, though for the life of me I can't remember a single one. But failing to remember specifics does not (I hope) mean that one's education was flawed. What we take from our schooling is an appreciation of what is important and a basic understanding of various bodies of knowledge that will help us navigate the world once we graduate, rather than specific facts and pieces of knowledge. Although I don't know any of the seventy-two (?) stages of meiosis, I do understand the scientific method, and I bet that Brother Tim Paul would be satisfied that at least I remember that.*

The fact is that facts can be looked up, if you know it's important to look for them. It is the deeper knowledge that is critical. I'm not really convinced by Prothero's examples of Waco and the murdered Sikh. Neither of these situations, it seems to me, would have come out any differently if our schools had just focused on teaching religious specifics. The problem in Waco was not that the FBI personnel running the siege operation didn't know the specifics of "end times theology," but rather that they didn't appreciate that a religious leader might have such a completely different perception of events that they should have sought expert advice from someone who did know these specifics. And I doubt very much that the murdered Sikh would still be alive if the post-9/11 killer had learned in high school that Sikhs, too, wear turbans. Perhaps nothing could have stopped this senseless murder, but if anything taught in school could have, maybe it would have been a lesson that conveyed something about how different adherents to the same general religious faith can hold very different views on political issues, or a lesson that stressed religious tolerance and understanding. That is why I think schools should focus on teaching more or less general characteristics of religion, including its crucial role in guiding human behavior and central place in the ordering of societies, rather than focusing on facts and specifics, like who gave the Sermon on the Mount.

---

*Well, maybe not. He was kind of a hard-ass.

Still, I agree with Prothero that it would be nice if more people knew a few more facts about religion. Maybe if our schools worried less about evolution and focused more on teaching students what they need to know to live in a world permeated by religion, a few more students would at least realize that Sodom and Gomorrah were not husband and wife.

A European Epilogue

I kept my promise to Adin Yutzy. I had intended to read Luke 16 ever since my visit to Ellsinore, but I didn't get around to it until I found myself in a hotel room in London about five months after giving my word. My family and I were on a little vacation from our semester abroad in Krakow, and I stupidly forgot to bring anything to read. When I noticed the Gideon Bible sitting in the little desk next to my side of the bed, I knew it was time to take a look at the passage about the rich guy going to hell and see what, if anything, it had to say to me.

I actually like reading the New Testament, and every once in a while I read part of it, even when I haven't made any promises to any plaintiffs from any famous religious freedom cases. As I mentioned in the last chapter, I find the Christian narrative fascinating, and there are even some ethical parts I find compelling. Some of the stuff from the Matthew passages Fanny urged on me, for example, is quite powerful. Who but a really mean person would not feel moved when Jesus says, "Blessed are the meek, for they will inherit the earth. . . . Blessed are the merciful, for they will be shown mercy"? But Luke 16? My goodness, what was Adin trying to do by pressing this chapter on me?

Luke 16 has two main parts. The first is a parable told by Jesus to his disciples about a master who fires his manager because the manager had wasted the master's possessions. On his way out, the manager, who fears he will have no job or money after he leaves, tries to make friends by calling in his master's debtors and reducing their debts without permission from the master. Luke 16:8 then says that "the master commended the dishonest manager because he had acted shrewdly. For the people of this world are more shrewd in dealing with their own kind than are the people of the light." Maybe it was a bad translation or something, but I seriously had no idea what this meant. I asked my wife to read it, and even though she grew up Christian, she had no idea what it meant either. In between visiting various London landmarks and eating lots of meat with dark gravy smeared all over it and trying to get our son to put on his pants, we talked and argued about the meaning of the passage for four days, and although we came to some tentative understanding (something about how people who care about money admire shrewdness in others, even if that shrewdness works to their disadvantage?), I still can't claim to really understand the point of the parable. I'm afraid I can't say that this confusing little story did much to make me want to convert.

The second main part of Luke 16 is the story of a rich man who "dressed in purple and fine linen" and a beggar named Lazarus, who was so poor that dogs came and licked his sores. When the two died, the rich man went to hell and the beggar went to heaven to hang out with Abraham. The rich guy was in such torment that he asked Abraham for pity. He pleaded with Abraham to "send Lazarus to dip the tip of his finger in water and cool my tongue, because I am in agony in this fire." Abraham refused, and he also denied the rich guy's fairly modest request that even if he had to spend the rest of eternity in hell, couldn't Abraham at least be nice enough to send Lazarus to tell his five brothers to repent so they wouldn't also have to live out the rest of eternity begging for water? "They have Moses and the Prophets," Abraham said, "let them listen to them."

Holy shit, was this supposed to convince me to live my life through Jesus? I can see how if you already believed that the Bible is the literal word of God, reading this passage would definitely discourage you from pursuing riches, but how could reading the passage ever appeal to someone who is skeptical about the Bible in the first place? It's so incredibly unforgiving and horrifying and cruel, it almost makes me want to cry. Not that I think rich people are great or anything, or that people who beg for food don't deserve sympathy. But how could I choose to believe in a religion that thinks if you dress in purple and fine linen, you have to spend the rest of eternity burning in hell while the virtuous stand in heaven and mock you? (I should probably reiterate here that I am not rich, which makes Yutzy's selection of this chapter particularly odd; for example, I rarely, if ever, dress in purple and fine linen, though I do own one pair of khaki linen pants from J.Crew.)

Thinking about this ugly passage, I was reminded of something else that Yutzy said to me during my visit. At some point at our conversation, he was talking about some of the modern trends that disturb him, and he lamented a decision made by some government body in California that would require schools to teach students about homosexuality. Yutzy thought this was a shame and that it would force a lot of religious parents to send their kids to private schools.

I'm sure that some people who have read the book up to this point, and who don't particularly like religion, will be thinking that in these pages, I have been too kind to religious belief. Isn't it religion, more than anything else, that encourages intolerance? Why should we give religious people a pass when so often they insist on making others conform to their reactionary ethical beliefs? Believe me, I have sympathy with this claim. Religion makes me angry sometimes too, particularly when it comes to this issue of gay rights. Thinking about the downright cruel reaction of many religious people to the Massachusetts Supreme Court's recognition of gay marriage makes me want to punch somebody. Sometimes I feel like we should just give up any effort at coexisting in an atmosphere of peaceful mutual respect. Screw it, I think: God stinks.

I don't know if the theorem has been mathematically proven yet or not, but it's when I find myself feeling angriest about religion that I try to remember that *two wrongs don't make a right.* Just as I wouldn't want to be judged based on the worst things about me, I try to resist judging religion based on the worst things about it. If Adin Yutzy indeed disapproves of gay lifestyles, then I'd have to admit I don't like this one aspect of him. But there would still be lots of things I do like about him. I wouldn't want to forget about his courageous fight for freedom, his generosity in talking about the case with me, and his lovely wife who made me laugh, just because he might happen to believe this one thing that I think is incredibly wrong-headed. This is not to say, of course, that nonbelievers should accept hostility to gay rights, or any other forms of intolerance that we reject. We should fight as hard as we can for those freedoms we believe in and resist the forces of religion (and of anything else) that stand opposed to them. But I don't think we need to condemn all of religion just because some religious people rely on their religious beliefs to take positions that we hate.

It's funny—being in Europe really makes you think

about religion. This was especially true for me in Poland, where I lived for six months while writing some of this book. Not that I'm any sort of expert in Polish history or church/state relations in Poland, but two things that came across pretty strongly from being in Krakow reinforced the feelings about religion that I've tried to express throughout the book. One is that this is a country that was devastated in the past century by two completely intolerant regimes—Nazi and communist—that were defined in large part by opposition to religion. Any thought that religion owns a monopoly on cruelty or intolerance is quickly dispelled here. The second is that it was the Catholic Church that provided solace to the Polish people during the communist era and whose authority may have been integral to the success of the Solidarity movement, which marked the beginning of the end of Soviet dominance in Eastern Europe. Not that the church in Poland has been completely benevolent—even today, there are some indications that forces in it are hospitable to anti-Semitism—but talking to Polish people gives one the strong impression that it is the church that kept this great country alive during an extended era of repression and economic hardship.

This last point, if indeed it is true, says a couple of things about religion and the relationship between church and state. For one thing, it is a strong modern reminder that religion can be a force for good. This is an obvious point, perhaps, but it is often ignored by those of us who are not religious and tend to be skeptical toward religion. The second point is that it shows the importance of keeping church and state separate. The church was able to provide solace to the Polish people, and then to lend its ethical authority to the nation's resistance to communism, because it was able to remain separate and apart from the communist state. Arguably, some churches in the United States were able to play a similar role during the civil rights movement because they, too, were highly independent from the state. Our government here in the United States may have done some pretty bad things in the last few years, but it hasn't been incredibly repressive, at least to most of us. In these conditions, it is sometimes difficult to remember that once in a while the state has to be called to account for its unjust behavior and that the best people and institutions to do this are often religious ones. But religious communities can perform this critical function only if they are substantially separate from the state that they seek to criticize. And that, as much as anything, justifies our vigilant protection of the sixteen short words that make up the first sentence of the First Amendment.

Well, that and how it's a complete abomination for the government to tell atheists that our beliefs are wrong.

Acknowledgments

I got so much incredible help and encouragement while I was researching and writing this book. I would like to acknowledge and send my heartfelt thanks to the following people for talking with me or otherwise assisting me in the course of my journeys: Aaron Agulnek, Dan Barker, Chaplain Barry Black, Erwin Chemerinsky, Richard Dawley, Mary Kay Dorn, Peter Etter, Annie Gaylor, Rabbi Les Gutterman, Sean Hecker, Carolyn Jennrich, Richard Katskee, Stacy Kern, Jay Kramer, Kathy Kuderer, Bishop Gideon Miller, Judy Nakasian, Nic Owen, Natalie Peterson, Joel Petlin, A.J. Picchione and his nice family, Ernesto Pichardo, Steve Pinker, Miriam Pogach, Meg Saunders, Abbot Shih Ying-Fa (and the worshippers who talked with me at the CloudWater Zendo Temple), Jesus Suarez and his family, Suna at the Grand Mosque in Parma, Sister Syed and the staff at the Al Ihsan School in Cleveland, Thomas Van Orden, Shamsuddin Waheed, and Adin and Fanny Yutzy.

Holly Lincoln and Nick Semanko were kind (and brave) enough to go to Game 4 of the Indians–Red Sox series with me. Holly's Indians hat (the one with the "I," not the offensive Indian mascot) probably saved my life. Thanks!

I received extraordinary institutional support from several universities, and I would like to thank all of them.

Boston University has been my work home for the past seven years, and I want to single out Dean Maureen O'Rourke for her support and encouragement. I also got tremendous research assistance from students Sally Gasper and Mark Dahl. Ken Westhassel provided superior help on all sorts of things, which was not easy, since I needed a lot of this help while working thousands of miles away. I wrote substantial portions of the book while teaching at Lyon 3 in France and while serving as a Fulbright lecturer at Jagiellonian University in Krakow. I would like to thank these schools, as well as the Fulbright program, Mathieu Cardon, Iwona Karwala, Maud Touquet, and Filip Wejman, for their invaluable assistance.

I'm sure that without the efforts of Brian Halley, my first editor at Beacon Press, and Ellen Geiger, my terrific agent, this book would never have happened. There are a lot of reasons why writing a constitutional law comedy travelogue was a bad idea. If you've made it this far, you probably can think of some of them. I owe Brian and Ellen for ignoring most of those reasons and supporting me throughout the research and writing of the book. Thank you also to everyone else at Beacon Press, particularly Helene Atwan, who took over editing the manuscript, kicked it into shape, and brought it to completion.

Finally, super-duper thanks to the members of my family for their support and encouragement while I was traveling and writing: my dad, Fred; my stepmother, Mary; my in-laws, Jim and Charlotte; my wife, Karen; and most of all, my son, Walter. Thanks for making this project so incredibly fun, and sorry, Walter, for living in a building with a bar.

This book is dedicated to my mother, Cheryl, who passed away in 2004. I can sense her presence on every page of this book. Thank you, Mom.

Notes

PROLOGUE

The official citation for Adin Yutzy's case is *Wisconsin v. Yoder*, 406 U.S. 205 (1972). Richard Dawley's book is *Amish Snowbirds in Pinecraft, Florida* (New Berlin, WI: Amish Insight, 2007). On America's religious diversity, see Diana L. Eck, *A New Religious America: How a "Christian Country" Has Become the World's Most Religiously Diverse Nation* (San Francisco: HarperOne, 2001), and the U.S. Religious Landscape Survey on the Web site of the Pew Forum on Religion & Public Life, http://religions. pewforum.org. The figure of 14 percent of Americans who have no religious beliefs at all is taken from the 2001 U.S. census, which can be found at www.census.gov. The book that makes the point about the key distinction between orthodox and progressive believers is James Davison Hunter, *Culture Wars: The Struggle to Define America* (New York: Basic Books, 1991). My article on intelligent design is "Of Pandas, People, and the First Amendment: The Constitutionality of Teaching Intelligent Design in the Public Schools," *Stanford Law Review* 49 (1997): 439–470. Steve Almond's book is *Candyfreak: A Journey Through the Chocolate Underbelly of America* (Chapel Hill, NC: Algonquin Books, 2004). Chuck Klosterman's book is *Killing Yourself to Live: 85% of a True Story* (New York: Scribner, 2005). Sarah Vowell's masterpiece is *Assassination Vacation* (New York: Simon and Schuster, 2005). If you'd like to read some of my fiction and humor, please visit my Web site at www.jaywex.com.

CHAPTER 1

I don't really know anything about *Beowulf.* I got all that stuff from Wikipedia. The citation for the case involving Grendel's Den is *Larkin v. Grendel's Den,* 459 U.S. 116 (1982). You can find the Declaration in Defense of Science and Secularism at the Web site of the Center for Inquiry, www.cfidc.org/declaration .html. On the influence of religion on abolitionism, the Civil Rights movement, and other liberal causes, see Stephen L. Carter, *The Culture of Disbelief: How American Law and Politics Trivialize Religious Devotion* (New York: Anchor Books, 1994). Carter's book, incidentally, should be required reading for anyone interested in religion, politics, and law in the United States, and although I do not agree with much of what's in it, I must acknowledge the influence it had on my career—I doubt I would have ended up writing this book if I hadn't read Carter's work back when I was in law school. On religion's influence on the Endangered Species Act, see John Copeland Nagle, "Playing Noah," *Minnesota Law Review* 82 (1998): 1171–1260. An interesting academic literature exists on whether people have some sort of moral obligation to avoid relying on their religious views when reaching important public decisions. For two excellent, readable accounts, see Kent Greenawalt, *Private Consciences and Public Reasons* (New York: Oxford University Press, 1995), and Michael J. Perry, *Religion in Politics: Constitutional and Moral Perspectives* (New York: Oxford, 1997). I got my information about the Rick's Place controversy from Jeff Golimowski, "Bar Fight Brewing: Rick's Place Faces Neighbor, Zoning Battles," *Lawrence Journal-World,* November 15, 2003. I got my information about the Wichita Adult Superstore controversy from Josh Funk, "Porn Store's Exit Elates Area," *Wichita Eagle,* June 5, 2002, and Jean Hays, "City, Adult Store Work Out Deal," *Wichita Eagle,* February 8, 2003. The Lemon test comes from *Lemon v. Kurtzman,* 403 U.S. 602 (1971). The quote about the zoning law under the Lemon test comes from *Amico v. New Castle County,* 101 F.R.D. 47 (D. Del. 2006). The Alabama moment of silence case is *Wallace v. Jaffree,* 472

U.S. 38 (1985). The Supreme Court case involving the Satmar in Kiryas Joel is *Board of Education of Kiryas Joel v. Grumet,* 512 U.S. 687 (1994). More on my Hebrew school experience (including a little bit of the language used here) can be found in my story "Champagne" at www.eyeshot.net/champagne .html. The anti-Semitic comments come from the online version of the *Times Herald-Record* at www.recordonline.com (the articles are "Five condo buildings are going up in KJ," June 18, 2007, and "Proposed KJ construction law aims to aid low-income families, boost community unity," June 19, 2007). On Ave Maria, see Alexandra Alter, "Pizza Multimillionaire Envisions Florida Haven for Catholics," *Miami Herald,* March 25, 2007.

CHAPTER 2

The State Department reports can be read on the U.S. Department of State Web site at www.state.gov/g/drl/irf. The citation for the Santeria case in the Supreme Court is *Church of the Lukumi Babalu Aye, Inc. v. Hialeah,* 508 U.S. 520 (1993). For more information about Santeria and the case, see David M. O'Brien, *Animal Sacrifice and Religious Freedom* (Lawrence, KS: University Press of Kansas, 2004) and Joseph M. Murphy, *Santeria: African Spirits in America* (Boston: Beacon Press, 1993). The Florida greyhound case is *Kiper v. State,* 310 So.2d 42 (Fla. App. 1975). For information about the police raid in Coral Gables, see Tere Figueras Negrete and Elaine de Valle, "For Santeros, Religious Freedom Is Anything But," *Miami Herald,* August 14, 2007, and Tamara Lush, "Death in the City Beautiful," *Miami New Times,* July 12, 2007. Lush's article also discusses the woman who claims to have found a dead chicken in the Pinewood Cemetery. The beard case is *Fraternal Order of Police Newark Lodge No. 12 v. Newark,* 170 F.3d 359 (3d. Cir. 1999). The bear case is *Blackhawk v. Pennsylvania,* 381 F.3d 202 (3d. Cir. 2004).

CHAPTER 3

To learn about scrutiny, and just about everything else involving constitutional law, the best and most readable book is Erwin Chemerinsky, *Constitutional Law: Principles and Policies*, 3rd ed. (New York: Aspen Publishers, 2006). My constitutional law professor was Gerald Gunther, and the article in which he wrote his famous quote was "The Supreme Court, 1971 Term—Foreword: In Search of Evolving Doctrine on a Changing Court: A Model for a Newer Equal Protection," *Harvard Law Review* 86 (1972): 1–48. The polygamy case is *Reynolds v. United States*, 98 U.S. 145 (1878). Adell Sherbert's case is *Sherbert v. Verner*, 374 U.S. 398 (1963). Most of the information about the controversy involving the Amish in New Glarus comes from a superb book about the case (the book that Jay Kramer was flipping through when we met): Shawn Francis Peters, *The Yoder Case: Religious Freedom, Education, and Parental Rights* (Lawrence, KS: University Press of Kansas, 2003). The great pamphlet about New Glarus is Millard Tschudy, *New Glarus, Wisconsin: Mirror of Switzerland, 1845–1995* (1995). Richard Dawley makes his claim about Jay Kramer to Adin Yutzy in *Amish Snowbirds* (see notes for prologue). Dawley's magnum opus on the Wisconsin Amish is *Amish in Wisconsin* (New Berlin, WI: Amish Insight, 2003). The pilot yarmulke case is *Goldman v. Weinberger*, 475 U.S. 503 (1986). The case involving the Forest Service is *Lyng v. Northwest Indian Cemetery Protective Association*, 485 U.S. 439 (1988). The case in which Scalia refused to address issues that were not briefed or argued is *Weiss v. United States*, 510 U.S. 163 (1994). The case in which he addressed issues that were not briefed or argued is *Employment Division, Department of Human Resources v. Smith*, 494 U.S. 872 (1990). Garrett Epps's book about *Smith* is *To an Unknown God: Religious Freedom on Trial* (New York: St. Martin's Press, 2001). Judge McConnell's article criticizing *Smith* is Michael W. McConnell, "Free Exercise Revisionism and the *Smith* Decision," *University of Chicago Law Review* 57 (1990): 1109–1153. The case that invalidated the Religious Freedom Restoration Act as it applies to the states is *City of Boerne v. Flores*, 521 U.S. 507 (1997).

CHAPTER 4

Accounts of the controversy at Sea-Tac Airport include Jonathan Martin, "Airport Puts Away Holiday Trees Rather than Risk Being 'Exclusive,'" *Seattle Times*, December 10, 2006, and Gene Johnson, "Christmas Trees Being Returned to Seattle Airport," *Christian Post*, December 12, 2006. The comments can be found online at www.topix.net/forum/holidays/hanuk kah/TJSHKRFDAQSK4U4LA and http://blog.seattletimes.nw source.com/comments/2006/12. The Pawtucket case is *Lynch v. Donnelly*, 465 U.S. 668 (1984). The menorah/Christmas tree case is *County of Allegheny v. ACLU*, 492 U.S. 573 (1989). The "interior decorating" comparison was made by Judge Frank Easterbrook in *American Jewish Congress v. City of Chicago*, 827 F.2d 120, 129 (7th Cir. 1987) (Easterbrook, J., dissenting). You can buy music from the Freedom from Religion Foundation at www.ffrf.org/shop/music. On the Alabama Ten Commandments controversy, see Jeffrey Gettleman, "Monument Is Now Out of Sight, but Not Out of Mind," *New York Times*, August 28, 2003, and *Glassroth v. Moore*, 335 F.3d 1282 (11th Cir. 2003). The Kentucky Ten Commandments case is *McCreary County, Kentucky v. American Civil Liberties Union of Kentucky*, 545 U.S. 844 (2005). The Texas case is *Van Orden v. Perry*, 545 U.S. 677 (2005). The thing about telling Chemerinsky to put it in his pipe and smoke it is meant in good fun—Erwin is a great lawyer and writer and scholar, and he put me in touch with Thomas Van Orden, for which I am grateful. Chemerinsky is now the dean at the brand new University of California at Irvine School of Law, which appears posed to achieve enormous success.

CHAPTER 5

For an account of the interruption of Rajan Zed's opening prayer, see Sally Phillips, "Protesters Shine Bigotry Spotlight on N.C.," *Charlotte Observer*, July 19, 2007. The protesting organization's press release can be found at www.christiannewswire .com/news/575363635.html. On Vermont and Indiana's practices, see Daniel C. Vock, "Legislative Prayer Stirs Church-State

Issues," www.stateline.org/live/details/story?contentId=78262.
The Supreme Court's decision upholding legislative prayer is
Marsh v. Chambers, 463 U.S. 783 (1983). The Indiana case is *Hin-
richs v. Bosma*, 400 F.Supp.2d 1103 (S.D. Ind. 2005), reversed for
lack of standing, 506 F.3d 584 (7th Cir. 2007). The Cobb County
case is *Pelphrey v. Cobb County*, 448 F.Supp.2d 1357 (N.D. Ga.
2006). The case dismissing Newdow's suit challenging congressional prayer is *Newdow v. Eagen*, 309 F.Supp.2d 29 (D.D.C.
2004). The religion professor's article is Sam D. Gill, "Prayer,"
in *Encyclopedia of Religion*, edited by Mircea Eliade (New York:
Macmillan, 1987). Chaplain Black's autobiography is Barry C.
Black, *From the Hood to the Hill: A Story of Overcoming* (Nashville, TN: Thomas Nelson, 2006). I came across the suggestion
about the poet laureate while reading a PhD dissertation about
the Senate chaplain. See Jeremy G. Mallory, "If There Be a God
Who Hears Prayer: An Ethical Account of the United States
Senate Chaplain" (PhD diss., University of Chicago, 2004). Mallory's dissertation is the most detailed and comprehensive account of the Senate chaplain's office that I came across in my
research.

CHAPTER 6

You can read Madison's "Memorial and Remonstrance" online
at http://religiousfreedom.lib.virginia.edu/sacred/madison_
m&r_1785.html. The New Jersey bus case is *Everson v. Board
of Education*, 330 U.S. 1 (1947). The field trip case is *Wolman v.
Walter*, 433 U.S. 229 (1977). The case involving the blind student is *Witters v. Washington Department of Services for the
Blind*, 474 U.S. 481 (1986). The case involving the deaf student's interpreter is *Zobrest v. Catalina Foothills School District*, 509 U.S. 1 (1993). The Cleveland voucher case is *Zelman v.
Simmons-Harris*, 536 U.S. 639 (2002). On the incident with the
car and the Grand Mosque in Parma, see John F. Hagan, "Man
Admits Guilt for Ramming Mosque," Cleveland *Plain Dealer*,
December 13, 2001. The story about the bus being diverted to
the police station is true. See the January 17, 1983, issue of *Time*

Magazine, available online at www.time.com/time/magazine/
article/0,9171,951858,00.html. Shamsuddin Waheed's online
forum, "Islam in View," is at http://islaminviewforum.com.
The case about the Louisiana computer donation program is
Mitchell v. Helms, 530 U.S. 793 (2000).

CHAPTER 7

The quote about the difference between government speech
endorsing religion and private speech endorsing religion
comes from *Board of Education of Westside Community Schools
v. Mergens*, 496 U.S. 226 (1990). The Long Island prayer case
is *Engel v. Vitale*, 470 U.S. 421 (1962). The Bible passage case is
Abington School District v. Schempp, 374 U.S. 203 (1963). The
Providence case is *Lee v. Weisman*, 505 U.S. 577 (1992). The
Texas football prayer case is *Santa Fe Independent School District v. Doe*, 530 U.S. 290 (2000). For more on my pathetic freshman football experience, you can read "Some Notes Regarding
My Stint as Second-and-a-Half String Center on My Freshman
Football Team, Circa 1983," at http://eyeshot.net/wexler1.html.
The Pledge of Allegiance is codified at 4 U.S.C. §4. The case
that allows students to refuse to say the Pledge is *West Virginia
State Board of Education v. Barnette*, 319 U.S. 624 (1943). This
case was decided on First Amendment free speech grounds
and had nothing to do with religion or the "under God" phrase,
which of course didn't exist at the time it was decided. Thus
students can always refuse to say the Pledge if they want (and
if they can ignore the pressure of their peers to say it). This has
nothing much to do, however, with the question of whether the
Pledge violates the establishment clause. The Supreme Court's
decision in Newdow's case challenging the Pledge is *Elk Grove
Unified School District v. Newdow*, 542 U.S. 1 (2004). Newdow's
Web site, where you can buy his CD, is www.restorethepledge
.com. For accounts of Newdow's oral argument, see Tony
Mauro, "Atheist's Stellar Performance May Not Translate Into
Win," posted at First Amendment Center Online, March 25,
2004, www.firstamendmentcenter.org/analysis.aspx?id=13011,

and Dahlia Lithwick, "One Nation, Under Hallmark, Indivisible," posted at Slate.com, March 24, 2004, www.slate.com/id/ 2097737 (giving Newdow's performance "five stars"). Trevor Morrison's comments about the Pledge case can be found on Leiter Reports: A Philosophy Blog at http://leiterreports.type pad.com/blog/2004/06/more_on_justice.html.

CHAPTER 8

The comments of the *Orlando Sentinel* readers can be found at http://blogs.orlandosentinel.com/news_education_edblog/ 2008/02/more-on-the-vot.html. On the controversy in Texas over the "FYI" e-mail, see "Texas Official Resigns, Cites Creationism Conflict," *USA Today*, November 30, 2007. For an extended discussion of the debate between me and Francis Beckwith at Harvard Law School, see Nick Matzke, "Who's Your Daddy? Intelligent Design Creationism at Harvard Law School," posted April 20, 2005, on the Panda's Thumb blog, www.pandasthumb.org/archives/2005/04/whos-your-daddy-1.html. The book in which Beckwith criticizes me is Francis J. Beckwith, *Law, Darwinism, and Public Education: The Establishment Clause and the Challenge of Intelligent Design* (Lanham, MD: Rowman & Littlefield, 2003). The Tennessee Supreme Court's decision in *Scopes* is *Scopes v. State*, 154 Tenn. 105 (1927). The classic work on the *Scopes* trial is Edward J. Larson's Pulitzer Prize–winning *Summer for the Gods: The Scopes Trial and America's Continuing Debate Over Science and Religion* (New York: Basic Books, 1997). The Arkansas case is *Epperson v. Arkansas*, 393 U.S. 97 (1968). The Louisiana "equal time" case is *Edwards v. Aguillard*, 482 U.S. 578 (1987). The Pennsylvania intelligent design case is *Kitzmiller v. Dover Area School District*, 400 F.Supp.2d 707 (2005). My own views about intelligent design are set out most comprehensively in Jay D. Wexler, "Darwin, Design, and Disestablishment: Teaching the Evolution Controversy in Public Schools," *Vanderbilt Law Review* 56 (2003): 751–855.

The article in which I take issue with Judge Jones's finding on the nonscientific status of intelligent design is Jay D. Wexler, "*Kitzmiller* and the 'Is It Science?' Question," *First Amendment Law Review* 5 (2006): 90–111. An example of the positive press this piece has received in the creationist/intelligent design community is Casey Luskin, "Anti-ID Scholar Jay Wexler Thinks Judge Jones Made Extraneous Findings," posted September 18, 2006, at the Evolution News & Views blog, www.evolutionnews.org/2006/09/antiid_legal_scholar_jay_wexle.html. I have previously made this point about the impossibility of neutrality in the school curriculum in Jay D. Wexler, "Intelligent Design and the First Amendment: A Response," *Washington University Law Review* 84 (2006): 63–98. It is probably worth noting that despite the fact that the curriculum cannot possibly be neutral, it still may not affirmatively promote religion; this, however, is because of the establishment clause's prohibition on such promotion, not because of any general "neutrality" requirement. The poll that ranked Steven Pinker the twenty-sixth top public intellectual was *Prospect* magazine's 2005 poll; Pinker rates fifty-seventh in the magazine's 2008 poll (the results of which were published in the July 2008 issue and can be found online at www.prospect-magazine.co.uk/article_details.php?id=10261). My article on teaching about religion, in case you want to be the eighteenth person ever to look at it, is Jay D. Wexler, "Preparing for the Clothed Public Square: Teaching About Religion, Civic Education, and the Constitution," *William and Mary Law Review* 43 (2002): 1159–1263. The study that showed that teaching about religion promoted tolerance is Emile Lester and Patrick S. Roberts, *Learning About World Religions in Public Schools: The Impact of Student Attitudes and Community Acceptance in Modesto, Calif.* (Nashville, TN: First Amendment Center, 2006), available for download at www.firstamendmentcenter.org/about.aspx?id=16863. Stephen Prothero's book is *Religious Literacy: What Every American Needs to Know—and Doesn't* (San Francisco: HarperSanFrancisco, 2007).

EPILOGUE

On the Pope's influence on the Solidarity movement, see Timothy Garton Ash, *The Polish Revolution: Solidarity*, 3rd ed. (New Haven, CT: Yale University Press, 2002). On anti-Semitism in at least one part of the Catholic Church in Poland, see Craig S. Smith, "Call to Punish Polish Priest for Anti-Semitic Remarks," *New York Times*, July 12, 2007.

KERRY BURKE

Jay Wexler is professor of law at Boston University, where he has taught courses on law and religion, the First Amendment, and environmental law since 2001. Recently, he has taught seminars on U.S. church/state law and U.S. constitutional civil liberties at l'Université Jean Moulin in Lyon, France, and Jagiellonian University in Krakow, Poland, where his research was supported by a Fulbright grant. After earning his JD from Stanford Law School, Wexler worked at the Department of Justice in the Office of Legal Counsel, and as a clerk for Justice Ginsburg at the U.S. Supreme Court and Judge David Tatel at the D.C. Circuit Court of Appeals. Wexler holds an MA in religious studies from the University of Chicago Divinity School, where he studied modern religious thought, theological ethics, Buddhism, and Confucianism, and a BA in East Asian studies from Harvard. In addition to his scholarly publications, Wexler's short stories, reviews, and humorous articles have appeared in *Spy* magazine and on McSweeney's Internet Tendency and other prominent blogs.